Jennifer Wayne Cushman

FIELDS FROM THE SEA

CHINESE JUNK TRADE WITH SIAM DURING THE LATE EIGHTEENTH AND EARLY NINETEENTH CENTURIES

Jennifer Wayne Cushman

FIELDS FROM THE SEA

CHINESE JUNK TRADE WITH SIAM DURING THE LATE EIGHTEENTH
AND EARLY NINETEENTH CENTURIES

STUDIES ON SOUTHEAST ASIA

Southeast Asia Program
180 Uris Hall
Cornell University, Ithaca, New York
1993

Cornell Southeast Asia Program Publications
640 Stewart Avenue, Ithaca, NY 14850-3857

Studies on Southeast Asia No. 12

Second Printing, 2000

Printed in the United States of America

ISBN 0-87727-711-7

Contents

LIST OF TABLES

LIST OF ILLUSTRATIONS

Figure

Map

PREFACE

In 1976, soon after Jennifer Cushman joined the Department of Far Eastern History at the Australian National University, she gave me a copy of her successful Ph.D. thesis, "Fields from the Sea," to read. It was a thorough piece of research which produced thoughtful and well-argued conclusions. We discussed what more needed to be done and when and where the work should be published. She felt strongly she needed to know more about the Chinese and their trading methods and organizations in Thailand and the neighboring countries before she embarked on a final revised version. Once started on that, she became increasingly fascinated by aspects of Sino-Thai family business, and examples of cooperation between Chinese and Western entrepreneurs. The new materials she found were so exciting that they led to a new book which she was just about ready to publish when she died. I know she meant to come back to "Fields from the Sea" when she was ready, and, after her book on the Khaw family's pioneering activities on the Malay peninsular, she knew she was ready. All her friends are saddened that she did not live to see her first book appear. They will be pleased to learn that Oxford University Press will publish the first, and that the Southeast Asia Program of her alma mater will bring out this earlier work as her second. She would have been happier if she had had the chance to look over what she had written with a wiser and more sophisticated eye, but her friends know that the original in 1975 was already a work of fine scholarship and nothing has appeared since to match what she had done.

Jennifer Cushman teased out a sharp portrait of the Chinese junk trade before modern times from a vast range of disparate sources. It was a heroic pioneering task and the authoritative results show, especially in chapters 2, 3, and 4 on the Chinese native maritime customs, on the ships trading with Siam, and on the character of Sino-Siamese trade. What had held her back was her own dissatisfaction with how little we know about individual operators of that trade, how little flesh and bone there was, so to speak. Her own rigorous standards refused to let her be content with the fact that the sources are deficient. She was convinced there was more to discover and, insofar as her work on the Khaw family led her below surface details, she was right. But her most original contribution she had already made: that the junk trade with Siam was successful because it was perceived and justified as an extension of Chinese domestic coastal trade. It was quite distinct from tributary trade, or foreign trade with the West, and can only be understood if we recognize its true function in Ch'ing maritime policy. She was determined to nail this down before publishing a revised version. She thought she could now do it. Having just re-read her work, I believe her thesis still stands even without her final touches.

Had she not been so modest, her early conclusions and insights would have been part of the region's general understanding of a vital part of Sino-Southeast Asian trading relations long before now.

We do not have Jennifer around now to ask the hard questions and insist on adequate evidence for what we say. That loss is complete. To see two books of hers appear, albeit both incomplete in her own eyes, is some consolation. But what is most satisfying to know is that many others will now share her with us.

Wang Gungwu
University of Hong Kong
July 12, 1990
The first anniversary.
Ithaca, NY

The fields are few
but the sea is vast;
so men have made fields from the sea.

Amoy Gazetteer:15:650

1

Introduction

To many of the inhabitants along China's southeastern coast foreign merchants with their commonplace or exotic wares were as familiar as the seasonal monsoons which brought them and which took them away. A succession of foreign traders—Malay, Persian, and Arab during the first millennium, followed by European merchants after 1500—had found accommodation within the economic life of the maritime provinces. But while Western merchants were importing the manufactured goods of Europe, furs from North America, Indian textiles and later opium in exchange for teas, silks, and porcelains, the Chinese were themselves trading with countries in Southeast Asia to obtain the raw produce, foodstuffs, and spices for which a demand in China was regularly expressed. The Chinese had begun to supersede Arabs as carriers of Sino-Southeast Asian trade from the eleventh and twelfth centuries.[1] They continued to increase their share of this trade while effectively thwarting attempts by European shippers toward the end of the eighteenth century to supply the China market with "Straits produce,"[2] the general term applied to Chinese imports from Southeast Asia. Siam became a principal market for the acquisition of Straits

---

[1] Kuwabara Jitsuzo, "on P'u Shou-keng a man of the Western Regions, who was the Superintendent of the Trading Ships Office in Ch'üan-chou towards the end of the Sung Dynasty, together with a general sketch of Trade of the Arabs in China during the T'ang and Sung eras," *Memoirs of the Research Department of the Toyo Bunko*, 2 [1928]: 55-56; O. W. Wolters, *Early Indonesian Commerce* (Ithaca: Cornell University Press, 1967), p. 257. See also Wang Gungwu, "The Nahai Trade," *JMBRAS* 31,2 [1958]; 1-135 for an overview of Southeast Asian contact with China prior to the Sung Dynasty.

[2] Michael Greenberg, *British Trade and the Opening of China 1800-42* (Cambridge: The University Press, 1951), p. 87. The junk trade was capable of meeting the demand in China for Straits produce so there was little room for European merchants to move into the field and even less expectation of their making a profit.

produce, with Chinese frequenting her ports in ever greater numbers from the eighteenth century onwards. The factors which encouraged and sustained the dominant role of Chinese merchants in Sino-Southeast Asian, and particularly Sino-Siamese, commerce from the middle of the eighteenth to the middle of the nineteenth centuries will be explored in this monograph.

Three distinctive features characterized the Chinese junk trade: it was carried in Chinese-style craft, the officers and crews were Chinese, and the vessels and the goods shipped in them were subject to a body of regulations designed to apply only to Chinese trade. All the junk trade to and from ports on the South China coast, or which entered under the heading of "native craft" (a term used by Westerners to designate Chinese vessels) was carried primarily in Fukien- or Kwangtung-style junks.[3] These were readily distinguished from Western ships by their rigging and overall construction. They were manned by Chinese who were usually native to the counties between Ch'ao-chou fu, Kwantung, and Chang-chou fu, Fukien, although some were enlisted from the emigrant communities in Southeast Asia. If both the vessels and their personnel were recognized as Chinese by Chinese port officials, the commercial regulations for native trade then became applicable. As we will see in the following chapters, the regulations governing Chinese junk trade were more liberal than those under which Western trade was administered. This served to facilitate the transactions of Chinese merchants over those of their Western competitors.

China's junk trade with Siam fulfilled the necessary conditions for inclusion under the rubric of native trade. With the exception of tribute vessels sailing to Canton, the junks and junk crews engaged in this trade were Chinese. Siamese seamen were not hired except for voyages terminating at Canton, and even on these vessels the crews were generally Chinese.[4] When foreign trade was confined solely to Canton after 1757, the use of Chinese sailors and Chinese-style vessels became imperative if trade at other ports on the coast was anticipated. Although tribute ships frequently carried goods for sale in the Canton market and in Peking besides those to be presented as acknowledgments of submission, tribute

---

[3] For a definition of the word junk see below Chapter III, p. 43. Junks from Kiangsu and Chekiang were occasionally used to transport goods, but the junks sailing to and from Siam were modeled principally after those from Fukien or Kwangtung.

[4] It was discovered, for instance, that most of the sailors on a tribute vessel at Canton in 1724 were Chinese, whereas one would have expected them to be Siamese: YCSL: 25, 20a-b

trade should not be confused with native trade. The foreign envoys who were sent on tribute missions to China as a token of their ruler's fealty to the Chinese Emperor were permitted to trade the goods they brought duty-free at the frontier markets or in the capital. In addition, a summer market was established at Canton to which the merchants from "countries beyond the seas"[5] were allowed to trade every year. While their merchandise, and presumably their ships, were subject to duty, it was calculated according to the rates paid by Chinese merchants.[6] The emissaries of the Siamese king could therefore trade during the triennial missions and yearly at Canton if they chose.

Native trade had no connection with that entering under the aegis of tribute missions. This trade was perceived by the Chinese authorities as an indigenous economic activity and was administered accordingly; hence the necessity of relying upon Chinese merchants as the agents and Chinese vessels as the carriers of this trade. Not only was Chinese trade to Southeast Asia considered native trade, but so also was much of the trade originating in Southeast Asian countries. The state trade of Siam, i.e. that sponsored by the Siamese king and nobility for the purpose of selling the goods they collected in taxes or from services owed, was thus a form of native trade, because it was shipped in Chinese vessels under the supervision of Chinese merchants. While all of the tribute trade from Siam was channeled through Canton, almost none of the native trade was directed to that port,[7] and the junk trade was not involved in the mechanisms for handling tributary trade.

By the eighteenth century, the *Nan-yang* or "Southern Ocean" had become the focus of China's overseas junk trade. Unfortunately, this region had not been defined precisely by Chinese geographers in the past. Where a country was placed within a specific ocean region appears rather to have been a matter of personal preference,[8] although continuities are

---

[5] John K. Fairbank and S. Y. Teng, "On the Ch'ing Tributary System," *Ch'ing Administration: Three Studies* (Cambridge: Harvard University Press, 1960), p. 172.

[6] Ibid.

[7] See below Chapter II, pp. 15-39, and Table 1.

[8] For example, in Chang Hsieh, *Tung-hsi yang-k'ao* [An Investigation of the Eastern and Western Oceans], 12 *chüan*, in *Ts'ung-shu chi-ch'eng* (Shanghai: Shang-wu yin-shu kuan, 1936, orig. pub. 1618), East Asia is divided into the Western Ocean (*Hsi-yang*), the Eastern Ocean (*Tung-yang*) and outsiders (*wai-chi* Japan and the Dutch). Brunei marked the point of separation between the two oceans (p. 67). He included most of what was later known as the *Nan-yang*, i.e. Siam, the Malay Peninsula, Sumatra, the east coast of Java, and the south coast of Borneo in the Western Ocean; and Luzon, Sulu,

evident in much of the literature. Yet it is important that the *Nan-yang* be distinguished from the Eastern and Western Oceans, for mention of one or another is often made in historical documents dealing with Chinese commerce. In one description of Chinese vessels, for instance, a junk from Chekiang was said to be ill-suited for traversing the deep waters of the Southern Ocean because of its flat bottom.[9] And in Kwangtung, the tonnage rates charged foreign vessels varied according to whether they came from the Eastern or Western Oceans.[10] For the purposes of this discussion, the *Nan-yang* should be conceived of as a circle encompassing the mainland Southeast Asian countries bordering the South China Sea

Marinduque, the Moluccas, and eastern Borneo in the Eastern Ocean. Several decades later, Lu Tz'u-yun based his geography, the *Pa-hung i-shih* [A geography of the world], 4 *chüan*, in *Ts'ung-shu chi-ch'eng ch'u-pien* (Ch'angsha: Shang-wu yhin-shu kuan, 1939), on the four points of the compass. He appears to have placed countries somehwat indiscriminately in each section, having included Holland, Aden, Burma, Portugal, Sulu, and Sumatra in the western section (*hsi-pu*) and Java, Cambodia, Siam, Malindi, Mecca, and Annam in the southern section (*nan-pu*). Hsieh Ch'ing-kao in relating his travels to Yang Ping-nan, who wrote them down c. 1820 in the Hai-lu (A maritime record, 2 *chüan*, in *Pai-pu ts'ung-shu chi-ch'eng*, Taipei: I-pao she, 1952, orig. pub. 1842), divided the world into the Southwest Sea (*Hsi-nan hai*), the South Sea (*Nan-hai*), and Northwest Sea (*Hsi-pei hai*). The countries of mainland Southeast Asia, the Malay peninsula, and the coast of India made up the Southwest Sea while the South Sea included Sumatra, Java, Borneo, Sulu, the Philippines, Marinduque, Amboina, the Celebes, etc. The Northwest Sea was made up primarily by the Western nations. Wei Yüan's *Hai-kuo t'u-chih* (60 *chüan*, 2nd ed., Yangchou: Ku-wei t'ang, 1847) designates Southeast Asia as the Southeast Ocean (*Tung-nan yang*), separating the countries according to island and mainland. Japan, Korea, and the Ryukyus are the eastern border and Sumatra the western. Hsü Chi-yü's *Ying-huan chi-lüeh* (A brief discussion of the ocean circuit), 10 *chüan* (n.p., 1850) makes the same division as the Hai-kuo t'u-chih between island and mainland countries, but all of Southeast Asia is included in the Southern Ocean (*Nan-yang*), i.e. from Luzon and Celebes to Sumatra. Although he says that Pahang and Singapore are the furthest reaches of the *Nan-yang* (ch. 1, p. 24a), he does include Sumatra (ch. 2, p. 27a ff.). With the exception of Lu Tz'u-yün, the other geographers divded Southeast Asia along similar lines. They chose different names to mark the divisions in the oceans to the East, South, and South-west of China, but tended to place the same countries in the same general region.

[9] *Wu-pei chih* [A treatise on armament technology], comp. by Mao Yuan-i, 240 *chüan*, 1664: 117, 11a.

[10] "The Hoppo Book of 1753," manuscript no. 9, the Hirth Collection, Staatsbibliothek Preussischer Kulturbesitz, Berlin, pp. 73-78; passim. I would like to extend special thanks to Dr. Wolfgang Seuberlich of Marburg/Lahn, Westr Germany, for locating this manuscript for me. My thanks also go to Dr. Kieter George of the Orientalishce Abteilung, Staatsbibliothek Preussischer Kulturbesitz, for making the manuscript available to me on microfilm.

and the Gulf of Siam, i.e. Vietnam, Cambodia and Siam, southern Burma, the Malay peninsula, Sumatra, western Java, and the north-east coast of Borneo.[11] The Eastern Ocean or *Tung-nan* included Japan, the Liu-ch'ius, the Philippines, Celebes, and other lands east of Brunei.

Siam was recognized as the largest country in the *Nan-yang* by the nineteenth-century geographer Hsü Chi-yü.[12] During the fourth decade of the eighteenth century Chinese merchants increasingly called there while trading in the Southern Ocean. Siam offered numerous inducements which enhanced her position as a Southeast Asian entrepot for the China trade. She produced such staples as rice and woods which were readily marketable in China and also served as a collection point for the goods native to surrounding countries. A large and growing Chinese community was present in Bangkok. These Chinese acted as contacts or agents for merchants from China or were hired to man the trading junks. Siam lay on one of the principal trade routes to the *Nan-yang* and was favored by excellent harbors with ready access to large supplies of ship-building materials. The Siamese king and nobility were themselves active participants in overseas trade, especially from the 1780s. They aggressively sought to promote trade with China and made special concessions to the Chinese merchants entering Siamese ports. The foreign commercial ventures sponsored by the Siamese elite were recorded and certain of these records have survived. Similarly, the Chinese were aware of Siam's role in supplying certain essential staples, and her trade is documented to a greater extent than that of many other *Nan-yang* countries. The primary source materials for Sino-Siamese trade shed considerable light, therefore, on its character and the manner in which it was conducted.

Modern Western scholarship has generally neglected to analyze the role of the overseas junk trade in China's economic development. The primary concern of twentieth-century historians has been with the expansion of Western commercial activities in China, which is a legitimate emphasis given the greater volume and monetary value of that trade. Works by Sargent, Wright, Greenberg, Pritchard, Dermigny, and Fairbank,[13] to name but a few, have sought to explicate the attempts by

[11] See J. V. G. Mills, Ma Huan, *Ying-hai sheng-lan, 'The Overall Survey of the Ocean's Shores'* [1433] (Cambridge: Cambridge University Press, 1970), pp. 227-29 for his essay on Chinese perceptions of the oceans.

[12] Hsü Chi-yü, *Ying-huan Chih-lüeh*: 1:29a.

[13] A. J. Sargent, *Anglo-Chinese Commerce and Diplomacy* (Oxford: Clarendon Press, 1907); Stanley Wright, *China's Struggle for Tariff Autonomy: 1843-1938* (Shanghai: Kelly &

Western merchants and the governments backing them to increase their trading opportunities in China and to protect their own interests. A further trend among historical economic writers has been to characterize the Chinese response to the Western commercial intrusion or Chinese attempts to modernize following Western models.[14] The junk trade has not come under their purview except in passing, although some useful general information can be obtained from these sources.[15] While adding to the excitement of exploring uncharted territory, the lack of previous attention to the native trade has increased the difficulties in locating relevant primary materials.

Pre-twentieth-century Western language accounts provide some of our most important information, both quantitatively and qualitatively. There was more of a tendency among Western observers than among contemporary Chinese writers to note the practical aspects of Asian trade, i.e. the volume of goods shipped between countries, their prices, fluctuations in the market, and so forth. Some of the most perceptive and observant accounts were written by missionaries and diplomatic emissaries who were prominent in Siam and China during the nineteenth century. Men like Crawfurd and Bowring were more than qualified to comment on the customs and habits of the Asian countries they visited.

Walsh, Ltd., 1938); Earl Pritchard, *Anglo-Chinese Relations during the Seventeenth and Eighteenth Centuries* (New York: Octagon Books, 1970); Greenberg, *British Trade*; Louis Dermigny, *La Chine et l'Occident: Le Commerce à Canton au XVIII Siècle 1719-1833*, 3 vols., 1 album (Paris: École Pratique de Haute Études, 1964); John K. Fairbank, *Trade and Diplomacy on the China Coast*, 2 vols. in 1 (Cambridge: Harvard University Press, 1969), orig. pub. 1953.

[14] Albert Feuerwerker, *China's Early Industrialization* (Cambridge: Harvard University Press, 1958); Hao Yen-p'ing, *The Comprador in Nineteenth Century China: Bridge between East and West* (Cambridge: Harvard University Press, 1970); K. C. Liu, "Steamship Enterprise in Nineteneth Century China," *JAS* 18, 4 (1959): 435-54; Chang Yu-kwei, *Foreign Trade and Industrial Development of China* (Washington: The University Press of Washington, 1956); Ellsworth Carlson, *The Kaipin Mines, 1877-1912* (Cambridge: Harvard University Press, 1971); J. K. Fairbank, A. Eckstein, and L. S. Yang, "Economic Change in Early Modern China: An Analytic Framework," *Economic Development and Cultural Change* 9, 1 (1960): 1-26; Stanley Wright, *Hart and the Chinese Customs* (Belfast: McMullan & Son, 1950).

[15] See especially Fairbank, *Trade and Diplomacy*, chs. 2 & 14; Evelyn Rawski, *Agricultural Change and the Peasant Economy of South China* (Cambridge: Harvard University Press, 1971), ch. 4; M. A. P. Meilink-Roelofsz, *Asian Trade and European Influence in the Indonesian Archipelago between 1500 and about 1630* (The Hague: Nijhoff, 1962), passim; Rhoads Murphey, ed., *Nineteenth Century China: Five Imperialist Perspectives* (Ann Arbor: The University of Michigan Center for Chiense Studies, 1972), papers 1 & 2.

Their curiosity led them to look closely at a wide range of activities, and as they were often concerned with establishing commercial relations, they paid special attention to the trade already in existence.[16]

The newspapers of the last century are particularly valuable for the quantitative information they supply.[17] Not only were articles written about Asian trade for the edification of a paper's European readers, but they also included commercial registers of shipping arrivals and departures, price currents, lists of imports and exports, and the provenance and destinations of the vessels in port. The *Singapore Chronicle* included junk trade in its *Register* and, while the figures were certainly never exact for the volume of their imports and exports, they at least give an impression of which goods were in demand and the location of the major centers of Chinese trade.

Material of a similar nature can also be found in the commercial guides and sailing manuals[18] which proliferated as a result of the nineteenth-century expansion of Western trade with China. These were compiled to aid merchants in their dealings with officials and their

[16] John Crawfurd, *Journal of an Embassy to the Courts of Siam and Cochin China*, orig. pub. 1828, 1830 (Kuala Lumpur: Oxford University Press, 1967); *History of the Indian Archipelago*, 3 vols. (Edinburgh: Constable, 1820); John Bowring, *The Kingdom and People of Siam*, 2 vols. (London: Parker, 1857); G. Finlayson, *The Mission to Siam, and Hue the Capital of Cochin China, in the Years 1821-2* (London: Murray, 1926); C. Gutzlaff, *The Journal of Two Voyages along the Coast of China, in 1831, and 1832* (New York: Haven, 1833); H. Malcom, *Travels in South-Eastern Asia Embracing Hindustan, Malaya, Siam, and China*, 2 vols. (Boston: Gould, Kendell and Lincoln, 1839); Arthur Neale, *Narrative of a Residence at the Capital of the Kingdom of Siam* (London: Office of the National Illustrated Library, 1852); Jean Baptiste Pallegoix, *Description du Royaume Thai au Siam*, 2 vols. (Paris, 1854); E. Roberts, *Embassy to the Eastern Courts of Cochin-China, Siam, and Muscat* (New York: Harper, 1837); *The Burney Papers*, 4 vols. in 5 pts. (Farnborough, Hants: Gregg, 1971).

[17] *Canton Register*, Canton, 1827-1841, vols. 1-14; J. H. Moor, *Notices of the Indian Archipelago and Adjacent Countries* (Singapore, 1837); *The Indo-Chinese Gleaner* (Malacca: Anglo-Chinese Press), no. 10 (1819), nos. 12-13 (1820), nos. 16-17 (1821), nos. 19-20 (1822); *The Asiatic Journal and Monthly Register for British India and Its Dependencies* (London: Parbury, Allen & Co.), vols. 1-28 (1816-1829), n.s., vols. 1-40 (1830-1843); *The Singapore Chronicle and Commercial Register* (Singapore: Singapore Chronicle Press, 1831-1833), n.s., vols. 1-3.

[18] H. M. Elmore, *The British Mariner's Director and Guide to the Trade and Navigation of the Indian and China Seas* (London: Bensley, 1802); J. R. Morrison, *Chinese Commercial Guide* (Canton, 1834, 1848); John Phipps, *A Practical Treatise on the China and Eastern Trade* (Calcutta: Baptist Mission Press, 1835); S. W. Williams, *A Chinese Commmercial Guide* (Canton: Office of the Chinese Repository, 1856, 1863); William Milburn, *Oriental Commerce*, 2 vols. (London: Black, Parry, & Co., 1813).

commercial representatives at Canton. They contain descriptions of the port, of Chinese products, tables of weights and measures, and coastal sailing directions, as well as the Chinese government's edicts on trade and the duties and fees merchants would be expected to pay. Although these guides would have more utility for the historian dealing with the organization or operation of Western trade in China, they do give brief summations of the junk trade. Moreover, China's imports and exports, including those carried by junk, are described, the Chinese terms for them are given, and the countries in which they originated and to which they were shipped are indicated.

Mid-nineteenth-century Siamese trade was carefully surveyed by an employee of the British East India Company, D. E. Mulloch. At the end of his essay[19] he compiled an exhaustive list of Siam's exports, whether they were native to Siam or tribute commodities from Siam's vassals, the countries to which they were exported, and the value and quantity of the exports. Siam's imports from China and their volume are also enumerated. This is one of the few really detailed sketches of Siam's trade. Malloch was no novice to the Asian scene, having traded in Siam from at least the period of the Burney negotiations in the 1820s. His account should be regarded as more reliable than those of some of his contemporaries.

Finally, the testimony of British merchants and travelers before the parliamentary committees making inquiries into the role of the East India Company, and the later parliamentary committee reports on the trade at the ports opened by the Treaty of Nanking, give hints about changes and developments in the junk trade. Much of the testimony presented before these committees dealt with the position of Western trade in China, but scattered references were made to native Chinese trade,[20] particularly where it came into competition with British interests. The Chinese Maritime Customs also issued reports on all aspects of maritime activity in China.[21] The decennial reports, first published to cover the years 1880

---

[19] D. E. Maloch, *Siam: Some General Remarks on Its Productions* (Calcutta: Baptist Mission Press, 1852).

[20] These appear in the footnotes in the text.

[21] China: Imperial Maritime Customs, I. - Statistical Series: no. 6, *Decennial Reports on the Trade, Navigation, Industries, etc. of the Ports Open to Foreign Commerce in China and Corea, 1882-91* (Shanghai: Statistical Dept. of the Inspectorate General of Customs, 1893); China: Imperial Maritime Customs, I. - Statistical Series: no. 6, *Decennial Reports on the Trade, Navigation, Industries, etc. of the Ports Open to Foreign Commerce in China and Corea, 1892-1901*, 3 vols. (Shanghai: Statistical Dept. of the Inspectorate General of

to 1890, discuss Chinese coastal shipping in some detail, describe the junks from each region, giving the number of crew members, how much the junks cost to build and other such useful information. As these reports were compiled after the junk trade to foreign countries had declined, only marginal use can be made of them.

Thai materials on the junk trade with China are not plentiful, but the ones surviving from the nineteenth century have proved essential in this study. Extant manuscripts are held in the National Library at Bangkok and catalogued under the heading *Chotmaihet* or official documents. Two deserve special attention. The first is a series of letters written by the captains of a junk convoy which sailed to China in the summer of 1813.[22] The names of the junks and the Chinese ports they visited are supplied. Not only does this manuscript tell us approximately what goods were in demand at the time, but it also gives an impression of how business was transacted. The letters further indicate the rather large profit margin expected on most of the goods exported to China.

The second document consists of manifests for twenty vessels sponsored by various members of the Siamese nobility which traded in Canton, Shanghai, and Ningpo during the 1844-1845 season.[23] The weight, tax, unit price, and total investment for the goods these vessels carried is furnished. In addition, the cost of sailing the vessel, including payments to the crew and other such expenses, is provided, as well as the amount of cargo space assigned to crew members. These documents have been used extensively in parts of the discussion which follows, perhaps more than such isolated accounts warrant. While some problems exist in interpreting them, they are unique in that they contain the kinds of statistical information so seldom found in Chinese or Western language sources, and reveal a good deal about the actual details of Siamese trade with China.

Although I have not used Japanese language sources, a few words must nevertheless be said about them. The Japanese appear to have dealt more fully with the Chinese economy prior to the nineteenth century than have Western or even Chinese historians, but they have not handled Sino-

Customs, 1904); China: Imperial Maritime Customs, I. - Statistical Series: no. 7, *Native Customs Trade Returns*, nos. 1-3 (Shanghai: Statistical Dept. of the Inspectorate General of Customs, 1904).

[22] CMH.R.2, #15, 1813.

[23] CMH.R.3, #49, 1844. Although this document is catalogued under the year 1844, internal evidence indicates that it should be dated 1845.

Siamese trade specifically, concentrating instead on the role of overseas Chinese or on Chinese trade with Japan. However, some articles have been written on the Chinese native customs administration, on junk transport, and on the formation of trade and shipping guilds.[24] These deserve more adequate coverage than has been possible here.

Twentieth-century Chinese historians exhibit the same bias toward concentrating on the Western presence in China or on Sino-Western relations generally as Western historians have shown. Many of the histories of Chinese maritime taxation or Chinese guilds were written in terms of how Western business firms in Canton were affected, but are not related to the Chinese junk trade.[25] The other tendency has been to write histories of China's relations with Southeast Asia that mention the commercial aspect only in passing.[26] While some modern historians have

[24] Inaba Iwakichi, "Shindai no Kanton boeki" [Canton trade in the Ch'ing period], *Tao keizai kenkyu* 4, 2 (1920): 239-74; 4,3 (1920): 359-80; 4,4 (1920): 591-612; 5,1 (1921): 103-113; Kato Shigeru, "Shindai Fukken Koso no sen'an ni tsuite" [On the shipping brokers of Fukien and Kiangsu during the Ch'ing dynasty], *Shirin* 14,4 (1929): 529-37; Negishi Tadashi, *Chugoku no girudo* [Guilds in China] (Tokyo: Nihon hyoron shinsha, 1953); Ota Tatsuo, "Shindai Kanton no koshio ni tsuite" [Trade in Kwangtung during the Ch'ing period], *Shigaku* 13,2 (1934): 105-119; 13,4 (1934): 83-109; Uchida Naosaku, "Shindai no boeki dokunsen koko" [The structure of trading monopolies during the Ch'ing period], *Toyo Keizaishi kenkyu*, ed. Uchida Naosaku (Tokyo: Chikura shobo, 1970), vol. 1, pp. 290-331.

[25] For example, in Chou Yü-ching's *Shang-yeh shih* [History of Trade] (Taipei: The Author, 1957) he surveys trade from the Chou to the Republican Period, but in dealing with the Ch'ing makes almost no mention of Southeast Asian or Chinese trade. See also: Wong Po-shang, "Ch'ing-tai Kuang-tung mao-i chi ch'i tsai Chung-kuo ching-chi shih shang-chih i-i" [The historical significance of Kwangtung trade under the Ch'ing dynasty], *Ling-nan hsueh-pao* 3,4 (1934): 157-96; T'ung Meng-cheng, *Kuan-shui kai-lun* [An essay on customs duty] (Shanghai: Shang-wu yin-shu kuan, 1946); Wang Kuang, *Chung-kuo yang-yeh shih* [A history of water transport in China] (Taipei: Hai-yun ch'u-pan she, 1955); Liang Chia-pin, *Kuang-tung shih-san hang k'ao* [A discussion of the thirteen hong in Kwangtung] (Nanking: Kuo-li pien-i kuan, 1937); P'eng Tse-i, "Ch'ing-tai Kuang-tung yang-hang chih-tu te ch'i yuan" [The rise of Cohong in Kwangtung during the Ch'ing dynasty], *Li-shih yen-chiu* 1 (1957): 1-24; T'ang Hsiang-lung, "Shih-pa shih-ch'i chung-yeh Yüeh hai-kuan te fu-pai" [The corruption of the mid-18th century Kwangtung Maritime customs], *Jen-wen k'o-hsüeh hsüeh-pao* 1 (1942): 129-35.

[26] Ch'en Ti-chiang, *Chung-kuo wai-chiao hsing-cheng* [The administration of China's foreign affairs] (Chungking: Shang-wu, 1945); Feng Ch'eng-chün, *Chung-kuo Nan-yang chiao-t'ung shih* [A history of commercial relations between China and the South Seas] (Shanghai: Shang-wu yin-shu kuan, 1937); Hsieh Yu-jung, *Hsin-pien Hsien-lo kuo-chih* [A new edition of the gazetteer of Siam] (Bangkok: I-pao she, 1953); Wang Chih-ch'un, *Kuo-ch'ao t'ung-shange shih-mo chi* [A complete account of the foreign trade with various countries by the Ch'ing dynasty], 20 *chüan* (Taipei: Wen-hai, 1966), author's preface 1880.

studied the native trade during the Ch'ing, most have explored facets of early Ming and pre-Ming trade. Fu I-ling, T'ien Ju-k'ang, Chang Te-ch'ang, and others[27] have made valuable contributions in their writings on economic development, but the quantity of published material still remains sparse. There has also been a tendency in modern Chinese scholarship to reproduce primary source materials verbatim without analyzing the implications of the data.

In contrast to this somewhat gloomy appraisal of modern Chinese historical writings, pre-twentieth-century sources provide ample material for investigating most aspects of China's native trade--both domestic and foreign. Although trade was seldom the focus of the Ch'ing compilations consulted in this study, many chroniclers recognized the utility of native trade to China's southeastern coast, and its administration has been widely recorded; so widely, in fact, that locating the relevant materials is often difficult. The sources are disparate and an extensive range should be referred to if a picture of how the Chinese handled their own trade is to emerge.

The published collections of Chinese official documents contain proportionately the greatest volume of material on Chinese trade and often in the most organized format. These include such compilations as the *Veritable Records* of the Ch'ing dynasty, the administrative statutes and precedents for the government as a whole and for the Board of Revenue, the historical documents from the late Ming and early Ch'ing, and the records of China's management of foreign affairs during the nineteenth century.[28] The statutes outline the regulations under which the native

[27] Chang Te-ch'ang, "Ch'ing-tai Ya-p'ien chan-cheng ch'en-chih Chung-Hsi yen-hai t'ung-shang" [Sino-Western coastal trade in the Ch'ing period prior to the Opium war], *Ch'ing-hua hsüeh-pao* 10 (1935): 97-145; Fu I-ling, *Ming-Ch'ing shih-tai shang-jen chi shang-yeh tzu-pen* [Merchants and mercantile capital in Ming and Ch'ing times] (Peking: Jen-min ch'u-pan she, 1956); T'ien Ju-k'ang, *Shih-ch'i shih-chi chih shih-chu shih-chi chung-yeh Chung-kuo fan-ch'uan tasi tung-nan Ya-chou hang-yün ho shang-yeh shang te ti-wei* [The place of Chinese sailing vessels in the maritime trade of Southeast Asia from the seventeenth to mid-nineteenth centuries] (Shanghai: Jen-min, ch'u-pan she, 1957); Ling Ch'un-sheng *et al.*, ed., *Chung-T'ai wen-hua lun-chi* [Essays on Sino-Thai culture] (Taipei: Chung-hua wen-hua ch'u-pan, 1958); Lu Chi-fang, "Ch'ing Kao-tsung shih-tai te Chung-Hsien kuan-hsi" [Sino-Siamese relations in the Ch'ien-lung period], *Li-shih hsüeh-pao* 2 (1974): 385-412.

[28] *Tai-Ch'ing li ch'ao shih-lu* [Veritable records of the Ch'ing dynasty], 4,485 *chüan* (Taipei: Hua-wen shu-chu, 1964), orig. pub. 1937-38; *(Ch'in-ting) Ta-Ch'ing hui-tien* [Administrative statutes of the Ch'ing dynasty], 80 *chüan*, 1813 [1818?]; (Ch'in-ting) Ta-ch'ing hui-tien, 100 *chüan* (Taipei: Ch'i-wen, 1963), orig. pub. 1899; (Ch'in-ting) *Ta-Ch'ing hui-tien shih-li* [Administrative statutes and precedents of the Ch'ing dynasty], 250 *chüan*,

trade was to operate, and the statutes were enforced. Both the *Shih-lu* and the *Ming-Ch'ing shih-liao* contain officials' memorials advocating specific policies for handling the junk trade and the Emperor's decisions in the form of edicts and rescripts. The organizational framework under which trade was administered and supervised, as well as bureaucratic attitudes and responses to changes in commercial life, are therefore well demonstrated.

A second group in the category of collected works are unofficial compilations. They consist principally of essays by officials and literati on economic, military, governmental, etc. topics, and also include some official documents.[29] These are valuable to the extent that the essayists elaborate upon current commercial thought, discuss the economic needs that trade would satisfy or the problems it might create. Essays were one of the literary forms through which the search for alternate solutions could be explored and expressed. They allow us a more intimate view of how certain Chinese approached the problems of their own time.

Late Ming and Ch'ing geographies[30] inform us, often indirectly, about China's trade with the *Nan-yang*. Some deal almost entirely with the internal political, economic, and social life of the countries they examine,

1733; *(Ch'in-ting) Ta-Ch'ing hui-tien shih-li*, 1,220 *chüan* (Taipei: Ch'i-wen, 1963), orig. pub. 1899; (Ch'in-ting) *Hu-pu tse-li* [The precedents of the Board of Revenue], 134 *chüan*, 1791; *(Ch'in-ting) Hu-pu tse-li*, 100 *chüan*, 1874; *Ming-Ch'ing shih-liao: keng-pien* [Historical materials of the Ming and Ch'ing periods, series G] (Taipei: Chung-yang yen-chiu yüan, n.d.); *Ming-Ch'ing shih-liao: ting-pien* [Series D] (Shanghai: Shang-wu yin-shu kuan, n.d.); *Ch'ou-pan i-wu shih-mo* [The complete account of our management of barbarian affairs], 260 *chüan* (Taipei: Wen-hai, 1970-71), facs. rep. 1930 ed.; *(Ch'in-ting) Ku-chin t'u-shu chi-ch'eng* [Imperial encyclopedia], ed. Ch'en Meng-lei *et al.*, 10,000 *chüan* (Shanghai: Chung-hua, 1934), facs. rep. 1726 ed.; *Ch'ing-shih kao* [A draft history of the Ch'ing dynasty], ed. Chao Erh-hsün, 534 *chüan* (n.p. Lien-ho shu-tien, 1942), orig. pub. 1928; *(Ch'in-ting) Chung-shu cheng-k'ao* [Regulations of the central administration], comp. by Ming-liang *et al.*, 32 *chüan* (Taipei: Hsüeh-hai, 1968), orig. pub. 1825.

[29] *Huang-ch'ao ching-shih wen-pien* [Essays on statecraft during the Ch'ing dynasty], comp. by Ho Ch'ang-ling *et al.*, 120 *chüan* (Taipei: Shih-chieh, 1964), orig. pub. 1873; *Huang-ch'ao chang-ku hui-pien* [Collected historical records of the Ch'ing dynasty], comp. by Chang Shou-yung *et al.*, 100+2 *chüan* (n.p. Ch'iu-shih shu-she, 1902); *Hsiao-fang hu-chai yü-ti ts'ung-ch'ao* [Collected texts on geography from the Hsiao-fang hu studio], comp. by Wang Hsi-ch'i, pt. 1: 12 *chih*, pt. 2 (supplement): 12 *chih*, pt. 3 (second supplement): 12 *chih* (Shanghai: Chu-i t'ang, 1877-97); Yen Ju-i, *Yang-fang chi-yao* [Essentials of maritime defense], 24 *chüan*, 1838; Yü Ch'ang-hui, *Fang-hai chi-yao* [Essentials of Coastal defense], 181 *chüan*, 1842.

[30] See the sources mentioned above in footnote 8 and also Ch'en Lun-chiung, *Hai-kuo wen-chien lu* [A record of things seen and heard in the maritime countries], 1 *chüan*, maps

mentioning the arrival of Chinese junks only in passing. Others, like those written by Wei Yüan and Hsieh Ch'ing-kao, treat Chinese economic ties with the *Nan-yang* in a more substantial fashion. Import and export commodities are listed, the procedures the merchant was subjected to at the ports he visited are discussed. All the geographic works are of value, however, for they trace sailing routes and distances from which the trading networks of the region can be drawn. Those geographies, most notably the *Hai-kuo t'u-chih*, which document Chinese contacts with the countries of the *Nan-yang* from earlier periods, enable one to make comparative assessments between Ch'ing commercial activity in the region with that of previous dynasties.

Certain works were written primarily as commercial handbooks for the officials who administered the Western and native trade.[31] If used in conjunction with the government's administrative statutes and precedents, particularly those of the Board of Revenue, they are invaluable as guides to the operation at the provincial level of the overseas junk trade. The three handbooks for Canton, listing import duties, tonnage dues, and other port regulations would have been applicable mainly to Western trade. But sections were devoted to the native trade and stipulated the amount of tonnage dues to be paid by native junks and the duty to be levied on the miscellaneous goods they carried up and down the China coast. Liang T'in-nan's important study of the Kwangtung customs administration[32] covers the entire range of maritime commercial affairs at Canton. Tariff rates, the officials supervising the system, the geographic location and functions of customs stations, the hong organizations, and notices of the foreign countries that traded at Canton are all set out. Again, much of the emphasis is on Western trade, but in the profusion of

1 *chüan* (Taipei: T'ai-wan yin-hang, 1958), author's preface 1730; Feng Ch'eng-chün, *Hai-lu chu* [A commentary on the "Record of the Seas"] (Peking: Chung-hua shu-chü, 1955); Hsiang Ta, *Liang-chung hai-tao chen-ching* [Two sailing manuals with compass bearings] (Peking: Chung-hua shu-chü, 1961); *Wu-pei chih*; Wang Ch'ao-tsung, *Hai-wai fan-i lu* [A record of the overseas barbarians], 2 ts'e, 1844.

[31] "The Hoppo Book"; *Yüeh hai-kuan cheng-shou ko-hsiang kuei-kung yin-liang keng-ting tse-li* [Amended regulations for harbor dues, taxes, etc. of the Canton maritime customs, arranged by places] (Canton, 1749); *Yüeh hai-kuan kuei-li* [Canton customs house regulations], 2 2 *pen* (Canton, 1760); *Fu-chien sheng-li* [Laws and regulations of Fukien province], 34 *chüan*, 8 vols. in 3 (Taipei: T'ai-wan yin-hang, 1964), orig. pub. 1752, repr. 1872.

[32] *Yüeh hai-kuan chih* [Gazetteer of the maritime customs of Kwangtung], comp. by Liang T'ing-nan, 30 *chüan*, 4 vols. (Taipei: Ch'eng-wen ch'u-pan she, 1968), orig. pub. 1838.

material he makes available, various dimensions of the junk trade are noted.

The final category of sources to be considered consists of local gazetteers (*fang-chih*).[33] It is in them that one finds the most detailed information about Chinese native trade. The gazetteers for Kwangtung and Fukien, from the provincial to the county levels, survey the organization of trade at the coastal ports, the shipping regulations specific to each administrative unit, brokerage activities, governmental directives pertaining to provincial or local trade, and memorials by prominent natives of the region about the commercial affairs of the province. While the material in the officially compiled collections mentioned above is frequently repeated from one collection to another, the gazetteers, because they are compilations dealing with local history and local events, include new information that would not normally appear in the larger histories, encyclopedias or collectanea. Of all the documents bearing on Chinese overseas commercial expansion, the gazetteers may ultimately prove the most influential in shaping the historian's understanding of this process.

No attempt has been made here to present a comprehensive history of China's junk trade with Siam. I intend, rather, to explore specific topics: the administrative framework under which this trade was carried on, the goods basic to the exchange process, the kinds of men who participated in the trade, and the government's attitude toward native overseas commerce. This approach should serve to make more explicit the economic needs that native trade satisfied and to indicate its importance to the regional economies of China's southeastern maritime provinces.

---

[33] The most important of these are cited in the footnotes throughout the text. Material can generally be found in the sections of the gazetteers headed maritime or coastal defense, customs passes, ship administration, and taxes. Maritime taxes most frequently appear toward the end of the general section on taxation.

2

THE CHINESE NATIVE MARITIME CUSTOMS ADMINISTRATION

China's native overseas trade was administered in much the same fashion as her domestic junk trade. Within the customs apparatus established by the Ch'ing dynasty to supervise Chinese domestic and foreign trade little distinction was made between the offices or collectorates in charge of maritime trade and those managing inland traffic.[1] The trade of Western nations with China, prior to the introduction of the Canton System, was controlled by the appropriate maritime collectorates at the ports where their business was transacted, and after 1757, by the Kwangtung maritime customs. Although both native and Western trade fell under the jurisdiction of the same administrative hierarchy and under the surveillance of the same bureaucratic hierarchy, they were not subject to the same regulations. Furthermore, whereas Western trade was confined to Canton after 1757, Chinese merchants who traded abroad continued to patronize the coastal ports under Maritime Customs' supervision. Chinese foreign and domestic or coastal trade should therefore be equated, not only because the two were subsumed under the same customs administration, but also because Chinese ocean junks frequently engaged in a carrying trade between Chinese coastal ports before proceeding to their ultimate destinations in Southeast Asia.

"Siamese" vessels trading to China were accorded much the same status as Chinese junks, particularly as Siamese merchant junks were manned by Chinese crews and were designed in conformity with the

---

[1] Fairbank, *Trade and Diplomacy on the China Coast*, p. 255.

specifications for Chinese ocean vessels.[2] Asian shipping in general was treated more liberally than Western, and if the aforementioned prerequisites were adhered to, the vessels from other Southeast Asian countries were able to benefit in the same manner as Siam's.[3] Siamese trade and Chinese native trade maintained relative parity in the Chinese customs organization, and any references to the application of customs regulations to native trade throughout this chapter can be assumed to apply to Siam's trade unless otherwise stipulated.

The historian of Ch'ing institutional development is confronted not only by the vast corpus of regulations delineating the functions of governmental departments, but also by the permutation and modifications of those regulations. Ch'ing institutions were not static but were adapted to meet localized needs. Hence, while the general pattern of customs organization for all the provinces was similar, the specific rules enforced at individual customs collectorates could differ from port to port. Since the following discussion will focus on the port administration in the various regional centers of Sino-Siamese shipping, it will be useful first to review the location of those centers.

Nineteenth-century Western observers noted that Siamese junks called at ports scattered along the entire coast of China from Hainan to Tientsin. The preoccupation of these writers with the Canton System, however, has distorted the overall picture for it has led them to portray Kwangtung in general, and Canton in particular, as the nucleus of all of China's foreign trade. The impression fostered by the majority of Western-language accounts is that approximately one half of the Siamese shipping engaged in the China trade repaired to one or another port in Kwangtung (see Table 1). John Crawfurd, for instance, stated that, of the total Siamese junk traffic to China, two-thirds sailed to Kwangtung, with most of that terminating at Canton.[4] Skinner's analysis of the nineteenth

---

[2] *FCSL*: 23:616; Great Britain: Parliament, House of Commons, Select Committee on the East India Company's Affairs, *Report from the Select Committee Appointed to Inquire into the Present State of the Affairs of the East India Company, and into the Trade between Great Britain, the East Indies, and China*, Gt. Br., Parliament, Sessional Papers, 1830, vol. 5 [H.C.] 655, p. 300.

[3] This was particularly true of the trade from Vietnam and Manila. "Trade to all the Ports of the Chinese Empire," Great Britain: Foreign Office, Papers in the Public Record Office, Series: Foreign Office 17, China #9, p. 13 (hereafter FO 17/9); *TCHTSL*:1899:234:9a-b; *TCHTSL*:1899:235:11a.

[4] Crawfurd, *Journal of an Embassy to the Courts of Siam and Cochin China*, p. 410. From a total of 83 junks, Crawfurd lists 55 as having sailed to Kwangtung, and 53 of these 55 sailed to Canton.

Table 1. Centers of Sino-Siamese Trade[a]

Kwangtung	Fukien	Chekiang-Kiangsu-Chihli
Hainan:	*Chang-chou fu:	Ning-po fu
*Ch'iung-chou	Hai-ch'eng	(Limpo)
(Kiungchow)	Chen-hai	
*Hai-k'ou	(Lin hai, Tin hai)	Shang-hai
*P'u-ch'ien		
*Ch'ing-lan	*Ch'üan-chou fu:	Su-chou fu
Fu-t'ien	T'ung-an	(Soochow, Souchou,
Yü-lin	*Hsia-men	Saochou)
	(Amoy, Hea-mun)	T'ien-chin fu (Tientsin)
Kao-chou fu		
	Fu-chou-fu	
Chao-ch'ing fu:		
Yang-chiang		

Kuang-chou fu:
*Canton
*Chiang-men
 (Kong moon, Kiang-mui)
 Hsiang-shan
 San-shui
 Nan-hai\Macao

Ch'ao-chou fu:
*Chang-lin
 (Chong-lim, Changlim)
 Chieh-yang
 Jao-p'ing (Japing)
 Nan-ao (Namoa) (Nan Gaou)
*Ch'eng-hai
 (Ching-hai, Tinghai)
*Hai-yang
 Shan-t'ou (Swatow)
 Tung-lung kang
 (Teng-leng)

Centers said to be in Ch'ao-chou:
 Hee (Kee) yang -
possibly Chieh-yang[b]
 Chang-yang?
 Soakah (Shan-keo)?

* Center of primary importance

[a] Geographical information can be found in the *Chia-ch'ing ch'ung-hsiu i t'ung-chih* (The Chiach'ing revision of the Imperial Gazetteer), 560 *chüan*, in *Ssu-pu ts'ung-k'an hsü-pien* (Shanghai: Shang-wu yin-shu kuan, 1934), *chüan*, 428, 429, 441-43, 446, 452-53. For the location of these places, see map, p. 19.

[b] Morrison, *Chinese Commercial Guide*, 1848, p. 74.

century ports of call redresses the imbalance to an extent by his inclusion of the Ch'ao-chou fu area, but he too ignored the Chekiang-Kiangsu ports.[5] Chinese and Siamese sources, however, indicate that, with respect to the Sino-*Nan-yang* trade, the ports of greatest activity were those from Ch'ao-chou to the north, rather than Canton itself. A partial list of the Siamese junks sailing to China in 1813 reveals that two-thirds called at ports other than Canton, and, even of the seven that sailed there, at least one was a tribute vessel.[6]

The Western-language accounts further disagree over where trade was conducted with the greatest facility; some ports being favored by one author while discounted by another. After declaring that fifty-three Siamese junks traded at Canton, Crawfurd then proceeds to report that the trade there was unprofitable, the duties were higher than elsewhere, and the "public officers more vexatious."[7] Similar charges were leveled at other major ports, notably Amoy, Ch'eng-hai,[8] and Namoa.[9] Amoy,

---

[5] G. William Skinner, *Chinese Society in Thailand* (Ithaca: Cornell University Press, 1957), pp. 41-42. The probable reason for his omission of the central and northern ports is that he is discussing the centers of emigration, and there was little to Siam from the ports north of Fu-chou.

[6] CMH.R.2, #15, 1813:

Canton	-- 7 junks
Kao-chou	-- 5 junks
Tung-lung kang	-- 3 junks
Namoa	-- 1 junk
Ningpo	-- 7 junks
Shanghai	-- 4 junks
Khui-tong & Kon-yong (?)	-- 6 junks

Ch'ou-pan i-wu shih-mo: Hsien-feng: 3:29a lists Ch'iung-chou and Yang-chiang as places where Siamese vessels traded; *Kuang-chou FC* [Prefectural gazetteer of Kuang-chou], comp. by Shih Teng *et al.*, 163 *chüan*, 1879, 74:14b states that all the Chinese junks sailing to Southeast Asia were to leave from Namoa harbor; *MCSL:KP*, vol. 6, pp. 561b, 565a-b: Siamese vessels were reported anchored at Tunglung kang, Wei-t'ou, and Amoy.

[7] Crawfurd, *Embassy*, p. 413.

[8] FO 17/9, p. 39. This may be either Ching-hai in Hui-lai hsien or Ch'eng-hai hsien. Although the spelling in the Foreign Office report corresponds with the former, Ching-hai was not a hsien, and the implication in the text is that a hsien is referred to (p. 33). Both were duty collection stations (*YHKC*: 6:4b, 10b), and both were coastal ports, but Ch'eng-hai is more frequently mentioned as a port of call for Chinese junks than Ching-hai. Either, however, might be the place referred to.

[9] Crawfurd, *Embassy*, p. 413; Gutzlaff, *Two Voyages*, pp. 71, 76: "The duties, as well as the permit to enter the river [at Namoa], are very high; but the people know how to elude the mandarins, as the mandarins do the emperor"; CMH.R.2, #15, 1813: the duties were said to be so high at Amoy that the junks went elsewhere.

The South China
Coast Showing
the Ports of Call
in the Sino-
Siamese Trade

however, was frequently depicted as the major emporium in the China-Southeast Asian trade network,[10] while Gutzlaff asserted that the trade of Ch'eng-hai "has always been brisk and advantageous."[11] A comparison of the duties at the provincial maritime collectorates is included (Table 2), but it is worth noting here that, since the enforcement of customs regulations depended upon who was in charge of a collectorate at a specific time, a fair degree of variation was possible in the encouragement to, or obstruction of, foreign trade at any given port. The disagreement among sources raises the further possibility that Chinese export trade may have been promoted more vigorously than the import trade, especially as those commenting on high duties and encumbrances were generally referring to trade which entered from Southeast Asia.

The question finally arises as to whether the trade originating in China passed through the same ports as that originating in Siam. Ch'ao-chou fu appears to have been a leading center for the trade of both, followed closely by the southern prefectures of Fukien. Hainan Island sent numerous small junks to Siam, but as they tended to bring less lucrative cargoes,[12] junks originating in Bangkok usually by-passed Hainan on their way to ports on the Chinese mainland. There seems to have been little direct trade from Canton to Siam,[13] although a good deal originated

[10] FO 17/0, p. 30; Crawfurd, *History of the Indian Archipelago*, vol. 3, pp. 522-23; Great Britain: Parliament, House of Commons, Select Committee on Foreign Trade, *Third Report from the Select Committee Appointed to Consider of the Means of Improving and Maintaining the Foreign Trade of the Country: East Indies and China*, Gt. Br., Parliament, Sessional Papers, 1821, vol. 6 [H.C.] 746, pp. 247, 253; Fu Lo-shu, *A Documentary Chronicle of Sino-Western Relations: 1644-1820*, 2 vols. (Tucson: The University of Arizona Press, 1966), vol. 1, pp. 158-59. Amoy and the Bogue were the only ports through which Kwangtung and Fukien junks were permitted to enter or leave the country, and this regulation would naturally have enhanced the position of Amoy and the small ports near the Bogue. The *Kuangchou FC* (see note 6) states that Chinese ocean vessels were to sail to Southeast Asia from Namoa which would appear to contradict the 1727 ruling cited above. It is possible that more latitude was permitted in the late eighteenth and nineteenth centuries as the number of vessels sailing to Southeast Asia increased.

[11] Gutzlaff, *Two Voyages*, p. 134. He calls Ch'eng-hai Ting-hae or Ching-hae-heen which is said to be in the vicinity of Namoa.

[12] Crawfurd, *Embassy*, p. 410; Friedrich Hirth, "The Port of Hai-k'ou," *The China Review* 1,2 (1872): 127: "Their size is commonly 100-159 tons, being the smallest, the poorest, but the most numerous, of all descriptions of Chinese junks carrying on foreign trade."

[13] Skinner, *Chinese Society*, p. 40. Skinner suggests that the reason for the dearth of trade from Canton to Southeast Asia was a lack of motivation by the Cantonese merchants. Foreign trade came to them and they were not forced to seek it out on a regular basis as were merchants from Fukien whose ports were not always open to foreign trade.

Table 2. Selected Hai-kuan Tariffs[a]

Product	Kwangtung	Fukien	Chekiang	Kiangsu
Pepper	0.4.0.0	0.8.0.0[b] 0.7.4.0	0.2.5.9 (0.3.2.0)[c]	0.8.0.0
Cloves	2.0.0.0	2.0.0.0	1.4.4.0 (1.6.0.0)	0.2.0.0
Sticklac	0.4.0.0	0.1.0.0	0.0.8.6 (0.0.7.2)	0.1.0.0
Putchuck	1.0.0.0[d] 0.7.5.0 0.5.0.0	0.4.0.0	X	0.3.0.0
Camphor, Baroos per catty	1.0.0.0 0.8.0.0 0.6.0.0	0.3.0.0	1.4.4.0[e] (1.6.0.0)	0.3.0.0
Cutch	0.3.3.3	0.3.3.3	0.2.1.6 (0.2.4.0)	0.3.3.0
Cardamom, Inferior	0.3.0.0	0.3.0.0	X	0.3.0.0
Lucrabau	0.1.0.0	0.1.0.0	0.0.7.2	0.1.0.0
Betel-nut	0.0.7.0	0.1.0.0	X	0.1.0.0
Ebony	0.1.0.0	0.1.5.6 0.1.2.3	0.1.0.8	0.1.5.0
Elephant Tusk	3.8.0.0 3.4.0.0 3.0.0.0	3.2.0.0[f] 2.5.0.0 2.0.0.0	0.2.3.4[g] 0.1.8.0 0.1.4.4	3.2.0.0 2.5.0.0 2.0.0.0
Deer Horn	0.6.0.0	0.3.0.0[h]	0.2.1.6[h]	0.3.0.0[h]
Buffalo Horn	0.1.0.0	0.0.5.0	0.0.3.6 (0.0.4.0)	0.1.0.0
Rhinoceros Horn	0.1.8.0[i]	0.0.6.0[j]	X	0.0.6.0[j]
Kingfisher Feathers	0.0.4.0[k]	0.0.4.0[k]	0.0.2.4[l] (0.0.3.2)[l]	0.0.4.0[k]

[a] These are the published tariffs of the Board of Revenue: *HPTL*: 1874:54, 63, 65, 69. The duty is calculated according to picul unless otherwise indicated.

[b] The top figure is the duty at Nan-t'ai and Han-chiang. The bottom figure is the duty at Amoy and Ch'üan-chou. The same applies to the duty on ebony.

[c] All figures in parentheses are the duties at Cha-p'u.

[d] These three sets of figures represent the duty on 1st quality, 2nd quality and 3rd quality putchuck—a fragrant root used in the manufacture of joss sticks. The duty on camphor is calculated in the same manner.

[e] The duty on camphor is per 10 catties.

[f] This was the duty at Nan-t'ai and Han-chiang. At Amoy and Ch'üan-chou, all grades were taxed at 2.7.0.0/picul.

[g] The duty on elephant tusk is per 10 catties. The three sets of figures represent large, medium, and small tusk. At Cha-p'u, the duty was calculated per picul: 2.5.6.0; 2.0.0.0; 1.6.0.0.

[h] The duty on deer horn is per 10 catties.

[i] The duty in Kwangtung was calculated per catty.

[j] The duty in Fukien and Kiangsu was calculated per pair.

[k] The duty in Kwangtung, Fukien, and Kiangsu was calculated per 100 *chih* (枝).

[l] The duty in Chekiang was calculated per 8 feathers.

at nearby Chiang-men. Junks from Ningpo and Shanghai reportedly traded with the Indonesian Archipelago and Singapore, but, with the exception of Gutzlaff's testimony that they arrived in Siam from February through April,[14] there is little evidence to suggest that Siam was a regular stop on their itinerary. On the other hand, junks frequently sailed there from Bangkok. Siamese junks proceeding to China appear to have traded at many ports along the entire coast, whereas most of the Chinese junks sailing to Siam departed from two main geographic centers—Ch'ao-chou/southern Fukien and Hainan.

China's internal and external native trade was taxed and regulated by customs collectorates (ch'ang-kuan) scattered throughout the empire. These collectorates, with the exception of five under the direction of the Board of Works, were supervised by the Board of Revenue which formulated commercial regulations and tariffs.[15] Foreign and coastal trade in the southern provinces were controlled by four provincial maritime customs administrations (hai-kuan) in Kwangtung (Kuang-chou), Fukien Chang-chou,[16] Chekiang (Chen-hai), and Kiangsu (Shanghai).[17] These collectorates were established in the latter part of the seventeenth century both to regulate and to tax maritime trade.[18] From each of the central

See also *The Foreign Trade of China Divested of Monopoly, Restriction, and Hazard, by Means of Insular Commercial Stations* (London: Effingham Wilson, 1832), p. 54.

[14] Gutzlaff, *Two Voyages*, p. 44; Crawfurd, *Embassy*, p. 410. Crawfurd states categorically, in fact, that no Shanghai or Ningpo junks sailed to Siam under the Chinese flag. Since these vessels were often owned by people from Fukien, when they arrived in Siam, Crawfurd may have then assumed them to be from ports in Fukien.

[15] E-tu Zen Sun, "The Board of Revenue in Nineteenth-Century China," *Harvard Journal of Asiatic Studies* 24 (1962-63): 194; Fairbank, *Trade and Diplomacy*, pp. 255-58.

[16] Fu, *A Documentary*, vol. 1, p. 61. When the collectorates were established in 1684, Chang-chou was said to be the seat of the *hai-kuan*, but the *TCHT*:1813:16:5a does not indicate that a *hai-kuan* was in existence there, and Fairbank (*Trade and Diplomacy*, p. 255) says it was at Foochow. Administrative changes between 1684 and 1813 may account for the discrepancy.

[17] A collectorate was established at Shanghai to handle duties on ocean vessels as opposed to that set up in Yün-t'ai to handle coastal trade. "General Description of Shanghae and Its Environs, Extracted from Native Authorities," in *Medhurst's Chinese Miscellany* (Shanghai: Mission Press, 1850), p. 131; Fu, *A Documentary*, vol. 2, p. 461; China: Imperial Maritime Customs, *Native Customs Trade Returns*, p. 46.

[18] The Kwangtung and Fukien customs administrations were set up in K'ang-hsi 23 (1684): Fu, *A Documentary*, vol. 1, p. 61; *MCSL:TP*, vol. 8, pp. 745-46. The Chekiang and Kiangnan administrations were established in K'ang-hsi 24 (1685): *Chen-hai HC* [County Gazetteer of Chen-hai], comp. by Yü Yüeh *et al.*, 40 *chüan*, 1879, 9:80a; *Chiang-*

administrative collectorates at the provincial level (ta-kuan)[19] radiated a network of prefectural-level collectorates (tsung-k'ou or hsiao-k'ou) at the county level. The chain of command between these three levels was ambiguous, and in Kwangtung it is difficult to ascertain whether all of the sub-stations in a prefecture were under the direct control of the prefectural collectorate, or whether some were controlled from the central provincial office in Kuang-chou. Figure 1, drawn from the Yüeh hai-kuan chih, indicates that only those sub-stations specifically designated as subordinate to the prefectural collectorate fell within its direct jurisdiction. Logically, however, one would expect that the prefectural-level collectorates would have had some supervisory role over all the stations within the prefectures where they were located.

Collectorates, and the sub-stations under them, were separately charged with three distinct functions. Some were authorized to collect the customs duties on imports and exports (cheng-shui k'ou), some registered vessels (kua-hao k'ou), while others were assigned inspection responsibilities (chi-ch'a k'ou). These three terms, as conveyed in the Yüeh hai-kuan chih, lack functional definitions,[20] but other sources suggest what the obligations of each type of station were. The inspection stations checked incoming and outgoing cargoes, presumably to prevent contraband goods entering or leaving the country.[21] They may also have looked into any irregularities involving the licensing or the illegal entry of foreign merchants to Chinese ports.[22] But the one function they definitely

---

nan TC [Provincial gazetteer of Kiangnan], comp. by Yin-chi-shan et al., 200+4 chüan, 1736, 79:20b.

[19] Of the four provinces in which maritime customs collectorates were situated, only Fukien did not seem to have a ta-kuan (TCHT:1813:16:5a), although the prefectural-level collectorate at Amoy was called a ta-kuan (大館): Hsia-men chih [Gazetteer of Amoy], comp. by Chou K'ai, 16 chün, 5 vols. in 2 (Taipei: T'ai-wan yin-hang, 1961), orig. pub. 1832: 7,197. The Hui-tien gives the impression that more autonomy may have existed within the Fukien maritime customs administration than in the other three provinces because the hai-kuan in Fukien were located at all the major ports, i.e. Nan-t'ai, Amoy, Ch'üan-chou, Han-chiang, An-hai, T'ung-shan, Shih-ma, and Min-an chen.

[20] I should point out that the same terminology was not used in all the texts dealing with the organization of the native customs administration. For instance, in the Hui-tien (TCHT:1813:16:5a-b; TCHT:1899:23:5b): cheng-shui kuei-yin = cheng-shui, kuei-yin = kua-hao, and hsü-ch'a = chi-ch'a. At Amoy, the designatory terminology for the collectorates was again different: ch'ien-liang = cheng-shui and ch'ing-tan =kua-hao (HMC: 7:196).

[21] HMC: 5:166.

[22] MCSL:KP, vol. 6, p. 561b.

	Customs collection stations	Inspection stations	Registration stations
Ch'ao-chou	9	0	10
Kuang-chou	2	5	9
Kao-chou	1 (2)	5 (2)	0 (2)[a]
Ch'iung-chou	10	0	0
Hui-chou	4	3	3
Lei-chou	2	8	0
Lien-chou[b]	2	1	0
Chao-ch'ing[b]	1	0	0

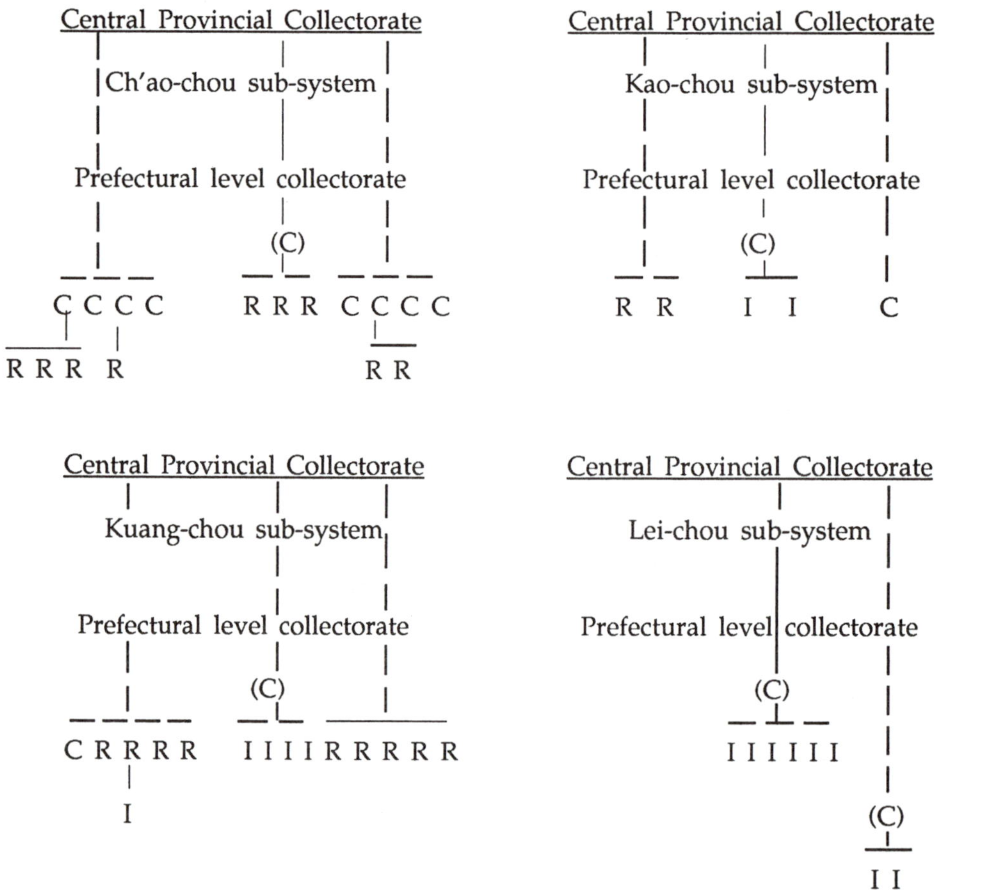

```
Central Provincial Collectorate
   |          |        |
   |Ch'ao-chou sub-system|
   |          |        |
   |          |        |
Prefectural level collectorate
   |          |        |
   |         (C)       |
 _ _ _      _ _ _ _ _
C C C C     R R R  C C C C
 _|_|_             _|_
R R R  R            R R
```

```
Central Provincial Collectorate
    |       |        |
    Kao-chou sub-system
    |       |        |
    |       |        |
Prefectural level collectorate
    |       |        |
    |      (C)       |
  _ _     _|_        |
  R R     I I        C
```

```
Central Provincial Collectorate
   |        |       |
   Kuang-chou sub-system
            |       |
            |       |
Prefectural level collectorate
   |        |       |
   |       (C)      |
 _ _ _ _  _|_ _ _
C R R R R  I I I I R R R R R
 _|
  I
```

```
Central Provincial Collectorate
            |        |
   Lei-chou sub-system
            |        |
            |        |
Prefectural level collectorate
            |        |
           (C)       |
         _ _|_ _     |
         I I I I I    |
                     |
                    (C)
                    _|_
                    I I
```

C = Customs collection station (*cheng-shui k'ou*)
I = Inspection station (*chi-ch'a k'ou*)
R = Registration station (*kua-hao k'ou*)

— — — = direct jurisdiction according to Liang
———— = unspecified jurisdiction

Figure 1. Kwangtung Maritime Customs Administration[c]

[a] The numbers not in parentheses represent Liang's original figures for the functional distribution of the Kao-chou collectorates (*YHKC*:5:1b). In *chüan* 6:20b-30b, however, he says that there were two of each (figures in parentheses).

[b] Neither Lien-chou nor Chao-ch'ing had prefectural-level collectorates.

[c] *YHKC*:5-6: passim. The *Hui-tien* records changes in the native maritime customs administration, and according to the 1813 edition (*TCHT*: 1813:16:5a), Ch'ao-chou rather than An-fu is said to be the Ch'ao-chou prefectural-level collectorate. Chia-tzu rather than Wu-k'an is mentioned as the prefectural collectorate in Hui-chou. Furthermore, Fu-shui kuan is omitted as a customs collection station and six registration stations are omitted. The 1899 edition (*TCHT*:1899:23:5b) adds Pei-hai as a prefectural-level collectorate.

did not perform was the collection of custom duty.[23] Registration stations issued permits or papers to junks. Vessels seeking permits from the Fukien government, depending upon their size, would obtain these papers from the prefectural-level collectorate or one of the county-level sub-stations.[24] These stations also checked a junk's papers upon entry and exit.[25] These three types of collectorates were not always located together in the same prefecture,[26] and the site of a given type of collectorate should provide some indication regarding the nature of that port's commercial activity. Such does not seem to have been the case, however. In Kwangtung, for example, one-third of the duty collectorates were on Hainan Island, while only two were situated in Kuang-chou fu.[27] Even more surprising were the eight inspection stations in Lei-chou fu, although they may have been established on the east coast of the peninsula to check incoming junks from Southeast Asia. This seems unlikely, since junks from the *Nan-yang*, unless coming from the Gulf of Tonkin, sailed around the east coast of Hainan.[28] The only indication of a relationship between collectorate location and commercial activity was the preponderance of registration collectorates in Ch'ao-chou fu and Kuang-chou fu. Since Ch'ao-chou was the center of Kwangtung's native export trade, and many junks were owned by Ch'ao-chou merchants, one would expect a large proportion of the licensing collectorates to have been set up there. Kuang-chou, as the administrative capital of the province, would likewise have been a reasonable location. The rationale behind placing a specific collectorate at a given port is otherwise somewhat obscure.

The multiplicity of collectorates appears to have been more conducive to red tape than to unobstructed commercial relations. The merchants of

[23] *Fu-chien TC* [Provincial gazetteer of Fukien], comp. by Ch'en Shou-ch'i *et al.*, 278+6 chüan, 1868:50:30b.

[24] *HMC*: 5:170.

[25] China: Imperial Maritime Customs, *Native Customs Trade Returns*, Amoy, p. 79.

[26] *YHKC*: 6:33a-40b, 45a-64b. In Lei-chou there were only duty collection and inspection stations, while in Ch'iung-chou only duty collection stations were established.

[27] Although the volume of trade to and from Hainan was not comparable to that entering and leaving Kuang-chou, the difference in the number of collectorates may simply reflect the greater number of ports of entry on Hainan. The trade to Canton was channeled up the river to one destination whereas junks could center a number of Hainanese ports.

[28] *Wu-pei chih*: 240:11a-b. On the other hand, these stations might have been set up to investigate the coastal traffic between Hainan, the mainland and the Vietnamese ports.

Amoy were said to have found it necessary to pay duty separately at a number of collectorates before they were allowed to continue with their business.[29] That the administrative system was so loosely coordinated, however, permitted local collectorates considerable freedom of action. For many years prior to 1807, Siamese junks had anchored at Tung-lung kang in Ch'ao-chou, even though it was not a central provincial collectorate with jurisdiction for regulating the handling of ocean ships. When this infraction came to the attention of the Canton authorities, an order was sent down that the practice was to be discontinued.[30] Yet even this ruling does not seem to have restricted the autonomy of the Ch'ao-chou collectorates, for Siamese junks persisted in stopping at Tung-lung kang in succeeding years.[31] Although province-wide regulations for the conduct of the customs collectorates were enacted, they appear to have been implemented largely at the discretion of the lower-level customs officials.

The commissioners or superintendents of the provincial customs administrations were not all of equal rank, nor were the functions they performed identical. Whereas the superintendent or hoppo at Canton[32] was a member of the Imperial family and this was his only official position, the superintendents elsewhere frequently were concurrent holders of other provincial offices. In Fukien, for example, the Governor-General also served as superintendent of customs, and at Shanghai the responsibility fell to the lieutenant-governor for a brief period.[33] Besides serving as an arbiter in commercial disputes, the superintendent could suggest changes in commercial policy, and he was expected to remit to Peking the revenue expected of the central collectorate in each province by the Board of Revenue.

The customs organizations were staffed by two categories of functionaries: licensed and unlicensed. Unlicensed, or petty, employees were usually local residents engaged by the collectorate to fulfill such tasks as examining and recording exports and imports for the customs house files,

---

[29] China: Imperial Maritime Customs, *Native Customs Trade Returns*, Amoy, p. 79.

[30] *MCSL:KP*, vol. 6, p. 561b. The implication was that the customs station at Tung-lung kang was authorized to handle only small vessels or native junks.

[31] CMH.R.2, #15, 1813.

[32] The Chinese title for the superintendent of the Kwangtung Maritime Customs was either the *Tu-li Yüeh hai-kuan-pu ta-jen* or the *Yüeh hai-kuan chien-tu*.

[33] Sun, "The Board," pp. 195-96; "General Description of Shanghae," p. 131; H. Brunnert and V. Hagelstrom, *Present Day Political Organization of China*, trans. from the Russian by A. Beltchenko and E. E. Moran (Shanghai: Kelly and Walsh, 1912), p. 413 (833b).

maintaining surveillance over cargo in transit between outer anchorages and the port to prevent smuggling, receiving the duties paid into the customs collectorate, and making periodic inspection tours of the sub-stations in a district.[34] The licensed employees maintained a quasi-official position, acting as intermediaries between foreign merchants and the government. The most important of these were linguists, compradores, pilots, and hong merchants. Linguists (*t'ung-shih*) obtained import and export permits, tallied the amount of duty owed, petitioned the government on behalf of foreigners, and prepared the necessary feast for the hoppo when he went to measure ships. Compradores (*mai-pan*) procured supplies for ships and arranged warehouse storage for imports. Pilots (*yin-shui*) reported the arrival of ships, their provenance, name, and the type of cargo they carried. Hong merchants guaranteed the monetary obligations incurred by the merchants they represented.[35]

After requesting a license for one of these positions from the local government, the applicant's financial standing and his dependability were investigated. Hong merchants, in particular, were selected only from among the wealthier merchants of a district. The appointment of merchants who were already well-established was necessary both because the cost of a license and the bribes entailed to acquire one could be high, and also because the hong merchant had to have sufficient resources to cover the duties and fees due on all shipping he was responsible for, even if the amount due was not immediately available for one reason or another.[36] The licensed positions were often handed down within families, provided suitable bribes were paid by the new holder in addition to the licensing charge. Hong merchants were licensed at all the ports handling both Western and native trade, but I have not been able to determine whether the other functionaries mentioned above were to be found in ports other than those visited by Western ships.

Hong merchants were the most prominent members of this semi-official port hierarchy. While the term hong (*hang*) can refer to an individual firm or merchant dealing in a specific commodity, e.g. a silk

---

[34] *Notices Concerning China, and the Port of Canton* (Malacca: Mission Press, 1823), pp. 30-35.

[35] Ibid., pp. 13, 30-34.

[36] George Staunton, trans., *Ta Tsing Leu Lee: being the Fundamental Laws, and a Selection from the Supplementary Statutes of the Penal Code of China* (London: Cadell and Davies, 1810), pp. 156-57; Le P. Guy Boulais, *Manuel du Code Chinois* (Shanghai: Catholic Mission Press, 1924), pp. 336-37; *Ta-Ch'ing lü-li* [The Statutes and Sub-statutes of the Ch'ing Dynasty], ed. San-t'ai *et al.*, 2 *ts'e*, 1740, *chüan* 13, section: *Jen-hu k'uei-tui k'o-ch'eng*.

hong or a tea hong, it has been used below to denote the cover organization to which a number of firms (*chia*) belonged. Hong merchants in Canton were divided into three such organizations. The first of these, and the most adequately treated by previous writers on China,[37] consisted of members of the ocean or foreign hong (*yang-hang*). In 1760 the foreign hong was charged with the sole responsibility for Western shipping[38] and changed its name to the outer ocean hong (*wai-yang hang*). At the same time two other hongs were formed: the *pen-kang hang*[39] to deal with the Siamese tribute envoy and with Siamese trade, and the Fu-ch'ao hang, formerly called the Hai-nan hang[40] to manage the Fukien and Ch'ao-chou native coastal trade arriving at and departing from Canton.[41] The hong merchants were also known as security merchants (*hang-shang* or *pao-shang*) since they were to serve as guarantors for the foreigners they represented. Their primary responsibility was to remit the import and export duties levied on the goods bought and sold by the merchants for whom they were commissioned to act, and to remit the measurement dues levied on merchant ships.[42]

Hong merchants or foreign and native trade brokers were not unique to Canton, but were to be found at all the trading ports (*hai-k'ou*) on the

[37] Perhaps the classic study is H. B. Morse, *The Gilds of China* (London: Longmans, 1909). In addition, scattered references to the Canton hongs can be found in all of the nineteenth-century Chinese commercial guides: Morrison, *Chinese Commercial Guide* (Canton: Chinese Repository, 1848), J. Phipps, *A Practical Treatise on the China and Eastern Trade* (Calcutta: Baptist Mission Press, 1835). In twentieth-century sources, the best coverage is provided by: Dermigny, *Le Commerce à Canton*, vol. 1, ch. 4; vol. 2, ch. 5; Ann B. White, "The Hong Merchants of Canton," (PhD dissertation, University of Pennsylvania, 1967); Liang, *Kuang-tung shih-san hang-k'ao*.

[38] Ling Ch'un-sheng, *Chung-T'ai wen-hua lun-chi*, p. 130. It was later known as the Co-hong (kung-hang).

[39] Since defining this hong as the Canton hong does not indicate its relationship to the management of Siamese trade and tribute, and might, therefore, be misleading, *pen-kang hang* will be used instead throughout the text.

[40] The function of the *Hai-nan hang* is obscure. It may have managed Hainanese trade previous to the formation of the *Fu-ch'ao hang* or it may have been in charge of coastal trade generally.

[41] YHKC: 25:1a-b, 10b-11a; P'eng Tse-i, "Ch'ing-tai Kuang-tung yang-hang," pp. 16-17; *Kuang-tung TC* [Provincial gazetteer of Kwangtung], comp. by Juan Yüan *et al.*, 334+1 *chüan*, 4 vols. (Taipei: Chung-hua ts'ung-shu, 1959), orig. pub. 1822, rep. 1864, 180:22.

[42] *Notices*, p. 34. In 1822 a regulation was enacted that the security merchant had to pay the measurement dues before the port clearance certificate would be granted. The

coast, reaching as far down administratively as the market town (*chen*).[43] At Amoy there were said to have been three security merchants[44] under the general designation of foreign hong,[45] and in Chiang-men, to the south-east of Canton, a north and south hong (*nan-pei hang*) to regulate inward junk traffic which operated under rules similar to those of the Canton hong.[46] Although licensed brokers had a virtual monopoly over the junk trade through their control of marketing, duty and wharfage collection, and the many other services required by merchants, they were probably restrained from abusing their power by fear of diminishing the traffic to their port. Furthermore, the tendency, during the nineteenth century, of Western merchants to deal increasingly with merchants who were not licensed to trade with foreigners[47] acted as a check on the brokers' power. Chinese merchants must have been even more clever at circumventing the hongs' stranglehold on trade than foreigners were.

Perhaps the most serious problem confronting all the brokerage firms[48] during the eighteenth and nineteenth centuries was their propensity to borrow money from foreigners at Canton for speculative purposes,

expectation was that such a move would prevent the hong merchants from owing huge sums to the government which they might not repay in the future; Andrew Watson, trans., *Transport in Transition: The Evolution of Traditional Shipping in China*, Michigan Abstracts of Chinese and Japanese Works on Chinese History, no. 3 (Ann Arbor: University of Michigan Center of Chinese Studies, 1972), pp. 18-19.

[43] Watson, *Transport*, p. 18; Great Britain: Parliament, *Report from the Select Committee*, 1830, vol. 5, p. 300; White, "The Hong," p. 92. White asserts, however, that there were no linguists or foreign hong establishments in Ningpo or Tientsin.

[44] Crawfurd, *History of the Indian Archipelago*, vol. 3, p. 170.

[45] *HMC*: 5:179-80. During the Chia-ch'ing period, the *yang-hang* in Amoy gradually ceased to function because merchants took their business to an unlicensed hong, and by 1813, only one *yang-hang* remained. But in 1821, the Amoy merchant hong (*shang-hang*) assumed responsibility for the *yang-hang*'s affairs. The three hong merchants mentioned by Crawfurd (footnote 44) were undoubtedly associated with this merchant hong.

[46] *Canton Register*, 6/21/1828; Watson, *Transport*, p. 19. These hong members were also called shipping brokers and may be equivalent to licensed *pu-t'ou*. See *TCLL*, *chüan* 15, section: *Szu-ch'ung ya-hang pu-t'ou*.

[47] These merchants were called shopmen (*tien-chia* or *p'u-chia*). Phipps, *A Practical*, p. 148.

[48] The member firms (*chia*) within a hong.

and their consequent indebtedness to Western merchants.[49] This borrowing was not done merely by firms in the foreign hong, but was also resorted to by those within the *pen-kang hang*, which managed Siamese trade. *Pen-kang hang* membership, demanding the solvency of all member firms at all times, fluctuated as it did within the foreign hong. In 1795, three brokerage houses, Ju-shun, I-shun, and Wan-chü, were dissolved because of their inability to discharge debts owed Siamese merchants. The foreign hong was ordered to assume responsibility for repayment of these Chinese debts, but the money was to come from the *pen-kang hang*'s consoo fund. The consoo fund had been established in 1780 to meet the debts of bankrupt hong merchants. In order to build up the fund, a charge of from 3 to 6 percent (*hang-yung*) was levied by the hong on a fixed estimated value of selected imports and exports. The largest sums were derived from the levy on tea and silk exports.[50] That the *pen-kang hang*'s consoo fund was sufficiently ample for member firms to anticipate borrowing against it indicates that the hong handled a reasonable volume of trade. But, as the volume of Siamese trade was by no means equal to that with the West, some discretion was required in taxing it to enlarge the hong's consoo fund. If it were undertaxed, the hong would have no surplus for meeting either demands by local bureaucrats or the needs of bankrupt members. If it were overtaxed, however, the Siamese could lodge complaints with the customs house officials, or they might direct their trade to other ports.[51]

The continuing inability of the *pen-kang hang* to fulfill its monetary obligations led to its abolition in 1795. Since the foreign hong was not willing to assume its obligations, the suggestion was made in 1797 that one firm be reopened as the *pen-kang hang* under the sole direction of a certain Ch'en Ch'ang-hsü. Chi-shan, then the hoppo at Canton, objected to Ch'en's monopolistic and inequitable practices and again abolished the

---

[49] Greenberg, *British Trade and the Opening of China 1800-42*, pp. 20-21, 50-74. Numerous examples are given of the failure of one firm or another in the foreign hong during the late eighteenth and nineteenth centuries.

[50] White, "The Hong," p. 162; John Davis, *China: A General Description of that Empire and Its Inhabitants*, 2 vols. (London: John Murray, 1857), vol. 2, p. 383; Phipps, *A Practical*, pp. 151-52. On page 157 he lists the estimated value of the goods on which the *yang-yung* was levied, but these estimated values may not have been applicable to goods traded by Chinese merchants.

[51] *YHKC*: 25:12b.

[52] *YHKC*: 25:11b-12a. On pages 13b-14a, Liang provides a schedule of the firm's names and the years in which they were to take charge of Siam's affairs.

hong, reassigning its duties to firms in the foreign hong on a rotating basis.[52]

Either people in the nineteenth century still remembered that the *pen-kang hang* had once existed or else it re-emerged following its dissolution by Chi-shan. For there is a Siamese record that in 1862, a "storekeeper" in Canton, referred to in Thai as "Pungan" and said to have been "in charge of affairs concerning Siam," sent letters reminding the Siamese to make up tribute missions they had neglected to send during the 1850s.[53] "Pungun" would seem to be a reference to the *pen-kang hang*, particularly since that organization had earlier managed the Siamese tribute and trade.[54] However, if a firm in the foreign hong had that responsibility in 1862, the "storekeeper" referred to was probably that firm. The use of the word "Pungun" may have been no more than an echo of earlier terminology.[55]

Brokerage organizations, the hongs, besides providing surety for foreigners trading in China, furnished the local bureaucracy with additional income in the form of fees. Fees were demanded when a hong merchant was licensed, when he died and was succeeded by a son, when he profited from securing a ship, and when he sought approval to retire from business. The Amoy hongs were expected to remit specific quantities of such goods as graphite and foodstuffs to the provincial treasury and to local officials.[56] These amounts were not inconsequential, and for the hong merchant to make a profit, the extra charges had to be passed on to the trader in one form or another. Because cargo duty was remitted to the customs treasury by hong merchants rather than by the traders

[53] Cawphraja Thiphakorawong, *The Dynastic Chronicles, Bangkok Era, The Fourth Reign, B.E. 2394-2411 (AD 1851-1868)*, 2 vols., trans. by Chadin Flood with the assistance of E. T. Flood (Tokyo: Center for East Asian Cultural Studies, 1965), vol. 2, p. 281.

[54] Although White, "The Hong," p. 54, says the eighteenth-century *pen-kang hang* was charged with the management of Southeast Asian trade and tribute, the *YHKC*: 25:1b, 10b, indicates that only Siam's trade and tribute were under its purview. The passage on p. 10b: "*Chi i-k'e mao-i*" might be construed as meaning Southeast Asian merchants, but as the Siamese are specifically referred to as *i* (p. 11b), it is likely that the hong dealt primarily, if not solely, with Siamese affairs; Lu Chi-fang, "Ch'ing Kao-tsung," p. 391 supports the latter interpretation.

[55] The tribute and trade of China's other vassals appears to have been organized in a similar fashion. At Foochow, for example, brokers were licensed to manage the commercial and diplomatic affairs of Liu-ch'iu and were said "to profit extensively from it": Fairbank and Teng, "On the Ch'ing," pp. 199-200.

[56] *HMC*: 5:179.

themselves, the firms in a hong could increase the amount collected as duty through "hidden" charges which were then incorporated in the price of goods imported and exported.

The revenue exacted from trade and the trade organizations can be divided into two kinds: duties and fees. Cargo duty as such was theoretically levied in accordance with the tariff determined by the Board of Revenue and was forwarded to the central provincial collectorate. Fees were the numerous miscellaneous charges levied by the customs house staff to supplement their official salaries, and were not reported to the provincial collectorate.[57] Fees had generally become established at customary rates so that merchants knew approximately how much they would be charged. Supernumerary fees were levied on junks entering port, they were paid to the sub-stations to acquire import, export, and re-export certificates, and they were paid on cargoes which would normally be subject to a high tariff rate to prevent these goods from being entered in the collectorate's books at their true value.[58]

The full amount assessed as duty also embraced other charges not included in the Board of Revenue's tariff, although not all of these additional charges were applicable to Chinese native trade. Export duty, for example, was based on a fixed valuation of goods, that valuation having been determined early in the eighteenth century.[59] A 6 percent *ad valorem* charge was superimposed on the export duty, and this represented the payment by a member of the hong for the right to sole management of a specific ship's cargo.[60] Goods shipped in native (or Chinese-style) vessels were not subject to the fixed valuation table,[61] and the export duty assessed on their cargoes was considerably lighter than the duty levied on goods exported in Western ships. Two other charges

[57] China: Imperial Maritime Customs, *Native Customs Trade Returns*, Amoy, p. 80. The collectorates in Amoy were said to collect $30,000 a year in fees and that these were distributed among the employees of the customs stations.

[58] Ibid., pp. 79-80, 111-112; Phipps, *A Practical*, p. 151.

[59] "Hoppo Book." Section three lists the goods exported (including imports which were later re-exported) and the value on which the export duty was to be levied in the early part of the eighteenth century.

[60] White, "The Hong," p. 38. The 6 percent *ad valorem* equaled the *fen-t'ou*; Kuan-cheng [Tariffs] (Nanking: Hsing-cheng yüan. Hsin-wen chü, 1947), p. 1: The export *cheng-shui* rate was originally set at 1.6 percent, but was raised to 2.6 percent at a later date. The *cheng-shui* is said to be the established duty for certain goods, i.e., that published in the central collectorate's tariff manual.

[61] *Canton Register*, 12/26/1833.

subsumed under duties were an additional 30 percent levied on the total amount of duty to defray the cost of converting foreign money into silver of the imperial standard, and a weighing charge assessed on all goods traded.[62] The import tariff was called imperial duty and the rates were published by the Board of Revenue. Amended lists were issued as new kinds of goods were imported. Section one of the Canton tariff sets forth the fixed duties on goods imported during the seventeenth century. As the trade at Canton expanded and imports became more diverse, section two was added, in which the value of the new imports was assessed in terms of items already listed in section one, in order to determine the appropriate charge. For example, in section two one large foreign musket was declared equivalent to one spy glass, to which a duty had been assigned in section one, while scissors, knives, forks, etc. were regarded as equivalent to pairs of eye glasses.[63]

In the commercial guides of the nineteenth century, duties were listed under two categories: "real" duties and "nominal" duties. Real duties, so designated because they were the amounts actually paid into the customs collectorate, included the imperial duty, the 30 percent levy for changing money, the weighing charge, and the 6 percent *ad valorem* charge on exports. Nominal duties, representing the total sum collected on any particular article of trade, included real duties plus the consoo levy and miscellaneous business charges.[64] When real duties were subtracted from nominal duties, the money remaining was given to the hong in charge of the cargo for its own benefit.[65]

Not all of the real duties collected during the year were remitted to Peking; a part was siphoned off by the customs house staff. Each central provincial collectorate was initially assigned a regular quota of duties (*cheng-o* or *o-shui*) to be sent to Peking. That figure, however, was only a fraction of the amount collected by the central provincial office, and, over time, an increasing proportion of the surplus (*ying-yü*) was also demanded by Peking. This surplus, added to the regular quota, com-

[62] Phipps, *A Practical*, p. 150.

[63] See the "Hoppo Book," all of section number two and Friedrich Hirth, "The Hoppo Book of 1753," *JNCBRAS* 17 (1882): 225.

[64] These charges, called *shih-li* or *szele*, were to reimburse the broker for his outlay in handling an article of merchandise. It was equal to the difference between the stated sale price of an article and the true price which a broker paid to the seller.

[65] For instance, if real duties on a picul of cotton were 0.3.4.5 and the nominal duties were 1.5.0.0, the difference of 1.1.5.5 ($1.61) was the amount retained by the hong.

prised the fixed annual quota (*ting-o*) required from the provincial level collectorate.[66] These quotas for the eighteenth century provide one index to the volume of trading activity in China. In 1729, for example, the regular quota for the Shanghai collectorate amounted to 21,480 *tael*, but between 1722 and 1749 the surplus revenue collected there quadrupled from 15,000 tael to 62,000 *tael*,[67] indicating either more efficient collection methods, or a considerable upsurge in coastal and maritime trade. Much of the money collected was required at the provincial level to provision troops, to support public works projects, and to meet other provincial needs. Rather than remit the entire sum to the Board of Revenue in Peking to be reappropriated for provincial use, the provincial-level collectorate was permitted to retain what it needed.[68]

The schedule of import and export duties as published by the Board of Revenue varied not only between provinces, but also between ports within the same province. The duty on sapan wood in Kwangtung, for instance, was a flat rate of 0.1.0.0/picul ($.14) with no distinction made for differences in size.[69] In Fukien, the duty at Nan-t'ai was 0.1.5.0/picul ($.21), at Ch'üan-chou and Han-chiang, 0.1.6.0/picul ($.22), and the same at Amoy, with the exception of sapan wood from Siam which was charged at the rate of 0.1.8.0/picul ($.25).[70] In Chekiang, however, the duty was lower while the deduction for tare, a percentage reduction of a commodity's weight on which the duty was calculated, was taken into account as well. The standard deduction for tare at Canton was 10 percent (*chiu-che*), i.e. goods weighing 100 catties were taxed on the basis of 90 catties.[71] In Chekiang, 20 percent was allowed for tare (*pa-che*) and large wood paid

[66] *TCHTSL*: 1899:234:8b: Kiangsu: regular quota: 23,980, + surplus: 42,000 = annual fixed quota: 65,980 *tael*. *TCHTSL*: 1899:235:9a, 10a, 15a: Fukien: regular quota: 73,549 + surplus: 113,000 = annual fixed quota: 186,549 *tael*. Chekiang (Chen-hai): regular quota: 35,908 + surplus 44,000 = annual fixed quota: 79,908 *tael*. Kwangtung: regular quota: 43,564 + surplus 855,500 = annual fixed quota: 899,064 *tael*. See also Fairbank, *Trade and Diplomacy*, pp. 356-57.

[67] "General Description," pp. 133-34.

[68] Fairbank, *Trade and Diplomacy*, pp. 256-57. These amounts are given under the heading "allotment retained for annual expenditure."

[69] (*Ch'in-ting*) *Hu-pu tse-li*: 1874:69:40a; Phipps, *A Practical*, p. 155: An additional fee was levied on sapan wood of $10/boat and the nominal duty was 0.6.7.0. The figure from the *HPTL* represents only Imperial duty.

[70] *HPTL*: 1874:63:18b.

[71] "The Hoppo Book," p. 66. The weight of the container was not to be subtracted before the 10 percent reduction was made, i.e. average tare.

0.1.4.4/picul ($.20), medium wood paid 0.1.0.8/picul ($.15), and small wood paid 0.0.7.2/picul ($.10).[72] One would expect that a port offering consistently lower duties could have attracted a greater volume of trade, and it becomes clear, therefore, why the merchants from Siam preferred trading in Chekiang over Canton or Amoy (see Table 2).

Native and native-style craft enjoyed certain advantages at Chinese sea ports. The duties levied on the imports and exports carried by these vessels were small, particularly if the junks entered and cleared for other ports on the coast.[73] Although Western observers noted that the duties on Straits produce, the general classification for Siam's exports to China, were high,[74] the Chinese carrying these goods had become adept at disguising the nature of their cargoes. They would transship the goods to a vessel whose cargo had already been examined, and declare that they carried only the more ordinary items, i.e. lumber, oil, charcoal, etc., associated with the coasting trade.[75] At some ports, however, special duty rebates were granted on the goods coming from countries in the Eastern Ocean and from Southeast Asia over and above the amount allotted for tare. At Chapu in Chekiang, for example, the duties on goods from the Eastern Ocean were reduced by 30 percent and those on goods from Annam, by 20 percent, while at the Chekiang provincial collectorate miscellaneous goods from those countries were taxed on the basis of a 30 percent tare, i.e. on 70 percent of their weight, with an additional 10 percent reduction in duty.[76] In Kwangtung, concessions were made for such bulk items as bricks, roofing tiles, jars, firewood, and charcoal, the duty being reduced to 50 percent.[77]

[72] *HPTL*: 1874:65:6a.

[73] FO 17/9, p. 40; Great Britain: Foreign Office, *Returns of the Trade of the Various Ports of China, down to the Latest Period*, Gt. Br., Parliament, Papers by Command, 1847, Foochow, p. 137; Gutzlaff, *Two Voyages*, p. 110. While Fairbank's description of the native tariff system (*Trade and Diplomacy*, p. 317) suggests that the accumulated duty on the cargoes carried in native vessels may have been high because an import, export, and re-export duty could be assessed on them, he nonetheless recognized that this succession of duties was often avoided through individual negotiation.

[74] Great Britain: Foreign Office, *Returns of the Trade*, Foochow, p. 137; Davis, *China*, vol. 1, p. 41.

[75] Great Britain: Foreign Office, *Returns of the Trade*, Foochow, p. 137.

[76] *TCHTSL*: 1899:235:10b-11a.

[77] "Hoppo Book," p. 99.

Port charges were not limited to duties and fees levied simply on cargo. The ships and junks entering and clearing were themselves subject to a similar array of charges. Western ships, however, paid consistently more than Chinese-style junks, both in measurement or tonnage dues, and in the additional fees levied by the employees of the customs stations. On Western ships there were four different port charges: measurement, cumshaw, pilotage, and fees. The two largest items in terms of cash outlay for the Western merchant were measurement and cumshaw or presents, of which the latter alone amounted to 1,950 tael ($2,730) per ship at Canton prior to 1830. Chinese vessels, however, were exempt from the cumshaw, and in tonnage dues were assessed only a fraction of the sum levied on Western ships. Measurement dues were figured according to a junk's picul capacity. This was determined by multiplying the length by the breadth of the junk, the product being the basis on which the dues were levied.[78] Tonnage charges, like customs duties, varied from province to province. Junks at Canton were divided into four categories. The first were Kwangtung junks of four different sizes which went abroad (*ch'u-yang*) to foreign countries. While each size paid proportionately less as its capacity decreased, all vessels in class 1, no matter how large, paid at the one rate of 15 *tael* per *chang*.[79] The second category was for junks

[78] China: Imperial Maritime Custom, *Native Customs Trade Returns*, p. 73. A more sophisticated example is given for Foochow:

Full length is measured and divided by 1.67 = length of cargo space (LCS).
Breadth of beam is measured at both ends and across the middle of the cargo space. The three were added, then divided by three = mean breadth (MB).
The depth was measured at both ends of the cargo space. The two were added and divided by two = mean depth (MD).
LCS x MB x MD ÷ 55.68 = picul capacity.
LCS x MB x MD ÷ 93.48 = capacity in tons.

The "Hoppo Book," pp. 62-66, 73-78 and the *TCHTSL*: 1899:234-35 calculate only on the basis of L x B.

[79] "Hoppo Book," pp. 62-64:

Class #1: junks with L above 7 *chang* 3 *ch'ih* (73 feet) and B above 2 *chang* 2 *ch'ih* (22 feet). L x B = 15 *tael*/*chang*

```
    7.3
  x 2.2              chang rounded off to nearest
    146              decimal = 16
   146                     x 15  tael
 16.06 chang                80
                            16
Total Measurement:        240  tael = $336.
```

which went abroad (*ch'u-hai*)[80] to trade in spices, and they paid a flat rate of three *tael* per *chang*. The last two categories were salt and coasting junks which were smaller than the vessels trading abroad. The charges on Chinese domestic junks were to be levied twice a year, whereas Chinese ocean-going vessels were theoretically to pay each time they entered port, as were Western ships.[81] According to the measurement charges listed for Western ships at Canton, Chinese merchant junks paid one-sixth the amount that the former were assessed; an obvious saving for those shipping in Chinese-style vessels.[82] In Kiangsu, ocean-going trading junks with a beam (breadth) of between one and two *chang* were charged one *tael* per *ch'ih*, i.e. on 10 to 19 feet they would pay 10 to 19 *tael* and up.[83] The charges at Han-chiang, Nan-t'ai, Ch'üan-chou, and Amoy were levied at the rate of five *mace* per *ch'ih*, based on the width at the beam. If a vessel measured between nine and ten *ch'ih* (9 to 10 feet) at the crossbeam, it was taxed on approximately 60 percent of its width. At this

Class #2: L = 7 *chang*
B = 2 *chang*   L x B = 13 *tael/chang*

Class #3: L = 6 *chang*
B = 1.8 *chang*   L x B = 11 *tael/chang*

Class #4: L = 5 *chang*
B = 1.6 *chang*   L x B = 9 *tael/chang*

[80] These vessels may have been smaller than those in the first category and have traded to countries in closer proximity to China (see Chapter III).

[81] Not only did they pay each time, but the Western ships were also measured each time. The Chinese believed that the space to be measured could be altered, and that by wedging the masts forward this distance would be shortened. Just such techniques were outlined in an early nineteenth-century sailing manual: Elmore, *The British Mariner's Directory and Guide to the Trade and Navigation of the Indian and China Seas*, p. 132.

[82] "Hoppo Book," pp. 76-77: The dues on Western Ocean ships of the largest type—comparable to class #1 of Chinese junks (see fn. 79):

L = 7 *chang* 4 - 5 *ch'ih*   7.5
B = 2 *chang* 3 - 4 *ch'ih*   x 2.4
                                   300
The duty would be 1,400 *tael*   150
as opposed to 240 tael for a   18.00 *chang* at 77.7 *tael/chang*
for a Chinese junk.

[83] *TCHTSL*: 1899:234:9a.

rate, a junk would pay three *tael*.[84] But if the vessel measured eighteen *ch'ih* or over (18 feet and above), it was taxed on only 40 percent of its width at the crossbeam.[85] Larger vessels were therefore taxed more lightly in proportion to their size than the smaller ones. The Fukien rates, taking into account the percentage deduction, were lower than the Kiangsu rates, and more on a par with those in Kwangtung. Since all of these rates were considerably less than the amounts applied to Western ships at Canton, however, the slight variation in provincial rates was not significant.

Asian shipping benefitted from reductions in tonnage dues much as native shipping did. Trading junks from Annam were granted a 30 percent reduction in Kiangsu, while dues on Eastern Ocean junks were reduced by 40 percent. An additional privileged exemption percentage (*yu-mien*) was superimposed on the above reductions,[86] making the total reductions for Annamese vessels 40 percent, and for Eastern Ocean, 50 percent.[87]

Besides customs duty and measurement fees, Chinese junk owners and masters were charged licensing and permit fees at the ports where their vessels docked, and especially at the county from which their papers were issued. Before a new junk was built, permission had to be secured from the county magistrate and guarantees of the owner's financial reliability provided by neighbors and local shippers. All details concerning the size of the crew, tonnage, number of masts, and the like were recorded, and the junk would then be registered according to its prescribed classification.[88] Every junk was required to carry registration papers (*p'ai-chao* or *ch'uan-chao*), and at the time of application a fee was

[84] The rate is calculated as follows:

  5 *mace* x 6 feet (60 percent of ten feet) = 30 *mace* = 3 *tael*.

[85] *TCHTSL*: 1899:235:9b.

[86] *TCHTSL*: 1899:234:9a-b.

[87] *TCHTSL*: 1899:234:9a-b. The benefits granted coastal trade were even greater. Kwangtung and Fukien junks trading to Kiangsu between the third and eighth months were given a rebate of 30 percent, but if they came from the ninth to the second months, the duties were cut by half. With the privileged exemption percentage added, their rebates would amount to from 40 to 60 percent, depending upon the months in which they arrived. "A General Description," p. 135: these reductions were said to have been levied on cargo rather than tonnage, but this seems to reflect a misreading of the Chinese.

[88] *Kuang-chou FC*: 1879:74:14a.

paid to the county from which they were issued. These licenses were to be renewed yearly, but because the licensing fees were substantial, the practice fell into abeyance. By the mid-nineteenth century few Chinese junks carried licenses that were up-to-date.[89] A junk was also issued papers before clearing port. These were to be produced at each customs station at the ports where the junk called, to be signed and sealed. When the voyage was over, and the junk had returned to its home port, the papers were canceled. New papers were issued upon payment of a fee before another voyage was begun.[90] In this way the movement of junks along the coast could be followed, since the arrival and departure dates as well as the composition of the cargo were entered on the papers.[91] Such a procedure was used for Siamese junks as well, if they were going from one Chinese port to another. When, in 1807, several junks requested permission to travel from Tunglung kang in Ch'ao-chou to sell sugar in Chekiang and Kiangsu, they were issued papers by a registration station in Ch'eng-hai hsien[92] enabling them to do so. By granting their request, the customs officer's action implied that Siamese vessels were considered identical to Chinese, and that they were to be treated as any other Chinese coasting junk.[93]

The foregoing discussion has been concerned with the institutionalized aspects of China's native overseas trade. Treatment at this level is a comparatively simple matter because of the numerous governmental compendia setting forth the structure of the customs administrative apparatus and the regulations it was to enforce.[94] A wide range of diversity was possible, however, even within as small an "institution" as

[89] China: Imperial Maritime Customs, *Decennial Reports on the Trade . . . 1882-91*, p. 599.

[90] Ibid., p. 403. At Wenchow in Chekiang it was reported that the magistrate received 1,300 cash ($1.82), the sub-prefect received 1,100 cash ($1.54), and the commandant of the city garrison received 600 cash ($.84).

[91] China: Imperial Maritime Customs, *Native Customs Trade Returns*, Foochow, p. 73.

[92] Tung-lung kang in Ch'eng-hai hsien was a duty collectorate, but there was also a registration station at Chang-lin which was directly under the jurisdiction of Tung-lung kang. It was undoubtedly from the Chang-lin station that the papers were issued to the Siamese vessels: *YHKC*: 6:12b.

[93] *MCSL:KP*, vol. 6, p. 561b; "General Description," pp. 135-36.

[94] At the functional level, however, there is little documentation describing the actual operation of the native trade. The only evidence I have been able to locate on Siamese shipping is a revenue statement from 1813 (CMH.R.2, #15, 1813) listing the duties and fees paid by Siamese vessels at Canton (see Appendix G). More evidence of this sort is necessary if a complete examination of the native customs is to be undertaken.

the native maritime customs. The provincial and inter-provincial variations attest to a degree of decentralization, possible perhaps only because of the seeming insignificance of maritime revenue to the central government in comparison with other forms of revenue. Freedom from a coherent, centrally imposed economic policy provided greater opportunities for developing a trade administration to best serve the needs of each province. The role of the native maritime customs organization and its functions within the framework of the Ch'ing state can be clarified only by further investigation of individual provincial networks, and of the rules and regulations appertaining to each.

3

Chinese Maritime Sailing

Chinese maritime trade was carried from earliest times in vessels referred to as "junks" by Europeans, despite the familiarity of Chinese merchants with the square-rigged ships used by Western merchants throughout the Asian maritime world. A "junk," as defined by Yule and Burnell, is "a large Eastern ship; especially . . . a Chinese ship."[1] The term is said to have been derived from the Javanese *jong* or Malay *ajong*, "a ship or large vessel."[2] While some doubt exists regarding its etymological base in Chinese, it is commonly equated with the Chinese word, *ch'uan*,[3] a non-specific designation for boats. All of the junks trading to Southeast Asia were called *ch'uan*, but they were representative of distinctive varieties. The general characteristics which distinguished a junk from a Western ship were its rigging, mat sails with bamboo stays, a rounded, keel-less bottom, bulkhead construction, and decorative motifs. Square-rigged vessels, with their greater cargo capacity and greater speed, should presumably have appealed to Chinese merchants, but junk carriage from China to Southeast Asia continued well into the nineteenth century. Southeast Asian, particularly Siamese, cargoes for the China market were also carried in Chinese-style vessels, even though these nations turned increasingly, from the 1840s, to the use of Western-style ships for other inter-Asian, and later Chinese, trade.

The preponderance of Chinese-style craft in the Sino-Siamese trade was related, in part, as noted in the previous chapter, to the concessions granted these vessels in both tariff and measurement fees at the Chinese

---

[1] H. Yule and A. C. Burnell, *Hobson-Jobson* (London: Murray, 1903), p. 472.

[2] Ibid.

[3] Ibid.; Joseph Needham, *Science and Civilization in China* (Cambridge: Cambridge University Press, 1971), vol. 4, pt. 3, p. 380; Ivon Donnelly, "Early Chinese Ships and Trade," *The Mariner's Mirror*, 11 (1925): 353-54; Crawfurd, *History*, vol. 3, p. 173.

and Siamese ports where they called. Junks sailing to Chinese ports were taxed at a lower rate than that collected on square-rigged vessels, while the cargoes they carried were generally subject to a less burdensome tariff than the goods carried in Western ships.[4] Furthermore, junks were free to trade at a larger number of Chinese ports and were not restricted to the one port of Canton as Western vessels came to be during the eighteenth century. A greater market was therefore available to Asian merchants shipping by junk. In the Chinese regulations for taxing ocean-going vessels, junks were classified according to their size, function, number of masts, and trading destination. If the proper specifications for native vessels were adhered to, foreign ownership and registry were of little importance in levying the tariff and port charges. Similar concessions were available to junks at Siamese ports, but they were not specifically related to the style of the vessel as they were in China. While a smaller measurement charge was levied on junks and a lower duty on their goods, and while Chinese merchants could purchase and sell their cargoes more conveniently than Westerners,[5] the purpose of these advantages was to maintain the good-will of the Chinese and to restrict the economic power of European traders.

From the fourth decade of the nineteenth century, however, the situation began to change and the junks engaged in the trade between China and Siam were gradually superseded, first by square-rigged vessels, and later by steamers. Events in both China and Siam were responsible for the shift away from junk transport. By opening Amoy, Foochow, Ningpo, and Shanghai to Western trade, article II of the Treaty of Nanking removed the necessity that Siamese merchants use junks to gain entry into those ports. In Siam, a growing awareness of the need to seek accommodation with the West culminated in the Anglo-Siamese treaty of 1855. The concessions formerly enjoyed only by Chinese were now extended to Western trade, and Chinese junks were soon quickly

[4] See Chapter II for a fuller explanation of the reductions. According to one source, the Dutch also took advantage of these concessions in the seventeenth century by shipping merchandise between Batavia and China under the Dutch flag, but in Chinese-style junks manned by Chinese: Saxe Bannister, *A Journal of the First French Embassy to China 1698-1700* (London: Cautley Newby, 1859), p. 148.

[5] Nineteenth-century accounts frequently mention the superior position of Chinese shippers in Siam's trade, for it was a source of great annoyance to the Western merchants of the time: *The Burney Papers*, vol. 1, Appendix C #19, Feb. 13, 1826, pp. 169, 177; Crawfurd, *Journal of an Embassy to the Courts of Siam and Cochin China*, p. 175; Crawfurd, *History*, vol. 3, p. 183; Moor, *Notices of the Indian Archipelago, and Adjacent Countries*, pp. 207 ff.

replaced by the speedier and more capacious square-rigged vessels. Junks continued to share in the trade into the twentieth century, but their numbers steadily diminished. Before the kinds of junks engaged in the trade between China and the *Nan-yang* are described, the Chinese classifications for junks and the regulations appertaining to each category will be discussed.

Junks were not classified uniformly in Chinese official documents, complicating any attempt to formulate a standardized terminology for these craft. The same term might be employed in a number of sources to describe several different kinds of vessels. While three fairly comprehensive terms—merchant, ocean, and foreign—gained currency in provincial maritime regulations and in provincial histories as a means of denoting vessels capable of engaging in ocean travel, they reflected extensive regional variation and local usage. In the *Hsia-men chih*, for example, merchant vessels (*shang-ch'uan*)[6] were defined generally as those which traded in the inner ocean, i.e. the sea between Taiwan and the coast of Fukien. Merchant vessels were then subdivided into two specific types: those which traded to Taiwan (*heng-yang ch'uan*)[7] and those involved in the coastal trade to the north and south of Amoy (*fan-ts'ao ch'uan*).[8] The junks classified as merchant vessels in Amoy would not necessarily have been so designated elsewhere, especially as their names were primarily an indication of the localities to which they traded and reflected Amoy usage only. In Kiangsu, for example, *all* vessels, with the exception of fishing craft, were described as merchant vessels[9] for the purpose of determining measurement fees. But the number of times a merchant vessel was to be taxed depended on whether it was classified

[6] *HMC*: 5:166. Merchant junks and fishing junks (*yü-ch'uan*) were often subsumed under the same rubric for regulatory purposes, even though the latter were smaller vessels (*HMC*: 5:172-75). Merchant vessels were also called *min-ch'uan* in contradistinction to official vessels (*kuan-ch'uan*): China: Imperial Maritime Customs, *Decennial Reports . . . 1882-91*, p. 487.

[7] Another type of *heng-yang ch'uan* was the *t'ang ch'uan* which transported sugar from Taiwan to Tientsin and was somewhat larger than the regular *heng-yang ch'uan*: *HMC*: 5:166.

[8] Those bound for Chang-chou, Namoa, and Kwangtung were called *nan-ts'ao* and those sailing to Wen-chou, Ningpo, Shanghai, Tientsin, and further north were called *pei-ts'ao*: *HMC*: 5:166.

[9] *TCHTSL*: 1899:234:9a. These were Annam *shang-ch'uan*, Eastern Ocean *shang-ch'uan* and Fukien/Kwangtung *shang-ch'uan*.

as one which sailed abroad or as one which merely engaged in trade.[10] The former undoubtedly traded once they arrived at their destination, so the distinction between the two probably was that the latter classification was applied only to junks engaging in coastal trade, although the regulations do not make this distinction explicit.

Ocean vessels (yang-ch'uan) were said to be the size of big merchant junks and to carry three masts made of foreign wood.[11] They were not square-rigged foreign vessels, but Chinese junks engaged in the longer ocean voyages such as those to the Nan-yang. Merchant vessels might also be classified as ocean vessels, but only if they sailed beyond Chinese coastal waters. The distinction between ocean vessels and sea vessels (hai-ch'uan) is somewhat more complex, however, and few sources provide a precise definition of the latter.[12] In the Kwangtung regulations, native junks were classified according to the destination of their voyage. They were therefore classified as either large junks going abroad to foreign countries (yang-ch'uan) or those going to sea to trade in spices (hai-ch'uan).[13] Again, the distinction between these two classes is not made explicit. Ocean vessels were apparently larger than sea vessels and the designation, ocean vessel, should perhaps be understood to refer to junks capable of making the longer sea voyages required in trade to the Nan-yang. Sea and merchant vessels, though they might trade to Hainan,

[10] *TCHTSL*: 1899:234:9a. *Shang-ch'uan* which went abroad (*ch'u-yang*) were taxed each time they left port while those engaging in trade (*mao-i*) were taxed twice a year. *Shang-ch'uan* was also a designation for vessels in Chekiang (*TCHTSL*: 1899:235:10a), but does not appear to have been used in reference to Kwangtung junks (*TCHTSL*: 1899:235:15b-16a).

[11] *HMC*: 5:177.

[12] *TCHTSL*: 1899:235:9b. The measurement for Fukien *hai-ch'uan* is provided, but the characteristics distinguishing them from small merchant vessels are not explained; Boulais, *Manuel du Code Chinois*, p. 444, #973. The punishment for people who built *hai-ch'uan* and then sold them to foreigners was the decapitation of the guilty party and the exile of his cohorts.

[13] *TCHTSL*: 1899:235:16a; "Hoppo Book," pp. 62, 64: "*Pen-sheng ch'u-yang fa-ko wai-kuo*" and "*Ch'u-hai mao-i hsiang-liao.*" The latter were also called *ts'ao-pai ch'uan*, and the similarity in name with the Fukien merchant vessels strengthens the identification of *hai-ch'uan* as merchant junks. Moreover, in Mayer's article, "Chinese Junk Building," *Notes and Queries on China and Japan* 1.12 (1867): 170-71, *ts'ao-ch'uan* were said to be the trading junks of Kwangtung. According to the *Kuang-chou FC*: 1879:74:24a, black and white *ts'ao-ch'uan* were used to transport passengers and goods. The trading vessels of Ningpo were also called *Wu-ts'ao*. See footnote 45 below.

Taiwan, and possibly the Gulf of Tonkin, probably should be understood to refer generally to carriers between Chinese ports.[14]

The basic feature differentiating junks from foreign sailing vessels (*fan-ch'uan* or *chia-pan ch'uan*)[15] was the latter's keel construction,[16] since a keel was seldom found on Chinese junks. The rigging, size, and overall construction of foreign sailing ships further marked them as non-Chinese vessels.[17] All Western shipping and certain of the Eastern Ocean craft were included within this category at Canton, but it is unclear whether the Eastern Ocean vessels were owned by Asian merchants or whether they were Western ships from the Philippines or Japan. For example, in the regulation book of the Kwangtung maritime customs collectorate, Eastern Ocean vessels are divided into four categories: large ships with keels (*ta chia-pan ch'uan*), other ships with keels and black and white merchant vessels (*chia-pan ch'uan* and *ts'ao-ch'uan*), and two categories of vessels for which the measurement fees are given, but no names.[18] This division may be peculiar to Kwangtung since the Eastern Ocean vessels sailing to Kiangsu and Chekiang do not seem to have been divided in a similar fashion. Kwangtung categories one and two, with the exception of the *ts'ao-ch'uan*, probably refer to Western ships from Luzon or Batavia, although they may well have been manned by Chinese.[19] The *ts'ao-ch'uan* and boats in categories three and four, on the other hand, were very likely junks, either owned by Southeast Asians or Japanese and manned by

[14] Lan Ting-yuan, in his essays on the *Nan-yang* (HCCSWP: 83:14a), offers further evidence that size and sea-worthiness were the primary features distinguishing ocean from merchant vessels. He argued that Chinese trade with the *Nan-yang* did not encourage piracy because pirate boats were not able to follow ocean vessels (*yang-ch'uan*), which were large and could sail against the wind, out to sea. Their victims were rather the merchant vessels (*shang-ch'uan*) trading between Chekiang and Kwangtung.

[15] *HMC*: 5:181; "Hoppo Book," pp. 73-74, 76-77.

[16] *HMC*: 5:181. Hence the alternative name of *chia-pan ch'uan* (boats with keels) which is equivalent to the *kampan* or square-rigged vessels mentioned in Thai sources: Chaen Patchusanon, *Prawat Kanthahanrüa Thai* [A history of Thai naval affairs] (Bangkok: Krom Saraban Thahanrüa, 1966), p. 46. *Chia-pan ch'uan* are also the "kea-pan" and "kapan" mentioned in nineteenth-century Western sources: Gutzlaff, *Two Voyages*, p. 87 and *Canton Register*, 12/26/1833.

[17] According to Lan Ting-yuan, foreign vessels were, moreover, stronger than Chinese, they cost less to build, and the Chinese themselves often bought foreign wood and materials for the vessels they built: *HCCSWP*: 83:14a.

[18] "Hoppo Book," pp. 73-74, 76-77.

[19] Chang Yu-kwai, *Foreign Trade and Industrial Development of China*, p. 2.

Chinese, or both owned and operated by non-Chinese.[20] Junks trading to the *Nan-yang* were always classified as ocean vessels. Their construction, and the rules to which they were subject, will be considered in the following pages.

Chinese junks trading throughout Southeast Asia in the nineteenth century were commonly described by contemporary observers as either "green-headed" (*lü-t'ou*) or "red-headed" (*hung-t'ou*) vessels.[21] According to a statute in the Fukien provincial regulations, all junk hulls from the bow to the crossbeam, and the upper half of the mast, were to be painted a certain color. The vessel's provenance, name, and registration number were to be engraved on both sides of the bow, then filled in using paint of a different color. Fukien junks were green with red characters and Kwangtung vessels were red with blue characters—hence the designation green- and red-headed.[22] Bow color provided a ready means of identification to the authorities at the ports where the vessels traded, and a junk's registration papers could be checked against this color. Although ocean vessels were in fact merely larger versions of merchant junks, they were permitted to exceed the construction and crew specifications governing the latter. The crossbeam of merchant junks was a measure eighteen feet or less and the crew was to be comprised of no more than twenty-eight men. Ocean vessels, on the other hand, could measure up to thirty feet total width, and would require a crew of eighty. Crew size was proportionate to the width of the vessel and as that decreased, so too

[20] That Eastern Ocean vessels were considered Asian vessels gains further credibility from the customs regulations of Kiangsu and Chekiang which granted reductions in their measurement charges and on the goods they carried. Such concessions were rarely made for Western ships. *TCHTSL:* 1899:234:9a, 235:11a.

[21] China: Imperial Maritime Customs, III.-Miscellaneous Series: no. 3, *Port Catalogues of the Chinese Customs' Collection at the Austro-Hungarian Universal Exhibition*, Vienna, 1873 (Shanghai: Imperial Maritime Customs' Press, 1873), p. 399; Henry Sirr, *China and the Chinese: Their Religion, Character, Customs and Manufactures*, 2 vols. (London: Orr, 1849); vol. 2, p. 137; Crawfurd, *History*, vol. 3, p. 180; *Singapore Chronicle*, 4/28/1831.

[22] *HMC:* 5:167-68: Junks from Chekiang were white with green characters and those from Kiangnan were blue with white characters. Boulais, *Manuel*, p. 448, #986; *Fu-chien sheng-li:* 23:616; Some junks apparently had the name and registration number painted on the sails: FO 17/9, p. 39. See also John Slade, *Notices on the British Trade to the Port of Canton* (London: Smith, Elder, 1830), p. 87. The entire bow was not solidly painted in the color designated. From later descriptions of these junks, it seems that the color was painted in a strip under the bulwarks to indicate provincial origin, and that additional colors were daubed about on the hull: G. R. G. Worcester, *Junks and Sampans of the Yangtze*, 2 vols. (Shanghai: Statistical Department of the Inspectorate General of Customs, 1947), vol. 1, p. 154.

did the number of sailors.[23] A further indication of the greater size of ocean junks was the number of masts they were allowed to carry. While merchant vessels were restricted to two, ocean junks could be built with three.[24] As we see below, however, junks trading abroad carried up to five masts, depending on the type of vessel involved, and the two or three mast regulation may refer only to Amoy, Fukien, or Kwangtung ocean junks. It becomes clear, nonetheless, that the Chinese appreciated that the longer distances involved in voyages to the *Nan-yang* or *Tung-yang* demanded more substantial, speedier vessels than were required for coastal trade.

Chinese reliance on natural products over manufactured articles was strikingly apparent in the materials used in junk construction. Neither cloth nor iron were relied upon to the extent they were in the construction of square-rigged vessels. Sails were usually made of rattan with bamboo stays, anchor cables were woven from palm fiber, the hull, nails, and anchor were cut from iron-wood, and a special caulking material was developed from a wood oil[25] mixed with limestone. Iron was not used on junks primarily to prevent damage to the lodestone.[26] The rudder, tiller, bulkheads, longitudinal wales, and other supportive members were generally fashioned from iron-wood because of its exceptional durability. The supply was limited, and junks were forbidden to sail abroad when the K'ang-hsi Emperor discovered they were sold to foreigners rather than returning to China.[27] Thereafter, supplies of wood for shipbuilding came to be imported increasingly from Siam, Annam,

[23] *HMC*: 5:166-67; *Kuang-chou FC*: 1879:74:14a. To gauge the size of a merchant vessel with a beam of 18 feet see the Foochow Pole junk in Worcester, *Junks*, vol. 1, p. 142. According to Fairbank (*Trade and Diplomacy*, p. 311), the crew was figured at 10 to 15 men per 100 tons.

[24] *HMC*: 5:166, 177.

[25] Friedrich Hirth, "The Geographical Distribution of Commercial Products in Kwangtung, *The China Review* 2,6 (1873-74): 379. Hirth states that the oil was from the Dryandra seed of the *Wu-t'ung* tree. The seeds actually came from the Dryandro Cordata or *Yu-t'ung* tree rather than from the *Wu-t'ung*, whose seeds were an ingredient used in the preparation of moon cakes: G. A. Stuart, *Chinese Materia Medica* (Shanghai: American Presbyterian Mission Press, 1911), pp. 156-57, 423.

[26] *Kuang-chou FC*: 1879:74:24b.

[27] Mark Mancall, "The Ch'ing Tribute System: An Interpretive Essay," in *The Chinese-World Order*, ed. John King Fairbank, (Cambridge: Harvard University Press, 1968), p. 88.

and Hainan, or the entire junk was built in Siam and subsequently sold in China.[28]

Ocean junks were permitted to carry weapons as protection against pirates, although the quantity and type were strictly regulated. For instance, one cannon, eight light guns, ten short swords, ten bows and arrows, and no more than thirty catties of gun powder were allowed on junks sailing to the Eastern and Southern Oceans.[29] The rationale behind limiting the quantity of arms was to prevent ocean junks themselves from turning to piracy. Examining officials at the customs collectorates were subject to stringent penalties if they failed to stop vessels carrying excessive weaponry.[30] They were also to ascertain upon a junk's return, whether it carried as many weapons as were recorded at its departure in order to prevent the sale of arms abroad or to off-shore pirates.[31] A further ordinance enacted both to protect and to control vessels trading abroad provided for their organization into groups of ten. Each vessel was held responsible for the others, with punishment directed against all in the group for an illegality committed by one, unless the malefactor was turned in to the local authorities by the remaining nine.[32]

In order to take advantage of the lower charges levied on native vessels at Chinese ports, junks were required to conform to particular forms of construction and rigging. Many Western writers were to observe that "the least deviation . . . would subject (them) at once to foreign charges and foreign duties, and to all kinds of suspicion."[33] Junks trading to China from Southeast Asian countries were accorded the same privileges as domestic Chinese trading vessels "if constructed and fitted out after the customary model."[34] The bias in favor of Chinese-style vessels apparently remained even after square-rigged ships were granted equal

[28] G. R. G. Worcester, "Six Craft of Kwangtung," *The Mariner's Mirror* 45 (1959): 134; Great Britain: Parliament, *Report from the Select Committee*, vol. 5, 1830, p. 299; Roberts, *Embassy to the Eastern Courts of Cochin-China, Siam, and Muscat* (New York: Harper, 1837), p. 311; Morrison, *Chinese Commercial Guide*, p. 164.

[29] *HMC*: 5:178.

[30] *Kuang-chou FC*: 1879:74:14b.

[31] *Kuang-tung TC*: 1822:180:3308.

[32] *TCLL*: 1740:20, section: *Szu-ch'u wai-ching chi wei-chin hsia-hai*: 3b; Boulais, *Manuel*, p. 445, #975.

[33] Great Britain: Parliament, *Report from the Select Committee*, vol. 5, 1830, p. 300; *Canton Register*, 6/17/1833.

[34] Great Britain: Parliament, *Report from the Select Committee*, vol. 5, 1830, p. 300.

access to the treaty ports, to the extent that the Siamese were said to attempt to disguise their square-rigged ships by attaching a woven bamboo mat, on which were painted two eyes, on either side of the bow. The port authorities, supposedly believing them to be junks or wishing to give them preferential treatment, let them enter and trade as junks from Siam had previously.[35] However apocryphal this example may be, it does indicate that Siamese merchants believed they must observe the traditional patterns of junk construction. Chinese junks were not all identical, however, and the various modifications in their build represented adaptations to the physical features of the localities where they traded.

While Chinese sources provide us with a broad spectrum of information regarding junks, describing the general aspects of their construction, the ocean regions in which they were best adapted to sail, the manner in which they were regulated, the composition of their crews and so forth, present-day writings in Western languages make more readily accessible data about the kinds of junks commonly used in China's native foreign trade, and the structural variations among them. It is to these accounts that we will now turn.

Chinese maritime vessels have been divided by Western scholars into two general categories: those which sailed to and from the north of Hangchow Bay—the northern type, and those sailing to and from the south of it—the southern type. Although both the northern and southern styles exhibited structural similarities, certain features were unique to each. Northern-style craft, with one exception, were rarely used in trade with the *Nan-yang*. Siamese junks were reported to have traded as far north as Tientsin,[36] but there is no evidence that junks from the Gulf of Pechili ever sailed to Siam. Junks hailing either from northern ports or trading principally in northern waters displayed the following characteristics: a flat bottom, a large, square rudder which could be raised or lowered beneath the junk's bottom to act as a stabilizer in the absence of a keel, decks flush with the hull (no bulwarks), a bluff box bow, a wide stern from which projected an upward stern gallery, three to five masts, square sail-peaks and leeches[37] (Figure 2) with a multitude of bamboo

[35] Anuman Rajadhon, *Tamnan Sunlakakon* [History of the customs department] (Bangkok: privately pub., 1939), p. 22.

[36] FO 17/9, p. 13; Gutzlaff, *Two Voyages*, p. 110.

[37] Peak: the upper outer corner of a lugsail; the upper outer end of a yard. Leech: the borders or edges of a sail which are more or less perpendicular. The fore-leech is generally called the luff.

battens to secure them, and few decorative motifs.[38] Such junks were well adapted to navigating the predominantly shallow estuaries of the northern waters for which a flat bottom and movable rudder were essential.

Junks trading from south of Hangchow Bay tended to have rounder bottoms, higher decks, a semi-keel-like construction off the centerboard, a rounder stern, a narrower and deeper, or fenestrated and rhomboidal rudder,[39] two to three masts, mat sails with four to five battens spreading fan-like over the sail, rounded sail-peaks and leeches, and numerous decorative motifs across the stern and along the hull. Bulkhead construction was common to both the northern and southern styles, proving particularly useful in trading vessels engaged in long overseas voyages since cargo could be transported with the knowledge that, if one compartment should leak, the others would remain dry. Junk construction was not restricted to one geographic region and the high degree of maritime coastal communication through trading and fishing led to numerous structural borrowings, with some northern junks adopting certain features of southern junks and vice versa.

One junk called either the Kiangsu or Pechili Trader[40] appears to have been the only junk conforming to the characteristics of northern-style vessels that traded with countries in the *Nan-yang*. Although more at home in the Yangtze estuary and shallower waters off the northern coast, it was capable of managing the hazardous conditions of the Southern Ocean.[41] Numerous references testify to its role in the Sino-Singapore trade of the nineteenth century,[42] but there is little indication that Siam was a frequent port of call. It was particularly noted for its five staggered masts and upward-projecting stern gallery.[43] The type of junk used by Cheng Ho for his fifteenth-century voyages has been suggested as the prototype of the Kiangsu Trader; the latter's bulkhead construction,

[38] Needham, *Science and Civilization*, vol. 4, pt. 3, p. 429; D. W. Waters, "Chinese Junks: The Antung Trader," *The Mariner's Mirror* 24 (1938): 50.

[39] Needham, *Science and Civilization*, vol. 4, pt. 3, p. 429.

[40] It was also known as the *sha-ch'uan*.

[41] *Wu-pei chih*: 117:11a.

[42] L. Audemard, *Les Jonques Chinoises*, 6 vols. (Rotterdam: Publicaties van Het Museum Voor Land- en Volkenkunde, 1957), vol. 3, p. 7; Worcester, *Junks*, vol. 1, p. 120; Gutzlaff, *Two Voyages*, p. 82; Needham, *Science and Civilization*, vol. 4, pt. 3, p. 402.

[43] Worcester, *Junks*, vol. 1, p. 114. The best discussions of the Kiangsu Trader are found in ibid., pp. 114-21; Needham, *Science and Civilization*, vol. 4, pt. 3, pp. 399-402; Ivon Donnelly, "Foochow Pole Junks," *The Mariner's Mirror* 9 (1923): 226-31.

capacity, and greater speed[44] would have made it a natural choice for distant overseas passages. The Kiangsu Trader was not the only ocean-going vessel native to the central provinces,[45] but the trade from this region, as well as that from Fukien and Kwangtung, was carried to Siam in junks of the predominantly southern-style.

Fukien ocean junks combined some features of both the northern and southern styles. Those trading with the countries of the *Nan-yang* had a 200 to 800 ton cargo capacity.[46] Their bulwarks were painted black with a green border and the sides of the hull were white.[47] The sails were reminiscent of those on northern craft, having a straight luff and leech.[48] The rudder was ordinarily solid rather than fenestrated, but the hull was more rounded than on junks found to the north. The bow piece was formed in the shape of a narrow, truncated wedge, the upper and lower halves separated by an inverted crescent (see Figure 3). Hull pictorial varied from port to port, but the oculus and *t'ai-chi*[49] were features common to nearly all Fukien junks.

The Foochow Pole junk or *hua p'i ku* is the most representative of the class of Fukien ocean vessels, and it was a junk of somewhat similar build, the Keying, which made a voyage to England in 1846. The Pole junk was noted for its tall, elliptical, transom-style stern on which were painted elaborate designs,[50] and for its recessed bow. From each side of the bow piece a wing arose "curving to a sharp point and sheering aft towards the poop, ... forming a fairly substantial bulwark" (Figure 4).[51] Capacity varied from 300 to 800 tons, the average length was 150 feet, and

[44] Worcester, *Junks*, vol. 1, p. 115. The large Trader measured 170 feet in length and had an average capacity of 400-600 tons. The greater number of sails increased its speed over that of the smaller two- to three-masted junks. See also the *Illustrated Catalogue of the "Maze Collection" of Chinese Junk Models in the Science Museum, London* (n.p., 1938) for a picture of the five-masted sea-going Shantung junk, and appendix no. 3, loc. cit., for specifications.

[45] The Ningpo Trader (*Wu-ts'ao*) and the Hangchow Bay Trader (*Shao-hsing ch'uan*) were the principal junks of ocean-going capability from Chekiang.

[46] Crawfurd, *History*, vol. 3, pp. 180, 182.

[47] Worcester, *Junks*, vol. 1, p. 154.

[48] Audemard, *Les Jonques*, vol. 2, p. 38. On fishing junks the sails were rectangular.

[49] See ibid., *Les Jonques*, vol. 3, pp. 7-22 for a full discussion of decorative motifs.

[50] Worcester, *Junks*, Plate #52.

[51] Ivon Donnelly, *Chinese Junks and Other Native Craft* (Shanghai: Kelly & Walsh, 1924), p. 98.

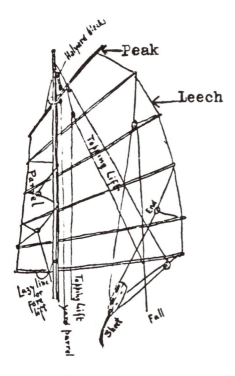

Figure 2. China Lugsail with Rigging

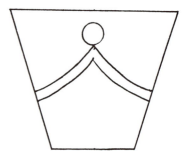

Figure 3. Bow Piece of a
Fukien Ocean Vessel

Figure 4. A Chinese Junk in Bangkok

it was an extraordinarily sturdy vessel with fifteen full bulkheads in the hull.[52] It was an ideal long-haul cargo carrier, particularly as its unusual maneuverability lent itself to navigation among the shoals and reefs of the *Nan-yang*.

The designs painted on the stern generally conformed to customary patterns, although the artist was permitted some latitude. A swallow was drawn at the top of the oval to symbolize the junk's speed and "indifference to the tempest." The characters for longevity, profit, and favorable voyages[53] were painted beneath the swallow, with the vessel's registration number written below this inscription. The eight immortals were drawn in a band across the middle, under which were flower medallions or animal figures. On the panels to the side of the stern the artist painted dragons or other designs that appealed to his fancy.[54] The hull and bulwarks were painted as well, in either a scroll-work pattern or with superimposed medallions of a different color, while a sea-serpent was portrayed swimming toward the bow or the stern. As on all merchant vessels, an eye was drawn on each side of the bow with the pupil looking forward so that the junk could find its passage on the open sea. On fishing junks, the pupil was painted to gaze downward into the water in order to locate schools of fish. Descriptions of the Chinese junks moored in Siam's harbors during the last century indicate that in build and design they closely resembled the Foochow Pole junk.[55]

The junks native to Kwangtung, ranging between 500 and 1,000 tons, were the largest Chinese ocean vessels (*yuang-ch'uan*) which sailed to Siam. A red band painted beneath black bulwarks gave rise to their appellation as "red-headed" junks, and these were said to carry four masts.[56] The *t'ou-meng*, sailing primarily from Chiang-men, and the *hai-po* from Ch'ao-chou were commonly used in ocean voyages. Their aver-

---

[52] Worcester, *Junks*, vol. 1, p. 140; E. Chatterton, *Sailing Ships, The Story of Their Development from the Earliest Times to the Present Day* (London: Sidgwick & Jackson, 1909, 1914), pp. 311-12; Donnelly, *Chinese Junks*, pp. 97-100.

[53] *Yung* (永), *li* (利), *shun* (順).

[54] Worcester, *Junks*, vol. 1, p. 141.

[55] Compare Figure 4 with Plate 52 in Worcester, *Junks*; Roberts, *Embassy*, p. 272.

[56] Audemard, *Les Jonques*, vol. 4, p. 58; China: Imperial Maritime Customs, *Decennial Reports . . . 1882-91*, p. 70. A junk classed as a Newchwang craft was also called *hung-t'ou*. This was probably the Chinchow Trader referred to by Donnelly, *Chinese Junks*, pp. 41-42. It traded in the Feng-t'ien-Shantung region and was much smaller than the Kwangtung ocean-going junks. It represented a conglomeration of regional styles with

age cargo capacity was 350 tons, although some might carry considerably less.[57] Ocean junks from ports in the prefecture of Ch'iung-chou were usually smaller than those from mainland ports, having a capacity of from 100 to 200 tons. Kwangtung junks were distinctive, particularly with regard to sail conformation. As one moves southward along the Chinese coast, the sail leech becomes progressively rounder, culminating in the sails of Kwangtung craft on which the shoulder of the leech is fully rounded. Additional features usually found on these vessels were a gently rounded bottom, an overhanging stern with a railed gallery, and fenestrated rudder.[58] The latter was probably developed to reduce drag on the vessel when directional changes were made in deep water navigation.[59]

Siamese vessels engaged in the China trade did not embody the characteristics of any one style of Fukien or Kwangtung junk, but rather combined in their build certain features of both. Most Siamese overseas vessels were indistinguishable from Chinese junks and, with Bangkok a center for the building of Chinese-style vessels, their sale to Chinese merchants, in Bangkok or in China itself, became common practice.[60] Several styles were prevalent in Siam and all were modeled after some form of Chinese craft. The few remaining Siamese junks presently trading

---

a bow piece similar to that of the Chekiang junks, an oval stern like the Pole junks but without its ornamentation or height, and the oculus, a design seldom found on northern vessels, was painted on the fore-hull.

[57] China: Imperial Maritime Customs, *Decennial Reports . . . 1882-91*, p. 632. The *hai-po* trading to Kiungchow on Hainan carried from 2,000 to 5,000 piculs and the *t'ou-meng* might carry as little as 400 to 800 piculs. Audemard, *Les Jonques*, vol. 4, p. 58, reports, however, that one *hai-po*, seen near Soochow, had a capacity of 1,000 tons.

[58] See Figures 1013 and 1044 in Needham, *Science and Civilization*, vol. 4, pt. 3, for illustration of these characteristics.

[59] D. W. Waters, "Chinese Junks—The Twaqo," *The Mariner's Mirror* 32 (1946): 162.

[60] CHM.R.2, #5, 1820: When a merchant vessel engaged in trade to Amoy became unseaworthy, an unsuccessful attempt was made to sell it there. Rather than dismantle it, however, the decision was reached to have it repaired and sold to Chinese customers in Bangkok. According to a Western report from approximately the same period, the junks of Siam were smaller, but were "constructed upon the same principle as those of Canton and Amoy": *The Asiatic Journal and Monthly Register* 10 (1829-30): 16; Crawfurd, *History*, vol. 3, p. 173; T'ien, Ju'k'ang, *Shih-ch'i shih-chi chih shih-chiu shih-chi chung-yeh Chung-kuo fan-ch'uan tsai tung-nan Ya-chou hang-yün ho shang-yeh shang te ti-wei* [The Place of Chinese sailing vessels in the maritime trade of Southeast Asia from the seventeenth to the mid-nineteenth centuries] (Shanghai: Jen-min ch'u-pan she, 1957), p. 22.

in the Gulf of Siam, if representative of nineteenth-century craft, closely resemble what Worcester has called the Hainan Trader.[61] The bow is pointed and the stern extended with a railed gallery,[62] but the stem post is much higher on the Siamese junk and the sheer from the stern to the bow is less pronounced than on the Hainan Trader.[63] Unlike the Trader the Siam junks carry only two masts and the hull does not exhibit the decorative devices standard on the Foochow Pole junk. The present-day junks seem to fit Poujade's description of the small Chinese-style junks which were primarily employed as coastal traders between Bangkok, Cambodia, the Gulf of Tonkin, and Hainan Island.[64]

Junks built in Siam were considered to be the cheapest and most durable,[65] having the upper portions of the vessels and the mainmasts, rudders, and anchors all constructed of Siamese teak.[66] Junks could carry from two to four masts, although two masts were the rule,[67] rigging was similar to that on Chinese junks, and the sails were of split bamboo matting supported by bamboo battens. Decoration, when present, followed the format of motifs on the Foochow Pole junk, and the oculus was painted on the larger vessels trading with ports on the Chinese mainland. Gutzlaff described one class of junk built in Siam which sailed as far north

[61] Worcester, "Six Craft of Kwangtung," p. 132, provides an illustration of the Hainan Trader. See also the model of a Hainan sea-going junk in the *Maze Collection.* The Siamese craft have also been called "Singapore junks" because they were capable of trading beyond the Gulf of Siam to Singapore: Jean Poujade, *Les Jonques des Chinois du Siam* (Paris: Gauthier-Villars, 1946), p. 5.

[62] Battelle Memorial Institute, Columbus, Ohio. *Blue Book of Coastal Vessels: Thailand* (Bangkok: Joint Thai-U.S. Military Research and Development Center, 1967), p. 323; Poujade, *Les Jonques,* p. 16.

[63] Battelle Memorial Institute, *Blue Book,* pp. 16, 322-24.

[64] Poujade, *Les Jonques,* pp. 5, 10, 16. Its small capacity, two masts, and absence of the oculus lend support to the validity of this comparison. The junk described by Poujade measured 12 to 20 meters and weighed 15 to 25 tons, which corresponds closely to the specifications of present Gulf of Siam cargo junks (12-25 meters; 18-40 tons). Poujade further argues that the oculus, appearing on all other junks of the Indo-China maritime region, is absent from the two-masted Chinese junks of Siam because their prototype, a two-masted coastal junk found between Hong Kong and Tonkin, was also painted without one. Note that none appears in the *Blue Book* illustrations.

[65] FO 17/9, p. 38.

[66] T'ien, *Shih-ch'i shih-chi,* pp. 23-24; CMH.R.2, #16, 1814.

[67] Poujade, *Les Jonques,* p. 10; Anuman, *Tamnan,* p. 24.

58

as the Yellow Sea, which was manned by men from Ch'ao-chou, and was called a "pak-tow-sun."[68] Donnelly identifies it as the Ch'ao-chou Trader[69] which was undoubtedly similar to the *hai-po*. It had a capacity of from 250 to 300 tons, three masts combining the rectangular northern-style sail with the rounded leech of the southern-style, a T-shaped bow, and a high elliptical stern. This vessel was said to have carried much of the trade between South China and Siam, but its regional scope was ultimately reduced to coastal transport because of competition from foreign steamers.[70] Junks were also built in Bangkok after the fashion of the Foochow Pole junk, and the transom stern with its profusion of birds and beasts has been cited as typical of these craft.[71] The junks built during Rama I's reign (1782-1809) were said to be "in the Chinese *tuakang* style," which has been tentatively identified as the twaqo of Singapore.[72] The present-day twaqo is far too small to undertake sea voyages and is used primarily for coastal cargo transport. It is, however, reminiscent of southern Chinese craft in its rigging, cut of sail, and decorative scheme.[73] The bow of the *tuakang* junk of the late eighteenth century was said to have been red or green—implying a junk modeled after those of Kwangtung or Fukien—with a bow piece measuring from 10 to 14 meters.[74] They were owned by royal princes, government officials, and merchants who were accustomed to selling the boat in China after the cargo had been disposed of.[75]

Rama III (1824-1851), fearing that trading junks would be replaced by Western-style ships, ordered a model erected at Wat Yannawa to stand

[68] Or "Pih-tow-chuen" (白頭船): Gutzlaff, *Two Voyages*, p. 44.

[69] Donnelly, *Chinese Junks*, p. 115.

[70] Ibid., pp. 115-16. The *pai-t'ou ch'uan* should not be confused with the *pai-ti ch'uan* which plied between Foochow and the north of Formosa: China: Imperial Maritime Customs, *Decennial Reports . . . 1882-91*, p. 424.

[71] Roberts, *Embassy*, p. 273.

[72] Chaen, *Prawat*, p. 45.

[73] D. W. Waters, "Chinese Junks—The Twaqo," *The Mariner's Mirror* 32 (1946): 156-57.

[74] Chaen, *Prawat*, p. 45. This may mean the crossbeam width which would indicate a junk of comparable size with the larger ocean vessels mentioned in the *Hsia-men chih* (see above pp. 48-49). Chaen's description is not sufficiently detailed to enable one to place these vessels in a specific category, but they may have represented a more capacious version of the twaqo.

[75] Ibid., p. 45.

as a reminder of the vessels that had once monopolized the trade between China and Siam.[76] Repairs and the substitution of stupa for masts have rendered the model somewhat unlike the original junk it was to represent. The bow and stern appear nearly level as opposed to most Chinese junks where the stern rises higher than the bow, and the bow has a curved, sword-like shape, the bulwarks joining together in a decided point at the stem.[77] A wedge-shaped bow piece, supposedly representing a lion's mouth, was inserted beneath the points of the bulwark as on many Fukien junks. The hull was rounded after the style of southern Chinese junks, but the bottom would seem to have a keel rather than being rounded.[78] The bulwarks were painted with a series of squares within squares which ended at the stern with its slightly raised and fenced gallery. Stern decoration consisted of the junk's name in characters, red circular motifs, and an eagle or swallow placed in inverted order from those painted on the Foochow Pole junk. The rudder conformed to the Kwangtung style, being fenestrated rather than solid. The rigging was identical with Chinese rigging and the mat sails flying from the two masts were strengthened by bamboo battens.[79] Anuman's description of this junk indicates that it embodied a conglomeration of Chinese styles, the builders perhaps adopting the most useful features during construction. If one makes allowance for the structural changes in the bow, a comparison of Figures 4 and 6 indicates the great similarity between the Siamese and Chinese vessels. The former would certainly have been recognized as a Chinese-style junk and admitted to Chinese ports on that basis.

The Siamese did not, however, rely solely on junks (*samphao*). They also employed Western-style ships (*kampan*) in some of their overseas commerce as well as for military purposes, but these did not enter the China trade until the middle of the nineteenth century. Dutch and English shipbuilders were hired to construct Western-style vessels from as early

---

[76] Anuman, *Tamnan*, p. 21.

[77] Ibid., p. 23. The original bow, shaped like the knives used in ancient times to shave monks' heads, broke off and was later replaced. The author states that the present bow is incorrectly formed, and indicates that the original resembled the bow in Figure 4 with wing-like bulwarks.

[78] There is no evidence that Siamese junks were built with keels, and the one in Figure 6 may be a misrepresentation, as is the bow.

[79] Anuman, *Tamnan*, p. 24.

as the seventeenth century.[80] The frigates, sloops, brigs, and galleys they built were to be used primarily to supplement the government's naval forces.[81] When Western-style ships were used in overseas trade, as occurred during the reign of Rama II (1809-1824), they sailed to such places as India, Macao, Penang, and Singapore, but not to ports under Chinese administration.[82] The displacement of junks by square-rigged vessels began to gather momentum in the 1840s and 1850s and was to alter decisively traditional commercial patterns. Prior to the opening of the Treaty Ports in China, however, the use of junks in Sino-Siamese trade was essential if the desired concessions were to be obtained.

Square-rigged vessels began to carry an increasing proportion of the China-*Nan-yang* trade once they were accorded equal status with Chinese-style vessels in major Chinese ports. Moreover, European and American trade with China and Southeast Asia expanded rapidly in the nineteenth century, particularly when Singapore's importance as an entrepot was recognized. As square-rigged vessels became more visible throughout the region, both the Chinese and Siamese recognized the advantages they afforded. Square-rigged vessels could make three trips per season between China and Southeast Asia as opposed to one trip by junk, their capacity was generally greater, and cargo insurance was available on the goods they carried.[83]

[80] Chaen, *Prawat*, p. 39; *Records of the Relations between Siam and Foreign Countries in the Seventeenth Century*, 5 vols. (Bangkok: Vajiranana National Library, 1915), vol. 1, Instructions to Mr. Edward Long, appointed chief merchant upon the Roebuck for Siam: Letter: Aug. 2, 1624, #82, p. 158, Mr. Head to be sent to build ships for the King of Siam; Henry Hawley *et al.* in Batavia to the Governor and Committees of the Company of Merchants of London Trading East India Company: Letters: Feb. 6, 1625, p. 170, Mr. Head would be detained a year longer.

[81] *Dutch Papers: Extracts from the "Dagh Register" 1624-42* (Bangkok: Vajiranana National Library, 1913), p. 13: On an expedition to Patani in 1634, the king's soldiers, ammunition, etc. were sent in "galleys, frigates, and junks . . ."; Pallegoix, *Description du Royaume Thai ou Siam*, vol. 1, p. 322. For an explanation of the differences between these kinds of ships see Chatterton, *Sailing Ships*, pp. 139, 171, 208, 219, 232-33, 258, 292, 300-01; Joseph Jobé, ed., *The Great Age of Sail* (Greenwich: New York Graphic Society, 1967), pp. 149-50; Stanley Spicer, *Masters of Sail* (Toronto: Ryerson Press, 1968), pp. 31-32.

[82] Chaen, *Prawat*, p. 46. Most of Siam's trade to Singapore, however, was carried by junk until the late 1840s.

[83] Great Britain: Board of Trade, *Abstract of Reports on the Trade of Various Countries and Places, for the Year 1854* (Gt. Br., Parliament, Papers by Command, 1856-[61?]), Swatow, 1854, p. 28; *Hunt's Merchants' Magazine and Commercial Review* 2 (May 1847): 302.

The Siamese began building Western-style trading vessels in the 1830s when they discovered that the junks engaged in state trade were not returning a profit. Rama III sent down an order that no more junks were to be built and that future state trading vessels were to be modeled on the European style.[84] Throughout the late 1830s warships and square-rigged merchant vessels were constructed at Chantabun and at Bangkok. By 1838 the Siamese had increased the number of Western-style sailing ships that were employed in their trade with Singapore.[85] During the Opium War, whether as an excuse or from real fear for their safety, Rama III recalled all his junks engaged in the China trade and ordered them to remain in port.[86] By the mid-1840s the king was sending his own square-rigged vessels, of which he possessed ten of 4,000 tons burden and two of three of a smaller size, to Canton. The Siamese use of junks had not as yet come to a standstill, for the trade in 1847 between China and Siam was said to be "much larger than that between China and Singapore . . . and was almost entirely in junks."[87]

The consignment of cargo to junks declined, however, once the implications of the Treaty of Nanking were realized. By granting Western ships equal status with Chinese at Amoy, Foochow, Ningpo, and Shanghai it was no longer necessary for Asians to ship goods to China by junk.[88] Moreover, since the treaty stipulated that a fair and regular tariff was to be enforced at the newly opened ports, merchandise carried in Western-style ships was no longer liable to the arbitrary exactions of local officials. The advantages previously enjoyed by junks were thereby nullified, and

---

[84] *The Asiatic Journal and Monthly Register* n.s., 23 (May-Aug. 1837): 122.

[85] *The Canton Press*, 4/28/1838, 4/23/1836; Bowring, *The Kingdom and People of Siam*, vol. 1, p. 252.

[86] *Asiatic Journal* n.s., 33 (Sept.-Dec. 1840): 117.

[87] *Allen's Indian Mail, and Register of Intelligence*, 84 (Sept. 1847), 527. According to Wong Lin Ken, "The Trade of Singapore 1819-69," *JMBRAS* 33,4 (1960): 276, eighty-one Chinese junks arrived in Singapore and fifty-five departed in that year. If China's trade with Siam were larger, one might suppose that well over a hundred junks were involved, especially as from 150 to 200 vessels were engaged in this trade when it was at its height (Chapter IV).

[88] Article 17 of the Supplementary Treaty signed in 1843, for example, declared that ships above 150 tons were considered large foreign ships and would be charged at the rate of 5 *mace* per ton. Those under 150 tons would be charged at the rate of 1 *mace* per ton. A 350 ton vessel, charged at the rate of 5 *mace* per ton would pay Sp. $245.00, a smaller levy than was applied to Chinese junks at Canton prior to the treaty (Chapter II, footnote 79).

many Chinese and Southeast Asian merchants found that loading their goods on square-rigged vessels subject to treaty regulations was more profitable.[89] The opening of these four ports had a particular impact on Siam's trade, for they were the major centers to which her trade had previously been carried. Although Siam had no treaty with China containing a most favored nation clause, the trading rights granted in China's treaties with Western powers were extended to nationals of other countries who frequented the Treaty Ports.[90] Siam was thus freed from reliance upon junk carriage, and the volume of trade consigned to her own square-rigged vessels slowly increased throughout the late 1840s and the 1850s.[91] The Chinese in Siam, quickly recognized the superior merits of square-rigged vessels, and by 1855 controlled four-fifths of those sailing under the Siamese flag.[92] Junks continued to call at the non-Treaty Ports, but with centers like Shanghai burgeoning into economic prominence, the trade at, and junk traffic to, the smaller ports went into a rapid decline.

The Bowring Treaty, negotiated between Siam and Great Britain in 1855, dealt a further blow to the junk trade by granting the British shipping parity with Chinese and Siamese in Siam.[93] Tonnage dues were abolished altogether and merchants were only required to pay the import and export duties on goods. On imports, a maximum of 3 percent *ad valorem* was fixed, while exports were to be charged at the same rate as the cargoes carried in Siamese and Chinese vessels prior to the treaty. Sugar, for instance, when exported under a European flag had paid 1.5 *baht* per picul, whereas that exported on junks had paid none. Pepper carried in junks was exported duty-free, but Europeans had paid from

---

[89] Wong, "The Trade," p. 123.

[90] T. R. Banister, "A History of the External Trade of China, 1834-81, China: Maritime Customs, I.-Statistical Series; no. 6, *Decennial Reports . . . 1922-31* (Shanghai: Statistical Department of the Inspectorate General of Customs, 1933), p. 20; Great Britain: Foreign Office, *Commercial Reports from Her Majesty's Consuls in China, Japan, and Siam, 1865* (Gt. Br., Parliament, Papers by Command, 1866), p. 36: nineteen Siamese square-rigged vessels are listed as having entered the port of Ningpo in 1865, six entered at Shanghai (p. 74), etc.; CMH.R.3, #49, 1844.

[91] *The Bangkok Calendar*, 1865, pp. 40-42.

[92] Wong, "The Trade," p. 149; Great Britain: Board of Trade, *Abstract of Reports*, p. 164.

[93] Bowring, *The Kingdom*, vol. 2, p. 220: Article VIII stated that "British shipping shall enjoy all the privileges now exercised by, or which hereafter may be granted to, Siamese or Chinese vessels or junks"; James C. Ingram, *Economic Change in Thailand Since 1850* (Stanford: Stanford University Press, 1955), p. 34.

3 to 6 *baht* per picul.[94] Moreover, the English were now allowed to transact business directly with local merchants rather than having to rely on the mediation of the king's factors. Prices, therefore, more closely approximated their real market value, while the Chinese ability to obtain lower prices was negated. Furthermore, all the Siamese trading monopolies, with the exception of that in opium, were revoked by the Bowring Treaty. During the reign of Rama III, an increasing percentage of the monopolies in tin, pepper, birds' nests, and the like, had been sold to Chinese, who were forced by their abolition to find new sources of income after the treaty went into effect.

Two other factors were instrumental in hastening the transition from junk to square-rigged and steamer carriage. The first was the upsurge in piracy off the China coast as Chinese political and military authority broke down under the onslaught of the T'ai-p'ing Rebellion. The disorder and dislocation arising from the unsettled conditions in the south produced an atmosphere conducive to piracy, and pirate raids on merchant junks did much to slow Chinese coastal and overseas trade.[95] Secondly, the political ties which had bound Siam within the Chinese tributary orbit had begun to weaken by mid-century, and there was evidence of growing discontent among members of Bangkok's modernizing elite with Siam's role in the tributary system. They believed that greater economic benefits could be gained through closer ties with the West, particularly as Siamese state trade with China had become increasingly unprofitable with the entrance of square-rigged vessels into the Treaty Ports.[96] When the king and nobility stopped sponsoring the junk trade with China, the obsolescence of these vessels was further hastened.

Junks continued to sail between China and Siam into the twentieth century, but they ceased to be significant carriers of Sino-Siamese trade. They were used increasingly for the transport of bulk goods like timber

[94] *The Burney Papers*, vol. 2, pt. 4, "Extracts from H. Burney's Report Respecting the Commerce of Siam," pp. 101, 106; CMH.R.3, #49, 1844.

[95] Tribute missions were affected by the disorder arising from the T'ai-p'ing Rebellion as well, and various tributary nations were excused from sending missions during the late 1850s and early 1860s on that ground: John K. Fairbank, "The Early Treaty System in the Chinese World Order," in *The Chinese World Order*, John Fairbank, p. 269.

[96] CMH.R.4, #113, 1854. The Siamese Minister of Foreign Affairs, in writing to John Bowring prior to the latter's mission to Bangkok, explained that, even though the trade between China and Siam was of long duration, the taxes on Siamese goods were now high and no profit was made. See also CMH.R.4, #98, 1856.

and rice and were similarly employed in Chinese coastal trade. Gradually, however, steam competition bit into this limited trade as well[97] and the great ocean junks of China's earlier foreign commerce fell into disuse.

[97] Mark Elvin, *The Pattern of the Chinese Past* (Stanford: Stanford University Press, 1973), p. 305. Elvin further states, however, that in comparison with junk carriage, steam transport provided little reduction in the cost of shipping goods, and that speed and reliability were the principal gains. See also China: Imperial Maritime Customs, *Decennial Reports . . . 1882-91*, p. 516.

4

IMPORTS AND EXPORTS: THE CHARACTER OF SINO-SIAMESE TRADE

Canton's emergence as an emporium of international repute during the late eighteenth and early nineteenth centuries arose from a growing European demand for tea and silk and the restriction of European trade to that port after 1757. By catering to the requirements of Europeans and Asians alike, the market at Canton was deluged by such an enormous range of merchandise that even the highly detailed Western commercial handbooks of the last century can give us only a hint of the goods available there. East India Company and Country ships[1] imported the manufactured wares and textiles of Europe and India as well as "Straits produce"—the animal, vegetable, and mineral products indigenous to the Malay Peninsula and Indonesian

---

[1] Country ships were those which carried the triangular trade between India, the Malay Peninsula and Indonesian archipelago, and China. The Country traders were licensed by the East India Company and provided the Company's treasury in Canton with the necessary funds to purchase the Chinese goods exported by Company ships to England. Because the Country traders brought goods to China of greater value than they took from China, the surplus revenue accumulated was exchanged for Bills on the Company which were readily sold in India. For a further discussion of this trade, see Greenberg, *British Trade and the Opening of China 1800-42*, pp. 11-17.

[2] Wong Lin Ken, "The Trade of Singapore," pp. 108-09. Goods from continental Southeast Asia will also be included under the heading of Straits produce in this chapter to distinguish them from European and Indian products. As Wong points out, the term became more inclusive as greater familiarity with these products developed, and one is justified in designating goods indigenous to Southeast Asia generally as Straits produce. Cowan seems to imply a more restricted definition with spices and minerals

Archipelago.[2] European shipping could presumably have supplied the existing demand in China for foreign goods, and yet an active trade in Straits produce was also carried by Chinese junks. That European and Chinese shipping were able to operate simultaneously was a function of the competitive advantage of Chinese junks over square-rigged vessels in the Southeast Asian and Chinese markets prior to the mid-nineteenth century (see Chapters II and III). During the Ch'ing, Chinese maritime trade was rarely carried beyond the confines of the *Nan-yang* and the Philippine Islands, where Chinese merchants monopolized the trade in Straits produce and in the miscellaneous Chinese products valued by overseas Chinese and native Southeast Asians. Their inability to compete successfully in this branch of inter-Asian trade led private European merchants to concentrate increasingly on the trade in Indian cotton and opium,[3] leaving the Chinese relatively free to develop the Sino-*Nan-yang* commercial links.

China's trade with Siam represented in microcosm the more extensive Sino-*Nan-yang* trade. The goods exchanged between the two countries differed little from those carried between China and the other countries of Southeast Asia.[4] Chinese exports to Siam consisted, for the most part, of such manufactured items for popular consumption as fans, textiles, preserves, and crockery. Siam, however, rarely exported manufactured goods,[5] supplying China with raw materials and unprocessed foodstuffs. Of the latter, rice was the most sought after and was traded with other Southeast Asian countries as well as with China. Since data reflecting the quantities and prices of the goods involved in the Sino-Siamese trade are not consistently available prior to 1850, no attempt has been made to ascertain the precise volume of this trade. I will consider instead why certain goods were in greater demand than others, how imports were utilized and for which segments of the population they had the most appeal, and how Siam's role as an entrepot contributed to the stability of the commercial relationship between the two countries.

By describing Singapore in the 1830s as "a mart for the exchange of the Merchandize and Products of Europe, India, China, &c. for the produce of the Archipelago and Neighbouring States—the Imports from

excluded: C. D. Cowan, "Early Penang and the Rise of Singapore 1805-1832," *JMBRAS* 23,2 (1950): 15.

[3] Greenberg, *British Trade*, p. 79.

[4] Crawfurd, *History*, vol. 3, p. 183.

[5] An exception were the iron pans exported primarily to Singapore.

one part, form(ing) the Exports to another, & vice versa,"[6] a writer for the *Singapore Chronicle* aptly typified the essential features of an entrepot. The development of collection centers for the transmission of European and Southeast Asian goods to China and Chinese goods to Europe and Southeast Asia was one of the distinctive characteristics of the traditional Sino-Asian commercial worlds.[7] While assertions of Siam's function as a Southeast Asian emporium are reiterated in nineteenth- and twentieth-century literature,[8] her unique position as an entrepot for the distribution of primarily Asian goods is seldom recognized in these works. Bangkok, unlike Canton, Malacca, or Singapore, was not primarily a center for the dispersion of European and Indian manufactures to other Asian states; rather, Bangkok supplied China almost exclusively with Straits produce obtained by Siamese coasting vessels[9] and the countries on her borders with the miscellaneous Chinese wares imported by Chinese junks. Siam began to import European and Indian textiles in greater quantities after Singapore's rise to prominence (Table 3), but, with the exception of those purchased by Lao and Cambodian merchants, most were consumed in Siam and were not re-exported to China.[10] Moreover, the growing impotence of the French, British, Portuguese, and Dutch trading establishments in Siam after 1700 tended to limit Siam's trade with Western nations and it remained insignificant until the mid-nineteenth century. Siam was in no position, therefore, to serve as the focus of an East-West commodity flow in the manner of Malacca or Singapore. A large Chinese community actively involved in Siam's commercial life, and the reciprocal advantages accruing to Siamese and Chinese vessels at the other's ports, encouraged Siam's development as an emporium for the China-*Nan-yang* trade. The Chakri kings' concerted efforts to expand Sino-

---

[6] *Singapore Chronicle*, 9/27/1832.

[7] O. W. Wolters, *Early Indonesian Commerce* (Ithaca: Cornell University Press, 1967); Wolters, *The Fall of Srivijava in Malay History* (Ithaca: Cornell University Press, 1970), ch. 1, 3-5.

[8] Skinner, *Chinese Society in Thailand*, p. 41; Ingram, *Economic Change in Thailand since 1850*, p. 26; Neale, *Narrative of a Residence at the Capital of the Kingdom of Siam*, pp. 176-78; Malloch, *Siam: Some General Remarks on Its Productions*, pp. 29-31; Crawfurd, *Journal of an Embassy*, pp. 413-15; Great Britain, Parliament, *Report from the Select Committee*, vol. 5, 1830, p. 311; T'ien Ju-k'ang, *Shih-ch'i shih-chi*, p. 26.

[9] Crawfurd, *Journal*, p. 413. Many of the goods exported to China had been sent to Siam by states under Siamese suzerainty as tribute, or brought to Bangkok by Asian merchants from neighboring countries. See Malloch, *Siam*, pp. 29-31.

[10] Malloch, *Siam*, p. 30; see also Appendix A, sec. 1.

Table 3. Sino-Siamese Junk Trade with Singapore 1831-1833[a]

Siamese Exports to Singapore

Product	1831	1832	1833
Salt	17,210	21,900	8,940
Oil	1,334	1,840	660
Sticklac	661	1,098	20
Sugar	14,010	9,600	4,780
Rice	13,890	240	420
Paddy	34 k	—	240
Sapanwood	1,000	1,160	980
Ebony	1,400	—	—
Iron pans	28,600 # / 200 c	32,000 #	8,100#
Tobacco (Siam)	44	—	20
Onions	60	15	70
Dried fish	250	2,020	150
China and earthenware	127,000 #	$450	—
Pigs	8 #	—	—
British textiles	40,000 yd	—	—
Beeswax	40	—	—
Rattan	300	—	—
Tamarind	50	—	—
China textiles	—	160 c	10 c
Gamboge	—	34	10
Pandan bags	—	3,000 #	—
Quallies casks	—	1,200 #	—
China paper	—	135 / $750	—

Siamese Imports from Singapore

Product	1831	1832	1833
Indian textiles	304.5 c	2,082.5 c	589 c
Cotton twist	49	223	278
British textiles	200,208 yd / 400 # / 41 c	108.75 c	282.5 c / 60
Rattan	1,090	954	200
Rattan mats	30 c	50 c	285 c
Beeswax	4	125	114
Opium	13 cts / 19 bls	4 cts	5 cts
Seaweed	150	—	—
Eng. iron	400	—	1,250
Chinese goods	57	15	—
Pepper	100	300	600
Gambier	—	100	300
Cowries	200	—	—
Birds' feathers	—	10,000 #	—
Lead	—	734	—
Sago	—	200	80
Betel-nut	—	200	—
Flints	—	20	200
Tin	—	—	100
Shells	—	—	800
Misc. goods	13.15	40	27
Spanish $$$	1,943 # / $250	3,400 #	20 #

Table 3. Continued

Product	Siamese Exports to Singapore			Siamese Imports from Singapore		
	1831	1832	1833	1831	1832	1833
Indigo	—	120	—			
Misc. Chinese goods	—	1.35	—			
Spanish $$$	—	1,000 #	—			

Product	Chinese Exports to Singapore			Product	Chinese Imports from Singapore		
	1831	1832	1833		1831	1832	1833
Earthenware	47,292 #	$120	$1,010	Tin	2,200	2,963	—
Chinaware	2,209,100 #	514,000 #	10 bxs	Pepper	4,270	3,385	—
	$15,750	$45,549	$11,275	Rattan & mats	6,750	7,923	—
Nankeens & cotton	5,948 c	64,325 c	110 c	Beche-de-mer	20 c	73.5 c	—
Raw silk & silk	57.5	30	6		1,644	2,460	50
		70 #		Mangrove bark	6,510	3,513	—
Ready-made clothing	210 c	70 #		Hides	460	153	—
		140 c		Seaweed	2.5 c	2.5 c	—
Tea	463.5	232	125		5,505	5,192	—
		670 bxs	450 bxs	Birds' nests	116.96	133.95	—
Salt	2,700	4,750	4,800	Opium	2 cts	20 cts	2 cts
Umbrellas	37,500 #	89,000 #	6,300 #	Ebony	4,240	5,700	—
Tiles, bricks, jars	89,300 #	11,200 #	1,000 #	Lakkawood	1,100	2,750	—
Paper goods	400	20	392	Sapanwood	1,100	1,800	—
	3,000 #	6 bxs	500 bds	Betel-nut	708	40	—
	19 bxs	$2,020	$1,150	Flints & lead	960	2,430	53 bls

Table 3. Continued

Siamese Exports to Singapore

Product	1831	1832	1833
Combs	82,400 #	5 bxs	—
Ceremonial goods	1,259 / 24 bxs	1,536 / $4,260	170 / $3,900 & / 200 bxs
Foodstuffs & preserves	4,300.5 / 400 j / 167 #	2,305.5 / 250 j / 10 # / 200 bsk	720 / 15 j / $300 / 300 bsk
Furniture/mats	645 #	—	—
Medicine/drugs	716	526	106
Tobacco	240	270 / 295 bsk	50
Sundries	$6,925	$1,786 / 4 cts	$4,576
Gold thread	15.1	345 bxs	28 bxs
Iron pans	—	—	500 #
Shoes/hats	—	4,000 # / 2 bxs	500 #
Misc. goods	150.5 / 100 #	212 / 10 kegs	20 / 5 bxs

Siamese Imports from Singapore

Product	1831	1832	1833
Misc. Straits produce	671.35 / 50 #	407	—
Indigo	400	—	—
Eagle wood	142	246	—
Sago	235	—	—
Rice	920	—	—
Gambier	220	—	—
Sundries	$524	—	—
European textiles	960 yd / 600	330.5 c	—
Cotton & cotton twist	83 / 50 bales	292	30
Spanish $$$	5,200 #	200 #	1,100 #

a All figures are from the **Singapore Chronicle Commercial Register** 1831-1833.

All quantities are given in piculs unless otherwise specified.

c = *corge* (20 piculs = 1 corge)
k = koyan (in Singapore 1 koyan = 40 piculs)
# = piece
cts = chests
bls = balls
bxs = boxes
j = jar
bds = bundles
bsk = baskets

Siamese trade after 1782 further stimulated this trend. Bangkok was even able to retain its status as an entrepot for several decades after Singapore had become the principal exchange mart in Southeast Asia. This probably occurred because Chinese merchants, long familiar with Siamese business practices, would have found operating in an accustomed setting more profitable and more convenient. Furthermore, many of the bulk items comprising the return cargoes of the Chinese junks were native to Siam, which made recourse to Singapore unnecessary.

British control of Singapore was initiated in order to facilitate Anglo-Asian trade. Expectations were high that an expanded market in China for Indian and British textiles and opium could be generated once a strategically located, duty-free port was established.[11] These expectations were not realized, because the China junks seldom carried back to China anything but Straits produce from Singapore and so failed to introduce European manufactures into the many Chinese ports to which they sailed. This is not to suggest, however, that the junk trade with Singapore was inconsequential, for the China-Singapore and Siam-Singapore traffic made up two of its most lucrative branches. Three quarters of the Singapore-Siam trade in 1833 was shipped in Chinese or Siamese vessels,[12] while, of the total Singapore-China trade in 1835, almost one half was carried by junk.[13] This trade was so critical, in fact, that a decrease in the number of Chinese and Siamese junks calling at Singapore during the 1832-1833 season was directly responsible for the stagnation of the entire market.[14]

China's trade with Singapore was an almost mirror image of her trade with Siam. Her exports included tiles, umbrellas, paper, earthenware, and the like, and her imports were primarily such Straits produce as rattan, pepper, seaweed, and woods (Table 3). Most of the Chinese goods exported to Singapore were then re-exported to other maritime Southeast

[11] Wong, "The Trade," pp. 23-34.

[12] *Singapore Chronicle*, 7/21/1831, 11/14/1833. The total value of the trade between Singapore and Siam was Sp. $462,973. The amount carried by square-rigged vessels was $128,506. The remainder, worth $334,467, carried by Siamese or Chinese junks.

[13] Wong, "The Trade," p. 106.

[14] *Singapore Chronicle*, 4/11/1833. Chinese junks were said to have been requisitioned by the government to transport troops to Formosa. The failure of Siam's rice and sugar crops in 1832 and the war with Cochin China explained the reduced number of Siamese junks entering the port.

Asian countries,[15] although some were shipped to India and Europe. Tea and the finer textiles comprised only a small proportion of junk exports to Singapore because these goods for European consumption were generally purchased directly at Canton by Western merchants. European and Indian imports to China were similarly obtained through the direct trade of East India Company and Country ships. Some Chinese and European goods were purchased at Singapore for export by junk or ship, but the hope that Singapore would replace Canton as the center of the Sino-European trade failed to materialize.

Siam's exports to Singapore are readily catalogued and were mostly such unprocessed staples as sugar, salt, and rice (Table 3). Although quantities of Chinese goods were available in Bangkok, almost none were re-exported to Singapore.[16] In discussing China's exports to Siam during the 1840s, Neale observed that many would be carried ultimately to Singapore, since "the richly-wrought silks and satins, the ivory and feather fans, and some portion of the preserves" were not in demand and "would be a dead loss, were it not for speculative merchants that trade with Singapore and Bombay."[17] The Singapore shipping registers and other contemporary sources do not, however, support this view. Silks, satins, and even velvets were in demand in the Bangkok market, while preserves and sweetmeats were purchased by Siamese and resident Chinese alike.[18]

British and Indian cottons and piece-goods formed the bulk of Siam's imports from Singapore, whereas Chinese junks returning to China took

[15] See the *Singapore Chronicle Commercial Registers*. Both European and native craft, i.e. maritime Southeast Asian vessels, took enormous quantities of Chinese goods to Batavia, Penang, the West and East coasts of Sumatra, etc.

[16] Malloch, *Siam*, pp. 50-51; T. J. Newbold, *Political and Statistical Account of the British Settlements in the Straits of Malacca*, 2 vols. (London: John Murray, 1839), vol. 1, pp. 291-342; *Singapore Chronicle Commercial Register*, 1831, 1832, 1833.

[17] Neale, *Residence*, p. 175.

[18] Malloch, *Siam*, p. 11: "The Siamese dress gaudily in silks, satins, and velvets, to attend marriages and festivals, and these articles of dress are mostly imported from China." On pp. 62-63 he states that 50,000 jars of pickled onion and garlic were imported from China along with great quantities of ginger preserves. There is no evidence that this was re-exported to Singapore (Table 3); Great Britain: Board of Trade, *Abstract of Reports on the Trade of Various Countries and Places, Siam, 1860*, p. 334; *Burney Papers*, vol. 2, pt. 4, Extracts from H. Burney's Report respecting the Commerce of Siam, Dec. 2, 1826, p. 80: "Not only the wants of these Chinese, but the wants of the Siamese themselves, who all use Chinese crapes, porcelain, teas and sweetmeats, render an intercourse with China as necessary as it is extensive."

only minute quantities of these commodities. The remaining Siamese imports were Straits produce and some miscellaneous Chinese goods, but these were insignificant when compared with the imports of European and Indian textiles.[19] Straits produce for Siam was normally supplied by coasting vessels directly from the small market ports dotting the Gulf of Siam or by itinerant merchants from Laos and Cambodia. Chinese goods were obtained by way of direct shipment from the Chinese maritime provinces. While Singapore was an exchange market only, for which European and Indian goods were essential and to which large numbers of European merchants repaired, Bangkok catered primarily to an Asian market, with European and Chinese imports earmarked for either internal consumption or for distribution to other states on the Southeast Asian mainland.

The Sino-Siamese commercial affinity was sustained by a sense of reciprocity: ". . . it is founded upon material wants not only of luxuries, but far more so, of the necessities of life."[20] These "necessities" included the rice, woods, cotton and sugar from Siam and the china- and earthenware dishes and bowls, the foodstuffs, and textiles from China. Traffic in bulk goods predated the Ch'ing[21] and was, perhaps, crucial to the underlying durability of the Sino-*Nan-yang* mercantile bonds. Such continuity suggests a stable demand and an economic utility which can be affirmed only by an examination of the products exchanged.

A salient feature of Siamese exports was their uniformity over time. Seventeenth- and eighteenth-century Western sources mention that rice, wood, salt, coconut oil, hides, brown sugar, tin, iron, copper and lead, indigo, cotton, sticklac, benjamin, wax, horns, and ivory[22] were the principal exports. While new commodities like pepper, white sugar, and

---

[19] *Singapore Chronicle*, 4/28/1831, 7/21/1831: the six junks clearing port for Bangkok took 97,540 yards of British cotton and 74.5 *corge* of Indian textiles, but only 300 piculs of rattan, 30 *corge* of Java mats and 30 piculs of seaweed. The commercial registers for the remainder of the export season show a similar trend. See also *The Asiatic Journal and Monthly Register*, n.s., 1 (Jan.-Apr. 1830): 16.

[20] FO 17/9, p. 44.

[21] Meilink-Roelofsz, *Asian Trade and European Influence*, pp. 48-49.

[22] Elmore, *The British Mariner's Directory and Guide*, pp. 307-09; *Dutch Papers: Extracts from the Dagh Register*," pp. 29-30, 67-70; John Albert de Mandelslo, *The Voyages and Travels of J. Albert de Mandelslo into the East-Indies 1638-1650*, trans. John Davies (London: Dring & Starkey, 1662), p. 130; *Records of the Relations between Siam and Foreign Countries*, vol. 2, pp. 9-18; Simon de La Loubère (*A New Historical Relation of*) *The Kingdom of Siam*, 2 vols. in 1 (1693. Reprint. London: Oxford University Press, 1969), pp. 94-95.

tobacco were introduced in the nineteenth century and others were dropped, Siam's export cargoes remained essentially unchanged.[23] Most nineteenth-century descriptions of Siam's trade failed to note the destination of specific merchandise. It is difficult, therefore, to ascertain where each of Siam's export commodities was shipped. Certain goods are known to have been exported to China (Table 4; Appendix A, sec. 1) but some of these may also have been exported to Siam's other trading partners. Since not all of Siam's exports were designated for the Chinese market, Siam's export trade with China can be delineated only if a distinction is made between those goods required for the China trade and those shipped elsewhere.

The Siamese products considered particularly desirable by the Chinese during the nineteenth century and regularly shipped there were rice, cotton, pepper, gamboge (a resin), sticklac (a resinous excretion from the lac beetle), sugar, sappan, red and agila woods, cardamom, tin, and hides.[24] While some of these, e.g. tin, cardamom, and eagle wood were high value per unit of weight (HV/UW) commodities, they were exported in smaller volume to China and more sporadically than the staples—rice, pepper, cotton, sugar, etc.[25] The dividing line between high or low value per unit of weight has been arbitrarily set at 15 *baht* for the discussion that follows. All goods with a cost below 15 *baht* are considered as low value per unit of weight (LV/UW) with those above 15 *baht* as HV/UW.[26] A further distinction must be made between bulk and non-bulk cargoes. A few of the bulk exports, such as tin, fell within the HV/UW category, but most did not. From Appendix B, sec. 1 (also Table 5), we

---

[23] Ingram, *Economic Change*, p. 25.

[24] See Appendix B.

[25] Ingram, *Economic Change*, p. 21; J. H. Van der Heide, "The Economical Development of Siam during the Last Half Century," *Journal of the Siam Society* 3,2 (1906): 6. Both authors maintain that Siam's exports were "items of high value per unit of weight." With the exception of tin, cardamom, and long pepper, the average price of the goods exported in the four vessels cited in Appendix B, sec. 2-5, were under 10 *baht* per picul and should not be classified as HV/UW.

[26] The wide range in price between high and low value goods becomes apparent after a glance through Appendix A. For instance, the price of cardamom could be as high as 400 *baht*/picul, depending on quality, of benjamin as high as 60 *baht*/picul, with ivory at 160 *baht*. The cost of low value goods like sapan wood varied between 4.5 and 1 *baht*/picul, sugar between 8 and 6 *baht*/picul, etc. Black pepper has been included here as a low value item because its average price at 12 *baht*/picul does not warrant its classification among such luxury articles as cardamom, gamboge, or birds' nests. The Siamese themselves considered it a low-cost item: CMH.R.4, #74, 1864.

Table 4. Composite Table of Siamese Exports to China 1800-1850[a]

Product	Siam: Cost[b] High - Low	China: Cost High - Low	Quantity Exported[c]
Bark: Mangrove Palong (Plong)	1.25 - .75	4.25 - 2.75	large quantity
Benjamin (Benzoin)	60 - 20	200 - 16	400
Betel-nut	4 - 2	7 - 4	large quantity
Beche-de-mer	65 - 14	160 - 10	650
Bones	7 - 1		23,000
Cardamom	400 - 20		650-900
Cotton	26 - 3		60,000
Cushions and mattresses	8 - .375#		504,000#
Fish	8 - 7		large quantity
Gamboge	60 - 30	120 - 100	600
Peltry	12 - 5.5		39,000
	1 - .18#		170,600#
Ivory	160 - 130	240 - 140	500-1,000
Pepper (black)	15 - 8	16 - 13	60,000
Rice	1.28 - .72	7 - 3	to meet demand
Shoes (Chinese-style)			200,000 pr.
Sugar	8 - 5		30,000-70,000
Tin	32 - 20	45 - 40	6,000
Wood: Agila	1000 - 50		920
Ebony	2.5	4	5,000
Red	1.5 - .75	5 - 3.5	40,000
Sandal	5#		a quantity
Sapan	4.5 - 1	9 - 4	100,000

[a] The figures in this table are from Appendix A, sec. 1.

[b] The cost is given in *baht* per picul or *baht* per piece (#).

[c] The quantity exported represents approximate annual exports and is given in piculs or pieces (#).

Table 5. A Composite Table of the Cargo Manifests of Four
Siamese State Trading Vessels Which Sailed to China in 1844[a]

Product	Weight[b]	Investment[c]
Sapan wood	12,450	28,013
Pepper	6,845	48,513
Redwood	8,867	16,075
Plong	1,600	1,755
Lac	156	1,542
Long pepper	353	4,231
Red cane sugar	200	750
Tin	162	4,806
Rhinoceros horn	.35	298
Cardamom (pursat)	10	2,349
Dried betel	15	53
Rudders	225	520
Anchors	240	252
Pradoo planks (Red sandalwood)	100	175
Total	31,223.35 piculs	109,332 *baht*

[a] The figures in this table are from Appendix B, sec. 1.

[b] Weight has been rounded to the nearest picul.

[c] Investment has been rounded to the nearest *baht*.

find that 75 percent of the total cargo weight of four vessels sailing to China in the early 1840s was made up by bulk items (sapan wood, redwood, plong bark, sugar, tin, and betel) and only 11 percent of the total cargo investment was attributed to HV/UW goods.[27] Although the aggregate manifest (Appendix B, sec. 1) includes goods exported on a Siamese square-rigged vessel, one finds that the same pattern holds true for the exports carried by the state trading junks (Table 6). For example, the Sunhong junk exported cargo weighing 6,886 piculs of which 75 percent were bulk goods and 98 percent were LV/UW. From a comparison of the junk manifests (Appendix B, sec. 2-4) with that of the square-rigged vessel (Appendix B, sec. 5), it is apparent that the kinds of goods exported by junk and by the Western-style vessel were similar. We might tentatively conclude, therefore, that the greater part of Siam's export trade to China was composed of LV/UW goods and that the HV/UW were shipped as excess cargo space became available. Furthermore, the high proportion of cargo space allocated to bulk transport indicates once again that junks were fully as capable of carrying this trade as the larger Western-style ships.[28] Finally, the preponderance of LV/UW products would suggest a certain demand for them in China; they were shipped because a profit was anticipated. Gutzlaff's testimony in the 1830s that a profit of 100 percent was made on pepper and sapan wood in China[29] must have been equally true for the 1840s, considering the quantities Siam exported.

Siam's exports should not be seen as marginal luxuries, but as staple products intended for either popular consumption or for the manufacture of consumer goods by the Chinese. The Chinese had little interest in acquiring vast stores of manufactured articles and therein lay the

---

[27] Long pepper, tin, rhinoceros horn, and cardamom are considered here as HV/UW even though the horn and pepper are listed below 15 *baht*/picul on the manifest since their average price was generally much higher (Appendix A, sec. 1). The lower prices for many of the goods listed in these cargo manifests probably reflect the vessels' official sponsorship. One would expect members of the royal family and high ministers to have been able to procure goods at reduced prices.

[28] Van der Heide, "The Economical," argues that it was only with the development of more modern transport that bulk commodities like rice and teak could be exported from Thailand. We have seen, however, that bulk transport was carried on throughout the nineteenth century and earlier by junks. He might, perhaps, have emphasized more strongly such factors as the new markets opened to Siamese goods with the expansion of Western trade in Siam after 1855 in considering why these particular articles of trade were not exported on a regular basis until later in the century.

[29] Gutzlaff, *Journal of Two Voyages*, p. 110.

Table 6. A Composite Table of the Cargo Manifests of Three Siamese Junks Which Sailed to China in 1844[a]

Product	Sunhung		Sunha		Cinli	
	Weight[b]	Investment[c]	Weight	Investment	Weight	Investment
Sapan wood	3,000	6,750	3,200	7,200	2,000	4,500
Pepper	1,700	12,113	1,700	12,113	1,400	9,975
Redwood	1,700	3,230	1,500	2,850	668	1,278
Plong	400	507	300	368	234	266
Lac	50	517	50	513	--	--
Long pepper	36	428	20	240	--	--
Red cane sugar	--	--	200	750	--	--
Rudders	--	--	140	360	--	--
Pradoo planks	--	--	100	175	--	--
Tin	--	--	--	--	102	3,026
Rhinoceros horn	--	--	--	--	.35	298
Total	6,886	23,545	7,210	24,569	4,404.35	19,343

[a] The figures in this table are from Appendix B, sec. 2-4.

[b] Weight has been rounded to the nearest picul.

[c] Investment has been rounded to the nearest *baht*.

strength of Straits produce over European exports in the Chinese marketplace. As one nineteenth-century observer noted: "they (the Chinese) have always declared they consider their own commerce with the Indo-Chinese islands as infinitely superior in every respect (to European). . . ."[30]

Demand for a given product can also be determined on the basis of increased productivity, particularly if the growth is continuous, thereby indicating a stable market.[31] The annual production of most of Siam's staple LV/UW exports appears to have increased from 1800 to 1850. Siam's cotton production showed a three-fold growth rate between 1825 and 1850, from 50,000 to 140,000 piculs.[32] While no figures are available for the quantity exported in the early 1800s, by 1850 cotton and cotton products accounted for 12 percent of Siam's total export investment.[33] The cotton trade must have been somewhat speculative, for its price in China fluctuated according to the abundance or dearth of the native crop. The increase of Siam's cotton output would seem to denote fairly constant Chinese demand as little or no cotton was exported to Singapore (Table 3).

China imported most of her pepper from Siam, and black pepper amounted to 14 percent of Siam's export investment in 1850. Pepper production increased only slightly between 1800 and 1850, but exports to China remained the same.[34] The acreage devoted to pepper cultivation

[30] Peter Dobell, *Travels in Kamtchatka and Siberia: with a Narrative of a Residence in China*, 2 vols. (London: Colburn & Bently, 1830), vol. 2, p. 165; Davis, *China*, vol. 1, p. 41: "The great industry and ingenuity of the Chinese causes them to turn nearly all raw produce to good account"; *British Relations with the Chinese Empire in 1832* (London: Parbury, Allen & Co., 1832), p. 15; "The Chinese Empire in Its Foreign Relations," *The Bombay Quarterly Review* 3,6 (1856): 234-35. All of these sources express the same idea, namely that the Chinese found more utility in importing unprocessed goods than manufactured goods.

[31] Of course, a sharp drop in the unit price of Siam's major export articles between 1800 and 1850 would have negated any increases in production. More would have needed to be produced and sold to bring in the same amount of revenue. The available figures are not adequate for this kind of analysis.

[32] *Burney Papers*, vol. 4, pt. 2, p. 106; Malloch, *Siam*, pp. 34-36.

[33] Ingram, *Economic Change*, p. 10; Malloch, *Siam*, pp. 34, 36, 40.

[34] Crawfurd, *Embassy*, p. 413: 60,000 piculs were produced annually and almost the entire amount was sent to China; Malloch, *Siam*, p. 44: 72,000 piculs were produced annually, 61,500 of which were exported to China; Crawfurd, *Embassy*, p. 381, states

in Siam was relatively small,[35] but it may, nonetheless, have been found sufficient to supply China's needs without expanding production.

Siamese sugar production was somewhat erratic during the 1840s following the king's imposition of a monopoly in 1839. Prior to that time, production and exports had been increasing, but when the selling price was arbitrarily raised so that all qualities sold for almost 10 *baht* per picul,[36] both began to fall off. Only toward the middle of the 1850s were sugar exports again approaching their pre-monopoly level, and in 1850 they were said to comprise 5 percent of Siam's export investment to China.[37] The trade in hides is not sufficiently well documented to make any assessment as to whether or not their export increased in the nineteenth century. A large profit was expected in the China market with the sale price there approximately four times the purchase price. Total peltry accounted for 7 percent of Siam's 1850 exports to that country.[38]

Sapan wood was, in terms of volume, Siam's largest single export, nearly all of which went to China where it was used principally for extracting a cloth dye. It and pepper were mentioned as the earliest and most important of Siam's exports in both Western and Chinese sources. Exports increased from 30,000 piculs in the early 1820s to 100,000 piculs in the 1850s (6.5 percent of export investment).[39] When the royal monopoly in sapan wood was abolished in 1839, revenue collection was farmed out to the highest bidder. Government receipts thereafter grew from 96,480 *baht* in 1851 to 152,480 *baht* in 1861,[40] denoting a continuing increase in production during the Fourth Reign (1851-1868). Redwood was the next most commonly exported wood after sapan, forming 1 percent of

that the government revenue collected from pepper was 400,000 *baht*, which was the same amount reported by Pallegoix (*Royaume Thai*), vol. 1, p. 310) in the early 1850's.

[35] Ingram, *Economic Change*, p. 11.

[36] Great Britain: Board of Trade, *Abstract of Reports*, 1854, Siam, p. 42:

> In 1822, 60,000 piculs were produced.
> In 1835, 135,000 piculs were produced.
> In 1840, 257,000 piculs were produced.
> In 1846, 150,000 piculs were produced (*Allen's Indian Mail* 84 [1847]: 528).

[37] Malloch, *Siam*, pp. 46, 50.

[38] Ibid., pp. 38, 44, 50.

[39] Ibid., p. 50; Crawfurd, *Embassy*, p. 413; Great Britain: Board of Trade, *Abstract of Reports*, 1854, Siam, pp. 43-44.

[40] Constance M. Wilson, "State and Society in the Reign of Monkut, 1851-1868: Thailand on the eve of modernization," (PhD dissertation, Cornell University, 1970), p. 636.

Siam's 1850 export investment. Its hardness and durability made it an ideal construction material and it sold for twice as much in China as it did in the Bangkok market.

Finally, stricklac was an article of trade with China as well as of tribute. It was not mentioned by Malloch as an export to China,[41] but in the 1820s, Crawfurd stated that 16,000 piculs were sent there,[42] presumably on an annual basis, and the 1844 cargo manifests also list it as an export (Appendix B, sec. 1). On the assumption that the quantity exported did not increase over Crawfurd's figure, it would have accounted for 3 percent of total export investment to China in 1850 if it sold at the average price of 12 *baht* per picul. Adding all the above percentages together, we find that the major LV/UW trade goods accounted for 48.5 percent of Siam's exports to China. If the goods which individually formed only a small proportion of the total, such as bark (2 percent), rice (2.5 percent),[43] and dried fish (2 percent) are included, over 50 percent of Siam's exports to China fell within the LV/UW classification.

Certain features of Siam's export trade can now be commented on. In the first place, Siam's export cargoes did not consist primarily of luxury or "fancy" foods. They were, rather, wood for building or for extracting dyes, products for food preparation or the food itself, the raw materials from which drugs were made, hides for farm equipment, cotton for the manufacture of wearing apparel, and so forth. Secondly, a rise in production concomitant with an increased export volume for most staples is indicative of a constant demand for these goods in China. Rising exports were perhaps linked to the growth of Chinese-controlled shipping during the first few decades of the nineteenth century. As we have seen above, the junk trade was monopolized by Chinese whose influence in Chinese and Siamese ports enabled them to undercut Western competition in the

---

[41] Malloch, *Siam*, pp. 44-45. According to his figures 18,000 piculs were exported, but all were shipped to Singapore and the Malay coast. Table 3 indicates that only a small proportion was carried to Singapore in the early 1830s and Malloch's figures could only be correct if the trading pattern changed radically in the intervening twenty years. It accounted for 1 percent of the cargo in Table 5 and 3 percent seems a reasonable compromise between that and Malloch's 5 percent.

[42] Crawfurd, *Embassy*, p. 413.

[43] Malloch, *Siam*, p. 42. He gives an export figure of 8,000 *coyan* (200,000 piculs) at 18 *baht/coyan*, but mentions that rice "may be had to meet any demand." In some years as many as 1,000,000 piculs (40,000 *coyan*) may have been exported (see Ingram, *Economic Change*, pp. 24, 29), which would have raised the proportion of rice to other exports considerably. See p. 94 below.

importation of Straits produce. Continuous demand and expanded shipping would have stimulated Siam's export trade. Finally the fact that this trade was carried in junks did not imply that the exchange was limited to only HV/UW cargoes. Transportation in bulk was not dependent upon Western-style shipping, but was an integral part of the junk traffic.

China's export trade was characterized by an infinite variety of manufactured consumer wares, or in nineteenth-century parlance, by "assorted cargoes." The largest categories of merchandise shipped to Southeast Asia were chinaware, earthenware, and textiles. Others were dried and salted vegetables and fruits, tiles, umbrellas, combs, herbs and medicinal preparations, and paper—relatively all LV/UW products (Table 7). China supplied Siam with most of her imported manufactured goods,[44] although competitive European and Indian textiles were imported from Singapore in greater abundance as Siam's trade with that port became established. While the most obvious market for China's exports was the overseas Chinese community in Siam, there is little question that the Siamese themselves had become accustomed to purchasing these goods.[45] We can see from Appendix A, sec. 2, that China's exports were not intended for only the Siamese elite, but for general consumption by all levels of Siamese society.[46]

Few comparative figures for China's junk exports to Siam are available, which increases the difficulty of determining whether or not this trade expanded during the first half of the nineteenth century. The increase in the number of vessels carrying the trade should provide some indication of any increase in the volume of exports. Here, too, the figures are inadequate, but from Crawfurd's estimate of 35,083 tons (including mainland and Hainan shipping) in the early 1820s,[47] the tonnage had

[44] Moor, *Indian Archipelago*, p. 226; Malloch, *Siam*, p. 27.

[45] Great Britain: Board of Trade, *Abstract of Reports*, 1854, Siam, p. 40. As was noted above, Chinese exports to Singapore were frequently re-exported for sale at other ports throughout the Archipelago. Chinese goods had undoubtedly gained wide acceptance among various groups in that region besides the Chinese.

[46] The goods desired by the nobility and king seem generally to have been ordered specifically, or purchased by agents sent to China on the king's behalf. He might also buy goods imported through the junk trade if they were of particularly good quality. Members of the royal family and the officials apparently did likewise. CMH.R.2, #5, 1820; CMH.R.3, #49, 1844; National Archives, Letter, King Rama IV-Yam Ap Toot, Jan. 30, 1853; CMH.R.4, #109, 1854; CMH.R.4, #88, 1857.

[47] Crawfurd, *Embassy*, p. 410.

Table 7. Composite Table of Chinese Exports to Siam 1800-1850[a]

Product	China: Cost[b] High - Low	Siam: Cost High - Low	Quantity Exported[c]
Ceremonial goods:			
Mock gold leaf		2	3,000 books
Gold leaf			large quantity
Artificial flowers			48,500#
Gongs		2#	15,000#
Joss sticks			large quantity
Incense rods			large quantity
Chinaware:			
dishes, pots, bowls, etc.		1 - .05#	880,000#
Copper-, Brass-ware:			
dishes, utensils, etc.		.75 - .125#	190,500#
Crapes: shawls	8 - 4#	6 - 5#	20,000#
Earthenware:			
bowls, bottles, jars, etc.		.125	1,010,200#
Fans: Paper		.063#	10,000#
Ivory		3 - .25#	20,000#
Foodstuffs/Preserves		6 - .5	4,000 piculs 50,000 jars 15,000 baskets
Glassware		20 - .02#	180,550

Table 7. Continued

Product	China: Cost[b] High - Low	Siam: Cost High - Low	Quantity Exported[c]
Metal goods: utensils, tools, lanterns, etc.		4 - .125#	155,500#
Nankeens	2 - .9#	20 - 1#	40,000#
Paper			a great quantity
Silk piece-goods	varies according to quality	varies according to quality	40,200# 1,630 rolls
Stones/Tiles/Pillars			a large quantity
Toys		15 - .25#	a large quantity
Umbrellas	.24 - .14#	1 - .125#	10,000#
Misc. wooden goods		.5 - .125#	30,000#

[a] The figures in this table are from Appendix A, sec. 2.

[b] The cost is given in *baht* per picul or *baht* per piece (#).

[c] The quantity exported represents approximate annual exports and is given in piculs or pieces (#) unless otherwise specified.

reportedly risen to 60,000 thirty years later.[48] Nineteenth-century approximations of the number of junks engaged in Sino-Siamese trade were based almost entirely on Crawfurd's estimates up to the period when junks were replaced by square-rigged vessels and steamers. Most sources covering the period 1820-1860, therefore, provide the same figures, i.e. 150-200 junks or 35,000-50,000 tons total burden. One writer, however, who described Chinese trade in the late 1840s, reported that "no less than forty large junks (from Amoy) annually frequent Bankah (sic.) . . ."[49] which was an enormous increase over the two mentioned by Crawfurd in the 1820s. Expansion of this magnitude is further reflected in a memorial of May 1840 to the Emperor of China discussing the illegal use of permits by Fukien junks. Seventy to eighty vessels were said to trade abroad, with Siam specifically named as a port of call.[50]

The growth of Siam's native and Chinese populations would have also provided the impetus for an expansion of trade between the two countries. Estimates of Siam's population during the first half of the nineteenth century ranged between a little less than three million to six million, with the resident Chinese population being reckoned at anywhere from 15 to 30 percent of the total.[51] As Skinner has pointed out, however, contemporary estimates of the Chinese population were mistakenly based upon observation of the centers of densest settlement, i.e. Bangkok and the towns along the Gulf of Siam.[52] If we assume that Skinner's figures are reasonably correct, the native and immigrant Chinese communities grew 30 percent between 1825 and 1850 compared with a total population growth rate in those same years of 9 percent.[53] One might expect, therefore, that the market for Chinese goods would have enlarged somewhere between the former and latter percentage. Moreover, while an immigrant population acted as a stimulus to an expanding trade, immigration itself

[48] Malloch, *Siam*, p. 28.

[49] Sirr, *China and the Chinese*, vol. 1, p. 138; *Burney Papers*, vol. 3, pt. 2, p. 353: In 1833 200 junks were said to be engaged in trade with China; Malcom, *Travels in Southeastern Asia*, vol. 2, p. 127: 200 junks come annually from China.

[50] *Ch'ou-pan i-wu shih-mo*; Tao-kuang:10:20b-21a.

[51] Crawfurd, *Embassy*, p. 452; Roberts, *Embassy*, p. 308; Pallegoix, *Royaume Thai*, vol. 1, p. 8; Bowring, *Siam*, vol. 1, pp. 81, 85; Skinner, *Chinese Society*, p. 68, Table 3, pp. 70-71, 79; Haü Chi-yü, *Ying-huan chih-lüeh*: 1:31b: The Cantonese in Siam ware said to account for one-sixth of the population.

[52] Skinner, *Chinese Society*, p. 72.

[53] Ibid., p. 79, Table 5.

was a part of the exchange process, "passengers form(ing) the most valuable importation from China into Siam."[54]

Goods other than the china-, earthenware, and textile staples were shipped in large quantities from China to Siam. Brass- and copperware made into boxes, dishes, or utensils, though generally LV/UW, yielded fairly high returns. This was true as well of the oranges, preserves, sugar candy, dried and salted vegetables, and the other edibles traded with Siam. The remaining Chinese exports were assorted LV/UW articles which were a significant factor in China's export trade primarily because of the volume in which they were exported. For example, in 1850, 500,000 writing books were exported and they sold in Siam for 62,500 *baht*; 40,000 boxes of dice and cards sold for 10,000 *baht*, and so forth.[55] In addition to merchandise and passengers, silver bullion was exported to meet the deficit arising from the trade balance in Siam's favor.[56]

Most of the merchandise exported to China's Asian markets was grown or produced in the southern provinces. The textiles shipped to Siam were manufactured primarily in Chang-chou or in the Canton delta.[57] Few of the costly fabrics in demand in European markets were exported to Siam by the junks engaged in the regular private traffic, but rather the poorer grades of cotton nankeens, linens, and silks. Fabrics of better quality were either supplied as gifts to the king and his envoys upon the completion of a tribute mission, or their purchase was specially commissioned by the more affluent members of Siamese society. China-ware was transported from Kiangsi to Canton where it was painted and

---

[54] Crawfurd, *Embassy*, p. 412.

[55] Malloch, *Siam*, pp. 61-62.

[56] Gutzlaff, *Two Voyages*, p. 44; Crawfurd, *Embassy*, p. 412; Wong, "Trade of Singapore," pp. 52-53: The same pattern seems to hold true regarding China's trade with Singapore, for in the thirty-two years between 1823 and 1855 China's imports from Singapore exceeded her exports to Singapore two-thirds of the time. Although the exportation of bullion was expressly prohibited during the Ch'ing, Western ships importing more valuable cargoes than they exported were permitted to take out 30 percent of the differences between their imports and exports in bullion. This practice was known as the "exportation of three tenths," and if one ship needed more than 30 percent in bullion, it was allowed to transfer the required amount from another ship whose imports and exports were equal: *Canton Register*, 2/26/1828; *Chinese Repository*, 5 (1837): 385-89.

[57] Evelyn Rawski, *Agricultural Change and the Peasant Economy of South China*, p. 66; Hirth, "Geographical Distribution," p. 307; Williams, *Chinese Commercial Guide*, 1863, pp. 114-15, 121, 128-29; *Kuang-tung TC*: 1911:97:9a, 10b, 12b-13a (repr. of 1822 ed.); *Chang-chou FC* (Prefectural gazetteer of Chang-chou), comp. by Shen Ting-chün, 50+1 *chüan*, 1877:39:2a; *HMC*: 5:177.

then exported, or Fukien-ware was exported directly from Amoy to Siam and the Archipelago.[58] As with fabrics, chinaware for the Siamese market was of the poorer qualities. The cups, dishes, and bowls were intended for daily use by the general public, and large amounts of broken ware were exported to be made into the mosaic designs adorning temple walls.[59]

Ch'ao-chou was famous for the quality of its sweetmeats and preserves, although oranges, lychees, and ginger were also preserved and bottled in Chang-chou and in and about Canton for the export trade.[60] Much of the stone and decorative material used in Siamese temple construction, as well as ceremonial objects, was manufactured near Canton or was quarried in Kwangtung and Yunnan. Marble and granite slabs and tiles were exported in vast quantities for courtyard pavement and for roofing. Griffins, peacocks, and Buddha images, posts and balustrades were carved from stone, often patterned after samples sent with commission agents from Siam.[61] Artificial and gilt flowers manufactured at Amoy, gold leaf, joss sticks, and paper from Canton were disposed of with equal ease in Siam.[62]

The Sino-*Nan-yang* trade was of some consequence to the economy of South China. Not only did it provide employment through shipping and its related activities (crews, brokers, and hong merchants), but it also helped to stimulate local handicraft industries and the production of cash crops. In some areas of Fukien, for instance, people cultivated rice less intensively because their rice needs could be met with only a part of the profit from home textile production or other activities to which the time saved might be devoted.[63] The local industries which grew up in response to the Sino-*Nan-yang* trade enhanced the prosperity of the region, providing alternative forms of employment. The *Chang-chou fu-chih* notes, in fact, that the exchange of local goods was a source of wealth for many

[58] *Fu-chien TC*: 1868:59:50a; *Chang-chou FC*: 1877:39:2b. Both mention that chinaware was produced in Chang-chou prefecture.

[59] Malcom, *Travels*, vol. 2, p. 122.

[60] Rawski, *Agricultural Change*, p. 66; Hirth, "Geographical distribution," pp. 376-77; Williams, *Chinese Commercial Guide*, 1863, p. 133.

[61] CMH.R.3, #49, 1844; Malcom, *Travels*, vol. 2, p. 122; Malloch, *Siam*, p. 60. Some of these goods were also purchased in Ningpo.

[62] Malloch, *Siam*, pp. 60-61, 63; CMH.R.3, #49, 1844.

[63] Rawski, *Agricultural Change*, pp. 47, 55-56.

of the people.[64] In Siam, on the other hand, land was abundant during the nineteenth century and the same incentives did not exist for developing handicraft industries as in South China. Siam's export trade in vegetable and mineral products was the reflection of an economy based almost totally on agriculture. China's export trade with Southeast Asia induced an element of greater diversification in her economy than did Sino-Western trade. Since, by the nineteenth century, Western porcelain and textile manufacturing techniques had become as good as, or superior to, those of China, the only Chinese commodity for which there was great Western demand was tea. The diversity characteristic of Chinese exports to the *Nan-yang* bolstered a wide range of lucrative enterprises which, in some instances, were totally supported by the requirements of the *Nan-yang* market place.

The importation of unprocessed materials from Siam further extended China's trade in that some were subsequently fashioned into Chinese export wares. The Chinese cabinet-work and furniture shipped abroad were frequently built from the redwood and ebony imported from Siam,[65] while other imports like sapan wood and mangrove bark yielded dyes for tanning or for dyeing the less expensive export textiles. Imported feathers were used in China as insignia of office, in theatrical costumes, etc., but they were also made into fans for export. Ivory was carved into models, balls, puzzles, and chopsticks, many of them for export to the West and Southeast Asia.[66] The Chinese economy thus benefitted from both an increased stock of goods for immediate consumption such as sugar, pepper, and rice, and from a supply of raw materials, some of which could be processed and re-exported to overseas markets.

Rice was the only commodity in the Sino-*Nan-yang* exchange for which the Chinese offered rebates to the merchants from those countries shipping it regularly to China. While Siam was but one of the foreign countries supplying China with rice in the nineteenth century, large quantities being imported from Manila, Java, Bengal, and Singapore as well,[67] Siam's rice, as we will see below, had achieved a reputation for quality and inexpensiveness, which made it a particularly desirable

---

[64] *Chang-chou FC*: 1877:39:1a.

[65] Williams, *Chinese Commercial Guide*, 1863, p. 120.

[66] *Chang-chou FC*: 1877:39:2b; *Fu-chien TC*: 1868:59:50a.

[67] Fu I-ling, *Ming-Ch'ing shih-tai shang-jen chi shang-yeh tzu-pen*, p. 204. The rice trade from Siam and Luzon was crucial to Amoy's development as a commercial center in the Ch'ien-lung period when Amoy's trade was at its peak.

import. The demand for rice was obviously greatest during those years when the China crop failed, but imports were often necessary in the best of times to provision the coastal population and military garrisons of Kwangtung and Fukien.[68] Rice could have been, and was at times, brought from the inland rice-producing regions of China, but the transportation costs were found to be less when carried, even from much further away, by sea.[69]

The importance of the overseas rice trade to China during the Ch'ing dynasty is best exemplified by the policies instituted to enlarge the volume of imports. Edicts enunciating concessions to foreign and Chinese merchants dealing in rice were sent down from the beginning of the 1700s. The state of the economy seems to have been a matter of concern as early as 1716 when the K'ang-hsi Emperor prohibited the export of rice from Kiangsu and Chekiang. Merchant vessels thereafter were allowed to take only that quantity required for the voyage.[70] Siam was known at the time as a rice-exporting country and was specifically mentioned in a number of edicts and memorials as a place where rice was plentiful and as one which sent rice-laden vessels to China. In 1722, deeming the rice trade beneficial to the southeastern coastal districts, the K'ang-hsi Emperor ordered 300,000 piculs carried from Siam and the taxes on it remitted.[71] Encouragement to rice-importing vessels was continued in

[68] *Hunt's Merchants' Magazine* 3,6 (Dec. 1840): 473: One sign of scarcity in the Canton region was that the price of rice was said to be double that in surrounding areas; H. Hinton, *The Grain Tribute System of China (1845-1911)* (Cambridge: Harvard University Press, 1956), pp. 9a-b, Table A, indicates that the Ch'ing did not levy rice tribute from Kwangtung or Fukien, suggesting that rice production may not have been as great there as elsewhere; Jane Leonard, "Wei Yüan and the Hai-kuo t'u-chih: A Geopolitical Analysis of Western Expansion in Maritime Asia," (PhD dissertation, Cornell University, 1971), p. 141; Mancall, *The Pattern*, p. 308: by the mid-eighteenth century grain prices were rising on a consistent basis because the rice yield per acre was no longer expanding to meet the pressure from growing population; *YHKC*: 21:26b.

[69] John F. Davis, trans., "Extracts from the Peking Gazette," *Transactions of the Royal Asiatic Society of Great Britain and Ireland* 2 (1830): 88-89: The Governor-General of Fukien-Chekiang suggested that the most efficient means of rectifying the high prices and rice shortages would be for Fukien merchants to import rice by sea from Chekiang; Mancall, "The Ch'ing Tribute System," p. 75.

[70] *KHSL*: 270:15b-16a; (*Ch'in-ting*) *Chung-shu cheng-k'ao* [Regulations of the central administration], comp. by Ming-liang *et al.*, 32 *chüan* (1825. Taipei: Hsüeh-hai, 1968), 22:21a-b.

[71] *KHSL*: 296:3a-b; *YHKC*: 21:21a-b; Hsieh Yu-jung, *Hsin-pien, Hsien-lo kuo-chih*, pp. 72-73; Mancall, "The Ch'ing Tribute System," pp. 88-89. Mancall maintains that the rice

the Yung-cheng period. In 1724, cargo vessels were granted tax rebates as long as they carried rice in addition to their other merchandise, while in 1729 Siam's envoys were allowed to buy horses and copper, the sale of which was generally forbidden, because of Siam's regular rice exports to China.[72]

A formal abatement procedure was begun under the Ch'ien-lung Emperor to be applied to all foreigners importing rice in succeeding years. The regulation was issued in response to a memorial of the Fu-chou Tartar General and acting Supervisor of Customs, Hsin-chu, who commented that, as certain Siamese junks had not brought the requisite 5,000 piculs of rice, the duty on the remaining cargo should not be forgiven out of hand.[73] The following year, the Emperor allowed the remission of cargo duties and tonnage dues since rice had formed a portion of the cargo, but maintained that certain procedures should be instituted to regulate the abatement of duty:

> Whenever foreign cargo vessels come to Fukien, Kwang-tung, and other provinces to trade bringing rice of 10,000 piculs or more, their cargo and ship duties are to be reduced by 1/2. If they bring 5,000 piculs or more, the reduction is 3/10. The purchase price should agree with the market price.[74]

By the late Ch'ien-lung and early Chia-ch'ing periods, the regulations under which duty was levied appear to have tightened up somewhat because of imagined or real abuses of the abatement concession.[75] The

imported was only to be carried on Siamese vessels. The citation he provides from the *KHSL* makes no mention, however, of transport in Siamese bottoms; Skinner, *Chinese Society*, p. 17.

[72] *YCSL*: 88:28a; Hsieh, *Hsien-lo*, p. 73; *YHKC*: 21:24b.

[73] *YHKC*: 21:25b-26a; Hsieh, *Hsien-lo*, p. 73.

[74] *YHKC*: 21:26a-b; Hsieh, *Hsien-lo*, p. 73; Bowring, *Siam*, vol. 1, p. 78. Note that the *YHKC* says the memorial (fn. 73) was sent up in CL 7, whereas Hsieh says CL 11.

[75] A rice shortage in Kiangsu and Chekiang in 1806 prompted an Imperial order that Chinese merchants were to trade abroad to purchase rice and that foreigners bringing rice and no other cargo would be excused the measurement, entrance, and exit fees: *CCSL*: 158:18b-19b. Western merchants quickly saw the possibilities inherent in the rice bounty, and by the 1820s had devised various methods to circumvent the prohibition against importing merchandise in addition to rice. Conflict developed between the Canton government and Western merchants over the interpretation of the exemption, but attempts at compromise were largely a failure. Western merchants continued to

Chinese government's preference for rice imports from Siam was force-fully exhibited by an order from the Ch'ien-lung period stating that merchants who returned with no rice but with only the other commodities Siam exported would be subject to twice the normal tonnage dues.[76]

Sino-Siamese rice trade was not as stable as the trade in such commodities as pepper and sapan wood, for the rice market was dependent upon the China crop and fluctuated accordingly. Rice was not cultivated in Siam specifically for an export market until after 1855,[77] but as the harvests were normally plentiful, some could be spared to meet the needs of other Asian countries when shortages occurred.[78] Moreover, Siamese rice was inexpensive and of good quality, being considered superior to rice grown elsewhere in Southeast Asia.[79] One estimate of Siam's total annual rice production prior to 1850 has put it at 20-23 million piculs, of which the proportion exported rarely exceeded 5 percent (1.0-1.5 million piculs), and was normally only 2-3 percent.[80] Rice could not be exported if there were a dearth in Siam or if a poor harvest was anticipated, and this rice traffic was monopolized by Asian merchants, the Burney Treaty having prohibited British export of the crop.[81] Fluctuating demand en-

complain about the illegal exactions of local officials, while the customs officers felt the merchants were doing their best to evade both the spirit and the letter of the law. For a complete discussion of these events see: Davis, *China*, vol. 2, p. 385; *Canton Register*, 6/18/1831; 1/10/1833; 6/17/1833; 8/5/1833.

[76] Lu Chi-fang, "Ch'ing Kao-tsung shih-tai te Chung-Hsien kuan-hsi," p. 389.

[77] Ingram, *Economic Change*, p. 41.

[78] Crawfurd, *Embassy*, pp. 420-21: "The certainty with which the crops of this grain are yielded from year to year, is probably of still more consequence than their occasional abundance. The conviction of this fact has produced a salutary influence even upon the jealous and arbitrary Government of Siam, which, in opposition to the practice of other Asiatic states, generally permits the free exportation of rice, no doubt from a long habitual experience of the safety of this policy."

[79] Moor, *Indian Archipelago*, p. 236.

[80] Ingram, *Economic Change*, p. 29. The *Singapore Chronicle*, 6/13/1833, however, estimates rice and paddy production at 1,696,424 *coyan* of 23 piculs each = 39,017,752 piculs.

[81] *Burney Papers*, vol. 1, pt. 3, p. 385; National Archives, Ledger copies of Ministry of War records, Fourth Reign, vol. 10, pp. 197-99, "A Proclamation announcing to the people that they are to begin planting paddy at the start of the monsoon," n.d. According to this proclamation, Siamese kings had previously prohibited Siamese and Chinese merchants from loading rice to sell externally. Moreover, Article I of the Commercial Agreement in the Burney Treaty implies that Chinese and Siamese merchants, as well as British, were forbidden to trade in rice. But as rice was exported

couraged speculation in rice, occasionally with disastrous results. Upon hearing that the Chinese offered exemption from measurement dues to rice-importing ships, huge quantities were sent from Calcutta to Canton in 1806, causing the already well-stocked market to collapse and the hong merchants to suffer a loss of $.50 per picul on the rice they handled.[82]

From 1820 to 1860 rice in China was purchased at an average price per picul of approximately 4 *baht*, while in Siam during the same period it averaged 0.75-1.25 *baht* per picul. Scarcity in both countries, however, elicited price increases. In 1831 the China harvest was poor and rice reached 6.66 *baht* per picul before the public granaries were opened. Junk imports of grain in 1833 contributed to a reduction and stabilization of the price.[83] The 1832 flooding in Siam caused prices to soar there to 4.5 *baht* per picul. Yet by 1834 they had declined to their normal level and rice was said to be plentiful and cheap.[84] Given the value differential between China and Siam, a 4,000 picul capacity junk (160 *coyan*) could clear a profit of 7,783 *baht* on one shipment.[85] But without an annual demand from China or other countries, profits such as this could not regularly be anticipated. The profit margin would, however, certainly

by Asian merchants after the signing of the treaty in 1826 just as it had been before, one suspects that the regulations were not enforced with any vigor.

[82] Greenberg, *British Trade*, p. 81.

[83] *Canton Register*, 6/6/1831; 10/24/1833.

[84] *The Asiatic Journal and Monthly Register* n.s., 11 (May-Aug. 1833), 27.

[85] According to the *YHKC*: 21:25b and Table 6, the average amount for one junk to carry was 4,000 piculs of rice (160 *coyan*.). While Yen Ju-i, *Yang-fang chi-yao* [Essentials of maritime defense], 24 *chüan*, 1838: 2:16a, says that the large Siamese junks carried 300 piculs and the medium 200, this figure is not supported by other sources and such an amount would not appear to justify a voyage to China. To establish the profit below, 160 *coyan* will be taken as capacity.

160	*coyan*
x 22	*baht* (18 *baht*/*coyan* + 4 *baht* tax)[a]
3,520	*baht* (Price in Siam)
160	*coyan*
x 100·	*baht* (4 *baht*/picul x 25 pl. = 100 *baht*)
16,000	*baht* (Selling price in China)
-3,318	*baht* (Port exactions at Canton)[b]
12,682	*baht*
-3,520	*baht* (Cost in Siam)
9,162	*baht*
-1,700	*baht* (Junk expenses for salaries, etc.)
7,462	*baht* (Profit)[c]

94

have tempted merchants to take advantage of the demand in China or elsewhere when it arose.[86]

Although rice exports have been figured at only 2-3 percent of total production and at 2.5 percent of total export investment, one cannot say that rice was of little importance as an article of trade. Various factors should be considered in assessing its role in Sino-Siamese commerce. As we have seen above, the unusual measures taken by the Chinese government to obtain rice from abroad emphasize its value as an import. It was in particular demand during the nineteenth century as the burden of over-population became increasingly apparent and civil strife restricted production in many places. No other product was as actively sought through legal channels by the Chinese as rice, and an awareness of this demand must have enhanced its importance to the Siamese as an export.

Secondly, in the years when Siam had a rice surplus, any quantity could have been exported depending on the demand. At certain times, therefore, more than the 200,000 piculs cited by Malloch would have been exported and the share of total cargo investment attributed to rice would have risen. Two and a half percent is strictly valid only for Malloch's estimates around 1850, and may, in fact, be too low.[87] Without other cargo manifests against which to compare it, however, it must be accepted as at least an approximation of average exports.

[a] Per *coyan* cost according to Malloch, *Siam*, p. 42. Tax according to CMH.R.4, #40, 1857. The tax may have been different during earlier periods, but this was the only figure obtainable.

[b] This is the highest possible figure according to the *Canton Register*, 1/2/1832. All rice ships were to pay a duty of Sp. $1,359 and if they exported cargo, an additional Sp. $300. Later estimates for the amount paid in fees varied considerably: *Canton Register*, 7/15/1833, says the fee was $470 per ship; *Canton Register*, 5/30/1837, says the legal duties were $873, but that the total charge was $1,189.50. As we have seen in the preceding chapters, Chinese-style vessels were exempt from many of the duties imposed on Western vessels or the duties were reduced. The 3,318 given above, may, therefore, be far too high for a Siamese junk, but has been included here to prevent calculating an overly generous profit since other variables cannot be taken into account.

[c] Freight costs have not been subtracted from the profit because Crawfurd's assessment that bulk goods were taken on speculation with no freight charges (*Embassy*, p. 412) has been accepted as accurate.

[86] *Singapore Chronicle*, 11/21/1833.

[87] If 500,000 piculs of rice were exported in one year, for example, and if total export investment maintained the level cited by Malloch (5,584,955 *baht*) or declined, the percentage of investment in rice to total investment would obviously have increased.

Finally, if the difference between the purchase price of rice in Bangkok and its sale price in China were maintained, the profit to be derived would have warranted its export, irrespective of volume. Linked to this aspect was that of production cost, i.e., the amount of labor and money expended by the farmer to obtain a specified yield. The rice fields in the Central Plain of Siam were irrigated by yearly rains and did not require the upkeep of the artificial irrigation systems prevalent in China. Furthermore, since rice was cultivated primarily to supply the family unit, any excess would have been seen as an unexpected profit to be bartered or sold. Thus, although hand transplanting and weeding were essential to rice cultivation, this represented labor that would have been undertaken in any event. The cost of rice to the producer, then, was presumably smaller than the cost of some of the goods obtained or grown specifically for the export trade.[88]

Sino-Siamese trade reflected certain aspects of the economic orientation of each country. Siam's abundance of unprocessed goods and raw materials was admirably suited to a Chinese market exhibiting a preference for just such products, while China's handicraft industries were able to supply Siam's need for small-scale manufactured goods. Neither country provided the other with products which were absolutely crucial to its survival, nor was the trade between them confined to superfluous luxuries. Although both countries could have obtained the other's wares through an indirect trade with centers elsewhere in maritime Southeast Asia, reciprocal trading concessions, coincident with Siam's role as an entrepot for Asian goods made a direct trade more profitable and more convenient.

---

[88] Birds' nests, for example, were not only difficult to locate, but demanded time-consuming cleaning procedures if they were not of the first quality. For the readily available lumber and bark, on the other hand, one would have had only gathering and transportation costs to consider.

5

THE OPERATORS OF SINO-SIAMESE TRADE

Sino-Siamese trade was not conducted by a homogeneous group of men constituting a merchant class as such. The people involved in the exchange of goods were of disparate backgrounds, represented various strata of the Chinese and Siamese social order, and fulfilled divers roles in the marketing process. Merchants were not the mere purchasers and sellers of wholesale commodities. They might, at the same time, also serve as junk captains, as brokers in Bangkok or Canton, or they might be members of the Siamese aristocracy. The term merchant will be applied throughout this chapter to any Chinese or Siamese who participated in the commercial intercourse between the two countries. Such broad categorization is necessary because the boundaries demarcating buyers and sellers from others involved with the subsidiary aspects of transportation and distribution are exceedingly vague.

The merchants have been arbitrarily cast, for convenience of discussion, into three major groups: carriers, consignors, and port personnel. The carriers, or junk crews, were predominantly Chinese,[1] were native to a limited geographic region extending from Ch'ao-chou fu, Kwangtung, to Ch'üan-chou fu, Fukien, and represented the more impoverished elements of the Chinese coastal population. Consignors were generally those people, either Chinese or Siamese, who invested money in foreign trade but who assumed little or no responsibility for

---

[1] On the junks sailing to Siam from China all members of the crews were Chinese. Junks trading to China from Siam were also manned by Chinese, although some Siamese were present on junks trading to Canton. Although Chinese tended to predominate in Siam's colonial or coastal trade (between Bangkok, the Malay Peninsula, and Singapore) as well, Siamese participation in this traffic was greater than in any other. See T'ien Ju-kang, *Shih-ch'i shih-chi*, p. 25; Crawfurd, *Embassy*, pp. 411, 415.

its actual management. They were often men of higher social status and greater wealth than carriers. Chinese officials and gentry, the Siamese king and nobility were among the foremost members of this group. It was a group for whom the proceeds from commercial ventures constituted one of many sources of income, whereas for carriers, overseas trade was often their sole means of support.

As we will see below, these two groups might occasionally overlap. For example, owners of the larger junks trading between China and Siam would normally be classified as consignors since they commonly hired others to transact business on their behalf in foreign ports. But on smaller vessels, the owner might also serve as captain. In this capacity he would be designated a carrier since he would ship his own goods for sale in addition to the goods of others.

The port personnel were merchants, in the sense that they derived their income from such trade-related activities as duty and wharfage collection or from arranging the purchase and sale of the commodities imported and exported by junk. The hong merchants in Chinese ports and the commission agents of the Siamese king and nobility were representative of this group. While they seldom acted as carriers in the junk trade, they did, upon occasion, invest in overseas trade, and at such times would be classified as consignors. By delineating the membership of these categories, it will be possible to judge the extent to which each group participated in, and contributed to, the advancement of Sino-Siamese commerce.

The Chinese were already famous for their business acumen in the nineteenth century, "being looked upon no otherwise than the Jews in Europe."[2] Chinese immigrants were said to have grasped more clearly than the native inhabitants the economic possibilities inherent in the Southeast Asian countries where they had settled, and to be readier to turn this knowledge into profitable channels.[3] This was certainly true of the Chinese settlers in Siam. They came increasingly to monopolize Siam's foreign trade from the mid-1700s and during the Third Reign

---

[2] Ivon Donnelly, "Historical Aspects of Chinese Junks and Maritime Trade," *The Orient* 5,10 (1955): 78.

[3] "I do not think they are exceeded by the natives of any country as a commercial people": *The Foreign Trade of China*, pp. 33-34, 37-38; Charles Gutzlaff, *A Sketch of Chinese History, Ancient and Modern: Comprising a Retrospect of the Foreign Intercourse and Trade with China*, 2 vols. (London: Smith, Elder and Co., 1834), vol. 2, pp. 193-95; Skinner *Chinese Society*, pp. 91-92, 94-95.

(1824-1851) began to play a more prominent role in the internal economy as well.[4]

The bulk of China's trade to the *Nan-yang* originated in eastern Kwangtung and south-eastern Fukien. Eighteenth- and nineteenth-century Chinese advocates of an unrestricted intercourse between China and the *Nan-yang* noted that, in Fukien particularly, reliance on foreign trade was the logical consequence of overpopulation and the scarcity of arable land.[5] While the reiteration of this theme not only revealed the perennial economic difficulties confronting China's maritime provinces, it was also indicative of the acceptable idiom through which overseas commerce could be justified. An insufficient agricultural base combined with the economic opportunities which foreign trade stimulated appear to have been important factors drawing the population of the south-east into mercantile enterprises, especially into the production of handicraft goods for foreign markets and into transportation.

On Western merchant ships, the crews' primary responsibility was toward the sailing of the vessel, whereas crew members of a Chinese junk were merchants first and sailors second.[6] Each member of the crew was permitted to bring a specific quantity of merchandise to sell during the voyage. If the junk was to touch at several ports before reaching its final destination, new goods might be bought for later sale after the original lot had been disposed of. During Gutzlaff's voyage up the China coast, his junk called at numerous ports to transact business before its arrival in Tientsin. These intermediate exchanges served both to introduce Southeast Asian products to a wider China market and to integrate foreign trade within the domestic trading network.[7]

Kinship connections were a major link among crew members and between the crew and officers of a junk. The selection of crew members depended upon affiliation with the captain's clan or on residence in the

---

[4] Wilson, "State and Society," pp. 620, 633-43; Walter Vella, *Siam under Rama III 1824-1851* (Locust Valley, N.Y.: Augustin, 1957), pp. 23, 27; Ingram, *Economic Change*, pp. 19-20.

[5] *HCCSWP*: 83:13b, 85:11a-b; *HMC*: 15:640; Ch'ing-fu, "Ch'ien-lung ch'ao wai-yang t'ung-shang an" [Cases on foreign trade in the Ch'ien-lung period], *Shih-liao haün-k'an*, 22 (Jan. 1, 1931): 803a-b; *Chang-chou FC*: 1877:33:64b-65a; *Canton Register*, 6/17/1833; Gutzlaff, *Two Voyages*, pp. 73, 75, 141; Skinner, *Chinese Society*, pp. 28-31.

[6] Gutzlaff, *Two Voyages*, p. 46. On East India Company ships the captain and officers were allowed "privilege tonnage," i.e. they were permitted to trade in goods on their own account. Sailors were not granted this allowance: Greenberg, *British Trade*, p. 19.

[7] Gutzlaff, *Two Voyages*, pp. 46, 74-103 *passim*; FO 17/9, p. 37.

districts where the junk traded or was registered.[8] The sailors of the *Shun-le* junk on which Gutzlaff took passage from Siam to Tientsin in 1831 were primarily from Ch'ao-chou fu, Kwangtung, the captain, Sin-shun, was a Ch'ao-chou man, his brother-in-law was the ship's clerk, and his uncle succeeded him as captain when he left the vessel at Namoa.[9] The personal ties between the seamen and the captain tended to foster a sense of paternalism in the organization of the crew, with the captain held responsible for the well-being of his subordinates.[10]

The men who were engaged on junks as sailors were generally of peasant stock[11] or, as one Chinese official remarked, they were the poor and indigent elements of coastal society, whereas the well-to-do became merchants, the captains of junks, or their owners.[12] But commerce also spawned a variety of trade-related business interests at the south China ports from which skilled, semi-skilled, and unskilled laborers could be drawn to man the junks.[13] There is nothing to suggest, however, that the rank-and-file junk personnel came from any but the most humble backgrounds, or that the income they derived from trade was used to gain entry into official or gentry circles. Gutzlaff observed, in fact, that sailors spent their money as fast as they earned it.[14] This is not to say that upward social mobility was never fostered by the wealth acquired through commercial pursuits. Often, however, such mobility was achieved by the

[8] Watson, *Transport in Transition: The Evolution of Traditional Shipping in China*, pp. 55-56, 60.

[9] Gutzlaff, *Two Voyages*, pp. 57, 70, 80.

[10] T'ien, *Shih-ch'i shih-chi*, p. 29; Watson, *Transport*, p. 59.

[11] Watson, *Transport*, pp. 60-61. Forty percent of the junk crews surveyed had previously been agricultural workers while the remaining 60 percent combined shipping with farm labor. Although the survey cited in Watson was undertaken toward the middle of the twentieth century, there probably was little difference from the situation that existed in the nineteenth century. One would expect, in fact, that by 1940 fewer junk operators and crewmen would have had connections with agricultural production than in the previous century, and the 60 percent of continued involvement may mean that an even greater percentage were so engaged earlier.

[12] *HCCSWP*: 85:11b.

[13] Skinner, *Chinese Society*, pp. 94-95.

[14] Gutzlaff, *Two Voyages*, pp. 73-73, 75.

more important merchants who amassed great wealth, rather than by the lower echelons of the trading community.[15]

Junk crews were roughly divided, according to the tasks they performed, into officers and hands. Officers were the more highly skilled, responsible members, fulfilling something of a managerial capacity, while the less demanding, repetitive chores were allotted to the hands. The Chinese terms used to designate the positions held by a junk's officers varied regionally, creating some confusion about the duties to which a specific term referred. For example, the captain in North China was called a *lao-ta*,[16] in the Shanghai area, a *tung-chia*,[17] and in the south, a *ch'uan-chu*.[18] Similar confusion also exists in the English terminology used, with the same title given a different translation by different writers. The role of crew members as actual traders would seem to warrant some description of their titles and duties, and of their share in the volume of cargo transported.

Chinese shipboard organization appears to have been somewhat informal, based largely on customary practice rather than dictated by legal obligations. There is no evidence that the social hierarchy among the crew of a Chinese junk was governed by a codified set of regulations as was true, at least theoretically, for merchant vessels from parts of the Malay maritime world.[19] Chinese commercial statutes do not enumerate

---

[15] Howqua (Wu Shao-yung) was representative of the former group and was reputed to be worth $25,000,000 upon his death: *Hunt's Merchants' Magazine* 10,5 (May 1844): 459. For a brief discussion of merchant mobility, see Maurice Freedman, *Lineage Organization in Southeastern China* (London: The Athlone Press, 1958), pp. 58-59.

[16] T'ien, *Shih-ch'i shih-chi*, p. 28; HMC: 5:178; Needham, *Science and Civilization*, vol. 4, pt. 1, pp. 280, 292; Gutzlaff, *Two Voyages*, p. 45. The navigator was also called a *lowdah*: China: Imperial Maritime Customs. I.-Statistical Series: no. 7, *Native Customs Trade Returns*, p. 63, which presumably is the same as the *lao-ta* given as the term for captain by Kosaka and Nakamura: Watson, *Transport*, p. 55. They say, moreover, that the *lao-ta* is in charge of navigation. As this is the only reference to the captain as navigator, it may reflect a northern peculiarity, since in the south the positions were definitely separate. In Thai, *lata* is given for the clerk or business manager and would seem to be a transliteration of the Chinese *lao-ta*. See below fn. 22.

[17] Watson, *Transport*, pp. 55, 59; Needham, *Science and Civilization*, vol. 4, pt. 1, p. 279: he is said to be called a *kang-shou*.

[18] T'ien, *Shih-ch'i shih-chi*, p. 27; Crawfurd, *Embassy*, p. 412. Crawfurd called him a *chinchu* which must be equivalent to the *ch'uan-chu*; HMC: 5:178.

[19] Meilink-Roelofsz, *Asian Trade*, pp. 40, 46-48; Richard Winstedt and P. E. de Jong, "The Maritime Laws of Malacca," *JMBRAS* 29,3 (1956); 51-59; Richard Winstedt, "Old Malay Legal Digests and Malay Customary Law," *Journal of the Royal Asiatic Society of Great*

the responsibilities of officers and crew on merchant vessels, and the system which evolved must have done so out of a concern for convenience and practicality. Nonetheless, we will see below that numerous parallels were evident in the pattern of trading activity and the structure of the crew on Chinese, Siamese, and Malay vessels, suggesting a well-integrated Asian mercantile community.

The captain, who was also the supercargo, was the senior officer on a Chinese junk. He was charged primarily with the management of the cargo and with obtaining the most favorable prices upon its sale.[20] He took no part in navigating the vessel, but was responsible for the crew and his subordinate officers. The captain was ordinarily either the sole or partial owner of the smaller junks engaged in the Sino-*Nan-yang* trade. The junk on which Gutzlaff took passage from Siam was owned and commanded by the same man.[21] The larger junks carrying more lucrative cargoes were frequently the property of several individuals, and the captain might be one of the owners or he might be a hired employee.[22] In either case, he would be allowed a share of the cargo. Because the success of any overseas venture depended to a great extent on the captain's ability to sell the goods shipped on his vessel at the most advantageous prices, kinship ties

Britain and Ireland (1945): 17-18, 25-26; Stamford Raffles, "The Maritime Code of the Malays," *JSBRAS* 3 (1879): 62-84.

[20] Gutzlaff, *Two Voyages*, p. 45; Crawfurd (*History of the Indian Archipelago*, vol. 3, p. 175) called the captain a commander "whose business it is to look after the crew."

[21] Gutzlaff, *Two Voyages*, p. 80.

[22] Watson, *Transport*, pp. 7, 15. On the large junks of 200 to 500 tons capacity, the captains and owners were seldom the same (p. 54). Although Kosaka and Nakamura's study depicts the situation in North China, evidence from Fukien on partnership operation suggests a similar conclusion. According to Meilink-Roelofsz (*Asian Trade*, p. 46), the captain (*nakoda*) on small Malay vessels tended to be the sole owner, and, on large vessels, the representative of the owner. She further notes that the titles in Malay for an owner and captain are interchangeable which is true also for the appropriate Chinese term *ch'uan-chu*. While the captain was also the supercargo on Chinese junks (FO 17/9, p. 37), a separate merchant (*mawla kiwi*) partially fulfilled this role on Malay ships. Under the Malay code, moreover, the captain was to consult with the chief supercargo before undertaking business transactions, whereas the captain of a Chinese junk had more autonomy in this matter. On Siamese junks, the captain or *junju* may have acted as supercargo, or this was possibly undertaken by the *lata*. The *lata* appears in the *Kotmai tra sam duang* [The Law of the Three Seals] (Bangkok: Khurusapha, 1962), vol. 1, p. 235 as equal in rank with the captain and navigator, and their names are mentioned along with the captain's in CMH.R.3, #49, 1844. He may, therefore, have been the supercargo, or of corresponding rank with the accountant on a Chinese junk (see fns. 33, 34).

were often the basis of his employment.[23] But outsiders, known for their competence, might also be engaged in this capacity by the larger "corporate" enterprises.

The captain received no wages but was permitted instead to ship 100 piculs of cargo on his own account, to sell cabin accommodations to passengers, and, as the agent for the principal consignors, to receive a commission of approximately 10 percent on the sale of their merchandise.[24] The captain's role as an agent on behalf of large-scale investors was as common a feature to the native shipping of East and Southeast Asia as it was to the trade of the Western Mediterranean from medieval times and is called the *commenda* system.[25] Since the captain and the investors he represented controlled the major share of the cargo shipped on Chinese junks,[26] his remuneration could be substantial. This was only just, for the risks inherent in a nineteenth-century sea voyage and the uncertainties of market conditions at both ends demanded reasonable compensation. The captains of junks engaged in the trade between Bangkok and Sin-

[23] Watson, *Transport*, p. 7; T'ien, *Shih-ch'i shih-chi*, p. 27; Gutzlaff, *Two Voyages*, p. 45; *HMC*: 15:652. In Fukien, the person who owned the largest proportion of the cargo was said to appoint his adopted son as captain, while the Chinese in Siam generally employed their sons-in-law. These men may have been chosen for adoption or as desirable marriage partners precisely because of their skill as junk captains.

[24] T'ien, *Shih-ch'i shih-chi*, p. 28; Great Britain: Parliament, *Report from the Select Committee*, 1830, vol. 5, p. 300.

[25] Meilink-Roelofsz, *Asian Trade*, p. 49. For an analysis of this system as it operated in the West, see Robert Lopez and Irving Raymond, eds., *Medieval Trade in the Mediterranean World* (New York: Norton, 1965), pp. 174-84. How closely the European and Asian *commenda* were related cannot be explored here, but the two had many similar features. In both East and West, for example, the captain or supercargo was responsible to the investor he represented for only one voyage, with a new contract, whether verbal or written, negotiated before the start of the next. The person borrowing money to invest had only limited liability, and was not expected to reimburse the lender if the voyage were a failure. Each received a percentage of the profits, 10 percent for the captain of a Chinese junk, and 25 percent for the supercargo under the European *commenda*.

[26] In her discussion of the Malay crews' share of cargo investment, Meilink-Roelofsz (*Asian Trade*, pp. 46-47) makes a distinction between their share in the tonnage, i.e. the right to a division of the hold (*petak*) and their share in the cargo, i.e. the right to a quantity of cargo by weight. The crew on Chinese junks trading to Southeast Asia were said to have been allowed to ship a certain number of piculs depending on their rank, although Crawfurd (*History*, vol. 3, p. 178) does note that merchants accompanying their cargo were given a compartment of the vessel which would be equivalent to tonnage. For the most part, however, the cargo shipped by the crew member of a Chinese junk was measured by weight rather than by a specific amount of bulkhead space (tonnage).

gapore were paid proportionately less since the voyage was not hazardous, the cargo was less valuable, and the trip was considerably shorter.[27]

The navigator or pilot (*huo-ch'ang*)[28] was second-in-command to the captain on Chinese junks. There might be one, or two if the size of the vessel justified it, and the chief navigator alone was responsible for charting the junk's course and maintaining the compass, while his subordinate announced and supervised the watch.[29] Navigators were of comparatively equal status with captains, particularly on the shorter runs. For the voyage between China and Southeast Asia, he was paid a salary of 200 dollars in addition to the right to ship 50 piculs of cargo. This was less than the captain was allowed, whereas between Bangkok and Singapore the two received equivalent reimbursement.[30] There were also helmsmen (*to-kung*)[31] on the vessel who managed the steering. They were of lowly rank, received no salary, and could ship only 15 piculs of cargo on their own account.[32]

Although the cargo was sold by the captain, the junk's accountants or clerks (*ts'ai-fu*)[33] supervised its loading and unloading and kept records of the payments received and of other financial aspects of its sale. The number employed seems to have been contingent upon the value and size of the cargo, with from one to three officers functioning in this capacity.[34] According to the pay scale, the accountant was the third-ranking officer, receiving 100 dollars in salary and the right to ship 50 piculs of cargo.[35] On Chinese junks there was also an officer in charge

---

[27] Great Britain: Parliament, *Report from the Select Committee*, 1830, vol. 5, p. 300.

[28] On Siamese junks he was called the *tonhon* (*Kotmai tra sam duang*, vol. 1, p. 235), and on Malay vessels, the *malim*.

[29] T'ien, *Shih-ch'i shih-chi*, p. 28. On Siamese and Malay vessels there were also first and second navigators who performed the same duties: Raffles, "The Maritime Code," pp. 64, 67; *Kotmai*, p. 235.

[30] T'ien, *Shih-ch'i shih-chi*, p. 28; Great Britain: Parliament, *Report from the Select Committee*, 1830, vol. 5, p. 300.

[31] Their Siamese counterparts were called *tai-kong*, and their Malay, *juromudi*.

[32] T'ien, *Shih-ch'i shih-chi*, pp. 27, 28; Watson, *Transport*, p. 55: The helmsmen were said to be the captain's principal assistants (*lao-erh* and *lao-san*) and the first assistant to be second in command of the vessel. This may have been the practice on junks sailing in the North, but their position on vessels trading with the *Nan-yang* seems to be lower than the navigator's if their salary is taken as an indication of rank.

[33] They were also called *tsa-shih*. On Siamese junks this position was probably filled by the *lata* (*Kotmai*, vol. 1, p. 235). There appears to have been no corresponding rank

of dividing the work among crew members, or, as Crawfurd called him, a captain of the hold (*tsung-han*).[36] He is not mentioned as having received a salary or cargo allowance,[37] but is listed in the *Amoy Gazetteer* together with the accountant and navigator. As officers were ranked according to some order of importance, we might assume that he was one of the senior officers of the vessel.

In addition to the senior officer, each junk was staffed by various petty officers in charge of the anchor,[38] the sail lines of the mainmast,[39] the lines for the remaining masts,[40] and repairs.[41] All but the last were allowed to carry 9 piculs of cargo.[42] The remainder of the crew were ordinary sailors who performed the less specialized tasks under the direction of the officers. Each of the hands could carry 7 piculs of cargo to trade.

That payment for service on junks was rendered not in cash but in the form of a specific cargo allowance clearly indicated the importance of individual trading by crew members. The practice was developed to an even greater degree on Malay vessels in that none of the officers received

on Malay vessels. See also T'ien, *Shih-ch'i shih-chi*, p. 27; Needham, *Science and Civilization*, vol. 4, pt. 1, pp. 279; Watson, *Transport*, p. 55: On northern junks he was a "senior officer (*ch'i-min*) responsible for business, liaison, and management when at anchor."

[34] Gutzlaff, *Two Voyages*, p. 45; *Kotmai*, vol. 1, p. 235: On board each junk there might be a clerk in charge of the lists of goods (*lata*) as well as two mid-level clerks.

[35] T'ien, *Shih-ch'i shih-chi*, p. 28.

[36] Great Britain: Parliament, *Report from the Select Committee*, 1830, vol. 5, p. 300. He was also called a boatswain (China: Imperial Maritime Customs, *Native Customs Trade Returns*, p. 63). On Malay vessels he was called the *tukang petak*, and on Siamese, the *tekkho* or possibly the *panju*.

[37] T'ien, *Shih-ch'i shih-chi*, p. 28. This may simply reflect insufficient data in the sources T'ien consulted. He probably did have a share of the cargo since all the other officers did.

[38] *I-ting, erh-ting*. On Siamese vessels he was the *thaoteng*, and the *jurobatu* on Malay.

[39] *Ta-liao, erh-liao*. He was called a *tualiao* on Siamese vessels. On Malay vessels the sailors handled the rigging and were supervised by the Chief Petty Officer (*tukang agung*): Raffles, "The Malay Maritime Code," p. 67.

[40] *I-, erh-, san-ch'ien*. How this position differed from the one before is not clear, unless these were the men who lowered the sails. On Siamese junks men in the equivalent ranks were the *itsian, yisian,* and *samsian* or "lowerers." They may also properly have handled the lowering of the anchor.

[41] *Ya-kung*. On Siamese junks he was an *aküng*.

[42] T'ien, *Shih-ch'i shih-chi*, pp. 28-29; *Kotmai*, vol. 1, p. 235.

a salary and "every person on board (had) some commercial speculation in view, however small."[43] Since most of the junks sailing between China and Siam ranged in capacity from 3,000 to 5,000 piculs (see Chapter III), the merchandise shipped by the crew accounted for only one-fifth to one-third of total capacity,[44] making the owners of the junk, those who consigned goods for sale, and any investors, the principal beneficiaries of the enterprise. They might be Chinese who shipped goods to Siam but who did not accompany their goods on the voyage, people who lent money for speculative purposes, or Chinese settlers in Siam, themselves trading to China or trading on behalf of the Siamese king and nobility. But in whichever capacity they functioned, the group I have designated as consignors were the most prosperous merchants engaged in Sino-Siamese trade.

Few of the Chinese participants in the junk trade, with the exception of those who were also intimately connected with the Western trade at Canton, have received any attention in Chinese sources[45] or in contemporary Western accounts. The picture one obtains is hazy because little specific information is available about individual merchants or their business activities. Nonetheless, certain generalizations are possible from the information that does exist. Fukien merchants appear to have played a dominant role in much of China's trade with Siam. It was managed, and to an extent monopolized, by men from T'ung-an and surrounding counties in Fukien. This was true also of China's coastal trade, as well as of the Canton-centered Western trade, many of the hong merchants having come originally from Fukien families.[46] Furthermore, the partnerships set up to finance junk construction and operation were for the most part initiated by Fukien merchants. The names of all junks sponsored under partnership organization were prefaced by the character *chin* (金),[47] and many of those recorded as having traded between China and

---

[43] Raffles, "The Maritime Code," p. 66.

[44] There were usually 90 to 100 crew members on board a junk trading between China and Siam. The officers and hands would have received approximately 1,000 piculs of cargo allowance on the basis of the amounts assigned to each of the positions mentioned above.

[45] The biases of the compilers of the local gazetteers toward merchant biographies is briefly discussed in Chang Chung-li, *The Income of the Chinese Gentry* (Seattle: University of Washington Press, 1962), p. 152.

[46] Henri Cordier, "Les Marchands Hanistes de Canton," *T'oung Pao* 3 (1902): 311; Gutzlaff, *Two Voyages*, pp. 75, 83, 141, 157; Chang, *The Income*, p. 164, fn. 41.

[47] HMC: 15:649; T'ien, *Shih-ch'i shih-chi*, pp. 27.

Siam in the early nineteenth century reflected their Fukien registry and ownership.[48] The larger joint concerns might own ten to twenty overseas junks or the ownership of a single junk might be divided among as many as fifty shareholders.[49]

Hong merchants, besides acting as middlemen at Chinese ports, were also known to have speculated on overseas trade. The involvement by member firms of the *pen-kang hang*, which managed Siam's commerce and tributary affairs at Canton, in Siam's trade has been recounted above (pp. 29-30) and the entire episode need not be again repeated. Certain aspects of the *pen-kang hang's* rise and fall do, however, highlight the problems surrounding the identity of the less influential merchants who managed Siamese trade. The *Yüeh hai-kuan chih* supplies the names of the firms and merchants[50] charged with this responsibility during the latter half of the eighteenth century only because of their repeated inability to maintain solvency. After Siam's business had been shifted to members of the foreign hong in 1800,[51] no further mention is made of the hong merchants who supervised that trade at Canton or elsewhere. While we have the names of the eighteenth-century *pen-kang hang* merchants, the primary sources never give a hint as to who their business associates were, their family backgrounds, or whether they had competed for and obtained official ranks as a number of the foreign hong merchants were to do.[52] The secondary literature is of equally little value in identifying these merchants more fully.[53]

---

[48] *MCSL*: KP, vol. 6, pp. 561b-562a, 565a-b *passim*: the *Chin hsieh shun*, the *Chin chü shun* and the *Chin kuang shun* are mentioned as having traded between China and Siam; CMH.R.2, #15, 1813: Of the twenty-odd junks named in this document as having sailed to China, eleven begin with the *kim* initial which is the Amoy pronunciation for *chin*.

[49] FO 17/9, p. 38; Watson, *Transport*, p. 7.

[50] Liu Ju-hsin of the *Ju-shun hang*, Hsin Shih-jui of the *I-shun hang*, and Teng Chang-chieh of the *Wan-chü hang*: YHKC: 25:11b.

[51] YHKC: 25:12a-14a: This duty was to be undertaken by different firms in alternate years. In 1800, the T'ung-wen and Kwang-li hongs were to handle the *pen-kang hang's* affairs. In 1801 the I-ho and I-ch'eng, in 1802 the Tung-sheng and Ta-ch'eng, and in 1803 the Hui-lung and Li-ch'üan. The cycle would then be repeated.

[52] Chang, *The Income*, p. 164.

[53] Liang Chia-pin, *Kwang-tung shih-san hang-k'ao*. Liang, for example, discusses the various hongs which took over after the abolition of the *pen-kang hang*, but only because their primary function was to serve Western merchants. His occasional references to the *pen-kang hang* are cited from the *YHKC*. See pp. 129, 147, 226.

A possible explanation for the difficulty one experiences in attempting to locate such detailed information is that, if hong merchants were members of the gentry, their merchant names as recorded in the *Yüeh hai-kuan chih* were not the same as their gentry names. Chang Chung-li has pointed out that gentry were forbidden to acquire hong licenses and frequently carried out their business activities under assumed names.[54] *Pen-kang hang* members were not necessarily gentry, although they too would have found official and semi-official connections advantageous as did hong merchants dealing with Western trade. Moreover, the expenses entailed in purchasing a hong license demanded a background of some wealth. Perhaps their minor status as secondary hong merchants is to blame for the paucity of documentation. In any event, only a thorough search of the available biographical material is likely to produce additional information concerning these men.[55] After the *pen-kang hang*'s business was assumed by the foreign hong, we learn nothing more of their management of Siamese trade primarily because Siamese affairs comprised such a small proportion of the hongs' total accounts in comparison with their Western trade.

Immigrants to Siam who later traded with China have also received little attention in Chinese primary sources. Occasionally their names were mentioned, particularly if they had in some manner contravened Chinese law. An example of this occurred during the early 1800s when the King of Siam was informed that he could not use Chinese merchants as his factors when trading with China. The Fukien Governor, Chang Shih-ch'eng, mentioned in a memorial of 1810 that two merchants from Fukien, Yang Yu and Wu Ching, and one from Kwangtung, Ch'en K'un-wan, had served in this capacity as well as trading on their own account at Canton. From the interrogation report on Yang and Wu we learn that they were from T'ung-an and Lung-hsi counties respectively, that business associates or family connections had recommended them to the King of Siam as men to whom he could entrust his business affairs, and that for an indefinite period they acted as his agents in the Sino-Siamese trade.[56] We

---

[54] Chang, *The Income*, pp. 164-65.

[55] Neither the biographical sections of the Kwangtung and Fukien Gazetteers nor any of the other standard Ch'ing biographical works contain biographies of the *pen-kang hang* merchants mentioned above. My search was conducted by using the names given in the *YHKC*, and if biographies are included in these sources they would appear under different names from those cited by Liang.

[56] *MCSL:KP*, vol. 6, pp. 565a-b.

remain ignorant, however, of the duration of their stay in Siam, who their contacts were in Bangkok or in Canton, how they used the money they earned, and whether they returned to China as merchants or took up other occupations.

Of all the merchants referred to in this episode, the only one for which additional information is available is Yang Yu, and even that is less than satisfying. His testimony reveals that he was from T'ung-an county, Fukien, and was recommended to the Siamese king for the position of captain on his junk, the *Chin hsieh shun*, by Huang Kuan. Huang was willing to make the recommendation because of his friendship with the Brigade-General of Su-sung, Yang Hua, who was related to Yang Yu.[57] Yang Hua attained moderately high positions in military service and was in charge of piracy suppression throughout the Pescadores. But his biographies do not mention that he participated in any commercial activities and his ties with Huang Kuan and Yang Yu remain obscure.[58]

Contemporary Western accounts have similar biases. Although they examine the economic role of overseas Chinese in the countries to which they emigrated and provide estimates of the immigrant populations in the host countries, individual merchants are lost in the composite view that emerges. Gutzlaff is more helpful in this respect, and we gain important information about the Chinese with whom he came into contact. Among the fellow passengers on his trip to Tientsin in 1831 was a captain Eo, who claims some of the missionary's attention despite his reputation as a practitioner of "wickedness and deceit."[59] Earlier on in his career he had commanded a Siamese tribute vessel but was impoverished when the vessel was wrecked at sea. He remained in Siam working as a painter and mechanic. By saving his money he was able to purchase 100 piculs of merchandise which he would attempt to sell in China. This accounts for his presence on the junk Gutzlaff traveled with. We never learn, however, whether he profited from his speculation, whether he bought goods with the proceeds from the sale of his 100 piculs, or whether he returned to Siam. It is seldom possible to follow up the basic data

[57] *MCSL:KP*, vol. 6, pp. 565b.

[58] For Yang Hua's biographies see: *T'ung-an HC* [County gazetteer of T'ung-an], comp. by Lin Hsüeh-tseng *et al.*, 42+1 *chüan*, 1929:30:11b; Ch'en Yen, *Fu-chien t'ung-chih lieh-chuan hsüan* [Selected biographies from the Fukien provincial gazetteer], 6 *chüan*, 3 vols. in 1 (Taipei: T'ai-wan yin-hang, 1964), 4:251-52. See also the *Chin-men chih* [Gazetteer of Quemoy], comp. by Lin K'un-huang *et al.*, 16 *chüan* (1774: Taipei: T'ai-wan yin-hang, 1960), 8:191, for a reference to Yang Hua's son, Yang Wu-chen.

[59] Gutzlaff, *Two Voyages*, pp. 56-57.

contained in either Chinese or Western accounts, because their concern is not with individuals but with events or with generalized impressions of groups of people, i.e. with the overseas Chinese as a whole.

Eighteenth- and nineteenth-century writers noted that Chinese living in Siam owned junks which they sent on yearly commercial ventures to China. Most of the junks dispatched from Siam were built there and had a Siamese nobleman as patron.[60] This made for close and visible ties between the Chinese mercantile community and the Siamese aristocracy, whereas in China such connections were more subtle. Chinese were also employed in Siam as tax farmers, remitting the government's share from the monopolies they held. In 1750, a Chang-chou man named Wu Yang emigrated to Songkhla and became a tobacco farmer. He was granted the monopoly in birds' nests by King Taksin in 1769 in return for a yearly payment of fifty catties of silver. In 1775, he was made Governor of Songkhla with the rank of *Luang* Suwansombat Senapati and his descendants retained important positions in the region.[61]

The case of Wu Yang raises the complex problem of how monopolists and merchants interacted in the Siamese economic system. Monopolists were to forward annually a set sum of money to the government for their right to the monopoly, and, to do so, they would have had to dispose of the goods on which they were granted monopoly rights. Prior to the Third Reign (1824-1851) the king retained the exclusive right to trade in certain goods, many of which made up Siam's exports to China.[62] But royal monopolies could apparently be farmed out as well, if the example of Wu Yang is reliable. While Chinese functioned as monopolists, they also served as middlemen in the interior to supply the Bangkok market with goods required for the China junk trade. And as Ingram has remarked, the ties between merchants and Siamese officials would have aided the Chinese in disposing of the goods they brought to market.[63] We might surmise, then, that, even though Wu Yang was not specifically stated to have been a merchant, his acquisition of the birds' nest monopoly could have been lucrative only if the birds' nests were subsequently exported. Moreover, to have sent fifty catties of silver to Bangkok is to imply that the nests were sold in China where the greatest demand existed. The role

[60] Ibid., *Two Voyages*, p. 59.

[61] Ling Ch'un-sheng *et al.*, ed., *Chung-T'ai wen-hua lun-chi*, pp. 273-74; Wilson, "State and Society," p. 779: A genealogy of Wu's (Hao Ying) family is provided.

[62] See Crawfurd, *Embassy*, pp. 380-81, for a list of the royal monopolies.

[63] Ingram, *Economic Change*, p. 20.

of Chinese in Siam as both monopolists and merchants, which can best be explored from Thai sources, has not been examined in the present study. It is reasonable to suppose, however, that the Chinese who came to control tax farms during the Third and Fourth Reigns combined these enterprises with overseas commercial activities.

The open espousal of, and participation in, overseas trade by the Siamese king and nobility distinguished them from their counterparts in China—the gentry and civil bureaucrats. Both Rama I (1782-1809) and Rama II (1809-1824) sponsored state trade with China, but they had not initiated the practice. Reports from the seventeenth century mention that the Siamese king was a merchant with factors throughout the Asian commercial world, but that they were principally found in China.[64] Rama III had been the head of the Harbor Department of the government under Rama II and supervised the junks engaged in the state trade with China.[65] When he came to the throne he abolished the royal monopolies, claiming that he would not be a "King-merchant."[66] The evidence indicates, however, that both he and Rama IV occasionally sent junks to China to purchase special items.[67] A major complaint levelled against Rama III by Westerners, in fact, was that free trade was impossible in Siam because the king, princes, and princesses all owned junks and had pre-emption rights over imports and exports.[68] Besides trading abroad, the king participated in the coastal trade in the Gulf of Siam. His junks were frequently employed to transport to Bangkok the tribute owed by vassal principalities on the Malay peninsula.[69]

[64] Mandelslo, *Voyages and Travels*, p. 130.

[65] Wilson, "State and Society," p. 611; Chaen, *Prawat Kanthahanrüa Thai*, p. 46. Rama III must have been fairly successful in this position for "he was called *caosua* (a person who becomes rich through trade) by his father."

[66] *The Burney Papers*, vol. 1, p. 51. Burney maintains that Rama III's decision was motivated by the losses incurred in the state trade, for they were subtracted from the king's share and Rama III had no intention of suffering in this manner.

[67] National Archives, Letter, King Rama IV to Yam Ap Toot, January 30, 1853. Rama IV had ordered that certain items be purchased for him in China, but they were sold to members of the royal family before he could claim them. He was, needless to say, disturbed by this usurpation of his prerogatives. For other examples of trade during the Fourth Reign see: CMH.R.4, #109, 1854; CMH.R.4, #88, 1857.

[68] Great Britain: Parliament, *Report from the Select Committee*, 1830, vol. 5, p. 311.

[69] Crawfurd, *Embassy*, p. 413.

As Walter Vella has pointed out, state trade began to decline from the Third Reign. Prior to the 1820s, state trade was necessary because the state's treasury had been submerged under payments in kind, in the form of taxes, tributary goods, and the products of the king's corvée laborers.[70] The most expedient method of disposing of payments in kind had been through the junk trade sponsored by the king and nobility. From the Third Reign the need for specie became more acute, however, as Chinese were hired to perform tasks for pay that had previously been required of corvée laborers, as the state's expenditures for religion and defense rose, and as the importation of Western goods increased.[71] With the government's revenue augmented through the conversion from payment in kind to payment in cash and through the sale of commodity monopolies,[72] state trade could be dispensed with.

The aristocracy, on the other hand, continued to sponsor junks in the Sino-Siamese trade, although they and the king also became involved in the development of square-rigged transport from the late 1830s. Patronage by a member of the Siamese aristocracy continued to be useful to Chinese merchants in Siam since it would have provided certain benefits and protection not otherwise afforded.[73] As was pointed out in the previous chapter, the returns from trade could be high, and the prospect of profits induced many aristocrats to pursue this as a supplementary avenue to wealth, especially as they received little salary for their government service. Fortunately, a mid-nineteenth-century Thai document survives listing some of the junks and a square-rigged vessel sailing to China in the early 1840s, the names of their patrons, and the value of the cargoes they sold. The picture that emerges from a study of this document is that the vessels laden with the most valuable cargoes were sponsored by the nobility of the highest ranks. For example, the square-rigged vessel, with a cargo investment of Sp. $19,358, was sponsored by *Camun Waiworanat* (Chuang Bunnag),[74] one of the most influential men of his

---

[70] *The Burney Papers*, vol. 1, p. 180.

[71] Vella, *Siam under Rama III*, p. 19.

[72] Chaen, *Prawat*, p. 55.

[73] T'ien, *Shih-ch'i shih-chi*, pp. 25-26.

[74] He was instrumental in promoting Monkut's ascension to the throne on the death of Rama III and became Minister of War and the Southern Provinces (*Kalahom*) during his reign. He was particularly interested in Western shipbuilding techniques. See David K. Wyatt, "Family Politics in Nineteenth Century Thailand," *Journal of Southeast Asian History*, 9.2 (1968, 220-21, and *passim*.

day, while the junk with the largest investment (Sp. $12,284) was owned by a son of Rama II, Phraongcao Thinnakon (1801-1856).[75] It would be imprudent to assert that these two examples typify the pattern of investment among the aristocracy without more extensive documentation, but if it could be shown that the upper nobility consistently speculated on the most lucrative shipping, the advantages to Chinese merchants of connecting themselves with such patrons would be clear.

Participation by members of the Siamese government and nobility in foreign trade is clearly spelled out by Thai and Western sources. As we have noted above, evidence of the involvement by Chinese degree holders and gentry is not as explicitly recorded. However, the large sums necessary for the construction and outfitting of junks, and the usefulness of local officials' support at the Chinese ports, suggest the possibility of collaboration between officials and merchants in promoting native trade.[76] The silence of Chinese sources on this point is perhaps a reflection of Siam's relatively low position as a trading partner. While imports from Siam were useful and marketable, the volume of trade never approached that exchanged with the West. The connection of Chinese bureaucrats with the Siam trade would not, therefore, have attracted as much notice as their participation in Western trade.

The endorsement by the Siamese king and nobility of foreign trade was probably grounded in economic considerations, of which few were applicable to the Chinese economy.[77] Whereas they were attracted to commerce at least in part by their recognition of its economic value to Siam, Chinese of comparable rank would not have regarded it as vitally important to China. It was precisely the involvement in Sino-Siamese trade by Siamese figures of political stature that elicited comment from

---

[75] CMH.R.3, #49, 1844.

[76] Chang, *The Income*, chapter 6 *passim*. Chang points out that several of the most important hong merchants had passed various levels of examinations and held official titles.

[77] Frank H. H. King, *Money and Monetary Policy in China 1845-1895* (Cambridge: Harvard University Press, 1965), pp. 8-10, 20. The eighteenth- and nineteenth-century Chinese economy was more complex than Siam's in the same period. Cash was needed by the government in China to provide a greater variety of services. The court, bureaucracy, and military had to be financed through cash payments in addition to maintaining public works. The land tax, the commutation of the grain tribute (see Hinton, *The Grain Tribute*, chapter 1 *passim*), levies on merchants and gentry, and the exploitation of government monopolies all served to provide the government with the necessary specie. Money was more commonly circulated in China than in Siam and reliance on trade did not, therefore, assume the same degree of importance in China.

foreign observers and which has also provided us with Siamese documents recording the government's participation. When trade was overtly promoted by the government, as it was in Siam, it became a matter for public record as it was never to do under the Ch'ing. Given the differing attitudes toward maritime trade held by these two governments, we might expect that Siamese merchants-bureaucrats would have more willingly espoused an active commercial policy than Chinese officials were apt to do. The question of the state's role and that of its representatives, the gentry and bureaucracy, in formulating maritime policy can now be examined.

6

The Foundations of Ch'ing Maritime Policy

Ch'ing maritime commercial policy was fashioned in conformity with the political, economic, and military requirements of the state. While the pronouncements regulating the activities of Chinese merchants trading with Southeast Asia were enunciated from Peking, policy itself was frequently formulated by provincial bureaucrats. The maritime world extending from China's southeastern borders was not perceived uniformly by the officials who were concerned with China's commercial activity in the *Nan-yang*. Some regarded it with hostility, believing that commercial intercourse contained the seeds of border disruption. Others held it in greater esteem, having realized that trade was an essential prop to the economic stability of China's maritime provinces. The factors considered by officials who advocated or opposed unfettered trade between China and the *Nan-yang* will be the focus of this chapter.

The notion that the Chinese government was opposed to private foreign trade gained currency during the nineteenth century. Western, and particularly British, merchants firmly believed that governments should remain aloof from the economic activities in which their subjects engaged. They also operated under the assumption that their prerogatives to trade at will throughout East and Southeast Asia must be admitted by the authorities with whom they dealt. They further believed that man should be free to provide for his needs and that the government's function was to support him to this end rather than to hinder him. A state relying solely upon agriculture was incompatible with the aims of a "free bourgeois state." As Adam Smith remarked,

116

those systems, therefore, which, preferring agriculture to all other employments, in order to promote it, impose restraints upon manufactures and foreign trade, act contrary to the very end which they propose. . . .[1]

John Bowring, a major figure in both China and Siam during the 1840s and 1850s,[2] held similar convictions. He was a friend of Jeremy Bentham, was associated with Richard Cobden in forming the Anti-Corn League, and was an ardent proponent of Utilitarianism. It is not surprising, then, that he should have applied these principles in his dealings with the Chinese and Siamese governments, or that the Anglo-Siamese Treaty of 1855 should reflect his deeply held belief in the salutary benefits arising from free trade.

The growing awareness among Western merchants and civil servants in China that the Chinese bureaucracy did not adhere to these same assumptions engendered frustration and hostility. A writer in the 1840s remarked that the Chinese government, on the advice of various officials, had consistently attempted to "put an end to all maritime intercourse." Chinese officials were said to "view the people engaged in this branch of industry (trade) . . . as a mere nothing, and . . . would never . . . admit the value of foreign intercourse."[3] Such sentiments were widely

[1] Adam Smith, *An Inquiry into the Nature and Causes of the Wealth of Nations*, ed. Edwin Cannan, 2 vols. (New Rochelle: Arlington House, 1966), book 4, pt. 9, p. 289. For Smith's views on China see pp. 282-84. Sentiments such as he expressed and those of other proponents of economic liberalism like Condorcet, Bentham, and Mill attracted a considerable following in the nineteenth century, and were influential in shaping the attitudes of the Western merchants who traded with China. For a fuller discussion of nineteenth-century economic thought see: Frederick Artz, *Reaction and Revolution 1814-1832* (New York: Harper & Row, 1963), pp. 82-97.

[2] Bowring was appointed British Consul at Canton in the late 1840s, he served as acting Minister Plenipotentiary during Sir George Bonham's absence in 1852-1853, and succeeded him as Minister Plenipotentiary to China, Japan, Siam, Vietnam, and Korea in 1854. It was during the latter tenure of appointment that he negotiated the Treaty of Friendship and Commerce between Great Britain and Siam.

[3] *The Canton Press*, 8/14/1841, first supplement. The writer believed that this line was followed because the officials in control of policy were in Peking and had little contact with the trade in the southeast, and that pride and ignorance hindered their acceptance of its usefulness. Similar views were advanced over a century earlier by Lan Ting-yuan in his "Discussion of proper policy regarding the Southern Ocean": HCCSWP: 83:13a-14a. He noted that bureaucrats in Peking were not conversant with affairs on the border and their ignorance had led to various prohibitions. He expressed the hope that his discussion of the countries in the *Nan-yang* would make clear the inutility of the

held and yet they failed to take into account the domestic concerns confronting Chinese policy-makers, nor did they distinguish between Chinese directives intended to regulate Western trade and those applicable only to the native junk trade.

Ch'ing maritime policy was not as rigid as its Western detractors asserted, although one can see a certain coherence in the idiom which was chosen to express it. The rules governing the Chinese junk trade with Southeast Asia were formulated in response to internal economic needs or external political threats. They were an expression of bureaucratic policy-makers' perceptions of the world around them. Consequently, policy statements could, and did, vary from reign to reign, and what was proclaimed in Peking might not be observed at the provincial ports. Provincial authorities were often requested to submit their opinions when the Court was debating the pros and cons of permitting Chinese to trade abroad. Several themes were common to nearly all their memorials and reflect a high degree of continuity from the Ming onward. Many of the examples of Ch'ing policy used in this chapter will be drawn from seventeenth- and eighteenth-century documents because the proposals advocated in the nineteenth century were based on those of earlier memorialists. While some vicissitudes are apparent in Ch'ing maritime policy, the fundamental arguments on which it was premised remained the same. The lineal development of Ch'ing policy can be understood only within the context of the policies advanced prior to the nineteenth century.

The maritime world referred to here is the *Nan-yang* (see Chapter I). This world was perceived in its entirety by policy formulators who seldom mentioned individual countries in Southeast Asia. Occasionally edicts considered the implications of commercial relations between China and another country but ordinarily they were directed at the entire region. While Siam was regarded as an important country in the *Nan-yang* and was known as a center of trade,[4] she was rarely singled out for special

prohibitions. For other nineteenth-century views on the government's attitude toward trade see: Crawfurd, *History of the Indian Archipelago*, vol. 3, p. 169; Phipps, *A Practical Treatise on the China and Eastern Trade*, p. viii; Gutzlaff, *A Sketch of Chinese History*, p. 192.

[4] See, for instance, Na-su-t'u's discussion of whether to allow Chinese junks to sail to the *Nan-yang*. He chose to mention only Siam and Johore as ports of call, indicating that he considered them established centers: *CLSL*: 176:6b; Fu, *A Documentary*, vol. 1, p. 174.

mention in policy statements. These were intended for application to the broader maritime scene and dealt with commercial relations generally. In discussing Ch'ing policy, then, Siam will be mentioned only when her activities were the topic of memorials or edicts. Otherwise, one should assume that all references to the *Nan-yang* include Siam.

The seemingly monolithic Chinese approach to foreign trade has been fostered not only by the biases of nineteenth-century foreign observers, but also by the Chinese source materials themselves. The formal regulations to which certain aspects of Chinese commercial activity were subject are contained in the Ch'ing Code.[5] These regulations are divided into statutes (*lü*) and sub-statutes (*li*) with appended commentary. Many of the statutes had been enacted during the Ming dynasty or earlier and were not pertinent to Ch'ing conditions. If the statutes were used alone to measure Ch'ing policy, one would gain a mistaken impression, for they were often ignored in the decision-making process. They must, therefore, be used in conjunction with the sub-statutes, i.e., the amended versions of the statutes. The sub-statutes were more reflective of the Ch'ing intent, having been "formulated for dealing with the problem of change within tradition."[6] In order to assess the kinds of commercial transactions proscribed or permitted by the Code, one would be advised to consult the sub-statutes and any commentary in addition to the statutes themselves.[7]

Commercial regulations also appear in the *Shih-lu* (collected imperial edicts), and these were usually of a more informal nature than the statutes in the Ch'ing Code. Imperial edicts, which became law until countermanded, provided the emperor and bureaucracy with a flexible medium for approaching contemporary problems. An edict was authoritative only as long as it was not rescinded by succeeding edicts, unless it was

---

[5] *Ta-Ch'ing lü-li*, 1740.

[6] Derk Bodde and Clarence Morris, *Law in Imperial China* (Cambridge: Harvard University Press, 1967), p. 64. See also pp. 63, 65-66; Sybille Van der Sprenkel, *Legal Statutes in Manchu China* (London: The Athlone Press, 1962), pp. 56-64. The sub-statutes were more up to date because they consisted of either edicts designed to answer a specific problem or of the Imperially endorsed decisions of the Board of Punishments.

[7] *Ta-Ch'ing lü-li t'ung-k'ao* [A comprehensive survey of the statutes and sub-statutes of the Ch'ing dynasty], comp. by Wu T'an, 40 *chüan*, 1886. Most of the statutes on commerce are in *chüan* 13 and 20. This source is particularly useful because the commentary following each sub-statute gives a survey of how the law had changed and the dates when the changes occurred. As Bodde points out, "the sub-statute system was necessary if any real effort were to be made to cope with a changing social environment." *Law*, p. 67; Van der Sprenkel, *Legal*, p. 60.

incorporated into the Ch'ing Code itself. Because edicts reflected imperial policy at one particular time, they should not be cited to document policy from another period until the sources have been thoroughly searched for any later edicts which may have nullified the earlier.[8]

Maritime regulations can also be found in the dynasty's administrative statutes and precedents (*Ta-Ch'ing hui-tien* and *Ta-Ch'ing hui-tien shih-li*)[9] and in the statutes of the Board of Revenue (*Hu-pu tse-li*).[10] These are comparable to the departmental regulations of a Western government, for they defined the functions of each department and the bases on which departmental employees were to undertake their duties.[11] The information contained in the administrative statutes and in those of the Board overlaps considerably. Moreover, the successful editions of the *tse-li* and *shih-li*a tend to duplicate the cases included in earlier editions. This is important in terms of retrieval, for if one edition cannot be obtained, an earlier or later one will generally provide the same material. Whereas the sub-statutes of the Ch'ing Code and the *Shih-lu* represent the flexible aspects of commercial policy, the administrative and Board statutes record the more conservative. Once the bureaucratic structure had been established to regulate such activities as assessing and collecting customs duty and licensing hong merchants, it retained much of its original form. It was this form that the administrative statutes described.

The intended scope of the regulations included in the sources mentioned above must be taken into account before they can be considered representative of commercial policy. A distinction should be made between comprehensive commercial law applicable to all Chinese

---

[8] For example, in KH 7 (1668) private (as opposed to tributary) trade was prohibited "in perpetuity": *KHSL*: 25:22a, while in KH 23 (1684) private trade was allowed and four *hai-kuan* were established: *KHSL*: 116:18a-b. Sources other than the *Shih-lu* must be consulted as well as if one is to locate all the changes in the law. Tung Chiao-tseng's memorial to the throne in 1818 requesting that Fukien ocean junks again be permitted to have cross beams measuring above 18 feet is not reproduced in the *Shih-lu* but only in his biography: (*Kuo-ch'ao*) *Ch'i-hsien lei-cheng ch'u-pien* [A classified compendium of eminent Ch'ing personalities, main series], comp. by Li Huan, 720 *chüan*, 1884-1890:194:20a where it has been condensed from the original. An English translation of the entire memorial is available in *The Asiatic Journal and Monthly Register* 3 (Nov. 1820): 443-44, and in *The Indo-Chinese Gleaner* 10 (Oct. 1819): 80-82.

[9] Trade regulations are found in the sections entitled "customs duty" (*kuan-shui*) and "customs regulations" (*shui-tse*). In the 1733 edition see *chüan* 52, in the 1813 edition, *chüan* 16, and in the 1899 edition, *chüan* 234-40.

[10] In the 1791 edition see *chüan* 56-57, 81, 83, 87. In the 1874 edition see *chüan* 38-72.

[11] Van der Sprenkel, *Legal*, pp. 56-57.

merchants and that meant only for the merchants of one or several provinces. The latter often mitigated the design of the former, increasing the hazards of portraying Ch'ing policy in general terms.[12] The directives emanating from the Court, moreover, were not always enforceable at the provincial level, particularly if they ran counter to the interests of provincial bureaucrats or of prominent merchants. The *de facto* situation must always be ascertained as well as the *de jure*.

Care must also be taken with the textual interpretation of commercial enactments. The occasional edicts prohibiting certain kinds of foreign trade were usually directed at people who evaded the law by operating outside the customs organization and regulatory framework maintained to control native trade. An expression common to nearly all imperial proscriptions is "those who clandestinely or illegally (*szu* 私) do . . .," with "illegally" the operative word.[13] The object in these cases was not to prohibit administered trade but to prevent abuse of the established system. To construe pronouncements specifically interdicting illegal activity as evidence of a restrictive government policy toward trade is to misread the intent of such decrees.[14]

---

[12] In 1727, for example, an interdiction was put on overseas emigration and this has been understood to show the hardening attitude of the Yung-cheng Emperor toward overseas trade: Mancall, "The Ch'ing Tribute," p. 89; Elvin, *The Pattern*, p. 218. But in the same year, the Governor of Fukien petitioned that trade should be allowed with the *Nan-yang* and his request was approved by the throne: *Ta-Ch'ing lü-li t'ung-k'ao*: 20: section, *szu-ch'u wai-ching chi wei-chin hsia-hai*: 4b; Fu, *A Documentary*, vol. 1, pp. 157, 193. On the one hand more restrictive measures were imposed, while on the other, the economic needs of the Fukien-Kwangtung region were recognized and dealt with. It might perhaps be wise to hesitate before asserting that these measures were indicative of an anti-commercial bias.

[13] *T'ou* was used interchangeably with *szu*. The following examples are illustrative of how the two words were used in legal enactments: "People who illegally go abroad without a pass" (*fan min-jen wu-piao szu-ch'u k'ou-wai che*): Boulais, *Manuel*, p. 438; "Locals who serve as guides to travellers and who help them to pass the frontier posts secretly (. . . *t'ou-yüeh pien-kuan*): Boulais, *Manuel*, p. 438; "(People who) illegally construct sea vessels" (*szu-tsao hai-ch'uan*): Boulais, *Manuel*, p. 444; "Merchants who secretly sell (boats) for profit" (*shang-jen she-li t'ou-mai*): KHSL: 270:15b.

[14] This is not to say that all suggestions regarding the conduct of native trade were favorable or permissive. Some officials may have believed that by imposing numerous restrictions on trade, even legal commerce would become impossible. The laws appear, however, to have been conceived in terms of defining the limits of trading activity rather than of prohibiting it altogether. The very existence of a body of laws governing native trade denotes governmental approval.

The Ch'ing court's sanction or proscription of Chinese overseas trade was founded on economic and security considerations. Whereas many aspects of Ch'ing policy were formulated in response to the practical requirements confronting the dynasty, certain elements were rooted in Ming and pre-Ming experience.[15] The proposals espoused by central and provincial bureaucrats were not conceived in isolation, but reflected the interdependence between economic needs and other matters of national concern. Memorials and edicts provide the medium through which this interdependence can best be explored. While occasionally resorting to stereotyped phraseology, they are nonetheless pervaded by a sense of pragmatism and flexibility.

Official communiques also reveal an interest in the merchants' welfare that has hitherto received scant attention. Thomas Metzger has observed that the merchant was considered a respectable figure in society. Such expressions as *"an-min t'ung-shang"* (pacify the people and encourage and facilitate the activities of merchants) and *"yü-kuo hsü-shang* (enrich the state while acting with sympathy for merchants) were common in the writings of Ch'ing officials.[16] Similar sentiments permeate the documents in which commercial policy was debated,[17] suggesting that the merchant may have been more highly esteemed than is usually recognized.

The advancement of the peoples' welfare—among whom merchants were certainly included—appears to have been surpassed only by the protection of China's borders as an issue in formulating maritime policy. Trade was acknowledged to be a convenient means of supporting the coastal population, particularly the population of Kwangtung and Fukien, and was promoted toward that end as long as it did not conflict

---

[15] Ch'ing memorialists consistently reiterated economic arguments similar to those common in Ming times. See below fn. 33.

[16] Thomas Metzger, "Ch'ing Commercial Policy," *Ch'ing-shih wen-t'i* 1,3 (Feb. 1966): 7.

[17] *KHSL*: 116:18a: "On the trade of the wealthy merchants levy a small tax, not to the point of distressing them"; *YCSL*: 10:4a-5b: The Emperor advised that greater kindness be shown to merchants travelling through the customs passes; Fu, *A Documentary*, vol. 1, p. 193: "Our law-abiding merchants will no longer feel deserted in a foreign land." The distinction between law-abiding and non law-abiding merchants is important in this context, for it was the former who were to be treated kindly. The latter group, or those who illegally (*szu*) carried out certain activities were to experience the full weight of Chinese law. See fn. 13 above and Fu, *A Documentary*, vol. 1, pp. 28-29, 167; Boulais, *Manuel*, pp. 351, 446-47.

with the maintenance of secure frontiers.[18] Upon lifting the interdiction on foreign trade in 1684, the K'ang-hsi Emperor argued that, because the people of Kwangtung and Fukien earned their livelihood through trade, its resumption would be of benefit to them as well as to the inhabitants of the interior who, with the increased imports of grain, could then reduce the amount of grain they were to provide for the coastal garrisons.[19]

The proponents of China's native foreign trade based their arguments on economic criteria whereas its opponents tended to view it from the perspective of its potential threat to border security. Government officials appear to have regarded trade favorably or unfavorably depending upon their own experience at the provincial level. Nearly all of the men who supported foreign trade most vigorously had served lengthy terms of office in the maritime provinces or were native to coastal prefectures and counties.[20] They were aware of the problems confronting this region and were able to draft proposals which often took into account both immediate economic goals and long-range security considerations. The Court usually accepted their suggestions unless the border was thought to be so precarious as to render trade restrictions a defensive necessity.[21]

Economic arguments were the ones most cogently advanced to excite support for Chinese trade with Southeast Asia. Late eighteenth- and early nineteenth-century memorialists urged, in rhetoric similar to that of their predecessors, that maritime trade was essential to the economic viability of the southeastern coast. Wang Chih-i's[22] essay entitled "A Discussion

[18] Jane Leonard, "Wei Yüan and the *Hai-kuo t'u-chih*," p. 40.

[19] *KHSL*: 116:18a-b; Mancall, "The Ch'ing," p. 87.

[20] Tung Chiao-tseng, Wang Chih-i, Ts'ai Hsin, Yang Lin, and others will be discussed in detail below. A common link among them was their personal participation in provincial economic affairs.

[21] *The Indo-Chinese Gleaner* 10 (1819): 81: The restrictions on the size of Fukien junks imposed in 1806 were said, by Fukien officials, to be "only what the circumstances of that time rendered necessary." Other examples will be given below.

[22] Wang was active during the late Ch'ien-lung and Chia-ch'ing periods. He was the Governor of Fukien from 1797 to 1801 and was appointed to the position of Min-Che Governor-General in 1810. He held this post an inordinately long time, until 1817. Throughout his career he was involved in financial matters, having served as the Su-sung Grain Intendant in 1791, the Kansu Financial Commissioner in 1793, the Chekiang Financial Commissioner in 1795, and the Fukien Financial Commissioner in 1797. During his tenure in Fukien he dealt with piracy off Chang-chou and Ch'üan-chou, as well as with problems arising from the activities of the Heaven and Earth Society. His financial responsibilities combined with the upsurge in piracy at the turn of the century

of the Seaport Situation,"[23] written while he was the Governor of Fukien in 1799, is one of the more perceptive analyses relating provincial economic needs to border security. People, he said, were not born pirates, but became pirates because the land could not support them. The solution to curbing piracy did not lie in prohibiting ocean trade, but in providing sufficiently for the public welfare.[24] He then discussed the ways maritime trade could contribute to the latter.

The population of Fukien, he maintained, was too large to make a living from the available arable land and had, therefore, turned to trade. The Chinese junks trading abroad could support a crew of 100 men and exchanged native goods for foreign rice and other products which they subsequently sold upon their return to China. This trade, he continued, had been conducted during the past 100 years or more, proving it to be profitable and the basis on which the people's livelihood depended. Trade had been permitted originally so that the profit obtained could be turned to supplying the province with the goods and revenue it lacked.[25]

With the recent increase in piracy along the coast, some officials were proposing that the foreign trade be halted. They believed that the heavily laden merchant junks offered too great a temptation to the pirates. They were also concerned with the possibility that merchants would supply the pirates with information, arms, and aid in disposing of their ill-gotten gains.[26] Wang contended, however, that there were junks in at least 360 bays and ports along the Fukien coast. It would be impossible to calculate accurately the number of people who benefitted, either directly or indirectly, from this trade. If it were abolished, these people would be out of work and impoverished. They would then become vagrants, robbers, and other undesirable elements. Trade enhanced local stability by providing employment to people who might otherwise resort to banditry or piracy. To prohibit trade would not bring about the desired ends, but

---

must have been important in shaping his perceptions of the maritime world. For his biography see: *CHLC*: 189:6a-13a; *CSK*: 363:1283.

[23] *HCCSWP*: 85:11a-12b.

[24] *HCCSWP*: 85:11a.

[25] *HCCSWP*: 85:11b.

[26] Ibid.

would, rather, increase disorder and poverty: "we must suppress piracy, but in so doing, must not harm the merchants and people."[27]

This recognition of the Fukien population's dependence on foreign trade was echoed in 1818 by Tung Chiao-tseng,[28] the Min-Che Governor General, in his memorial requesting the removal of restrictions on Fukien ocean vessels. He noted that, when merchants were permitted to build large junks, they could transport more goods and thereby increase their profits. The merchant population expanded, the goods and provisions they imported grew, and the people of Chang-chou and Ch'üan-chou were able to support themselves. After the size of Fukien junks had been limited in 1806, mercantile houses had failed from lack of business. Provincial grain supplies were considerably reduced because the newly regulated junks could carry only half as much grain as the older ones. Tung believed that, since ocean junks from the other coastal provinces had not been subject to the limitation, it was unjust to apply it only to Fukien vessels. Piracy had, moreover, been quelled and he felt the people should once again be permitted to construct larger, more sea-worthy junks.[29]

Besides providing employment for the coastal population, trade was also linked to increased provincial revenue and to the supply of staple goods. Wang noted that goods were traded from province to province or exchanged for foreign merchandise. The loss would be incalculable were such communications to end, and would certainly lead to a reduc-

---

[27] *HCCSWP*: 85:12a. Wang's analysis of the connection between trade and border pacification is uncommonly acute. He was one of the few memorialists to have recognized that encouraging private trade was one of the more feasible ways of ensuring tranquility inland as well as on the sea. While other memorialists described the unfavorable economic consequences of an interdiction on trade, they seldom made the connection between trade and internal security as Wang did.

[28] Tung spent much of his career either holding office in Peking as a Secretary of the Board of Civil Appointments (1790), a second-class, and then senior Secretary (1797-1798), or in the interior as the Szechuan Provincial Judge (1800), the Szechuan Financial Commissioner (1804), the Governor of Anhwei (1808-1810), and as the Governor of Shensi (1810-1813). From 1813 to 1817 he was the Governor of Kwangtung and in 1817 replaced Wang Chih-i as the Governor-General of Fukien-Chekiang until 1821. He did not serve in the coastal provinces as long as Wang, but he was concerned with eradicating piracy during his tenure as the Min-Che Governor-General. His defense of foreign trade was written at that time. For his biography see: *CSK*: 363:1284; *CHLC*: 194:15a-21a.

[29] *The Indo-Chinese Gleaner* 10 (1819): 80-82.

tion in tax revenue.[30] Tung also touched on these points, remarking that with the decline in trade, the customs houses were collecting less in duty and fees.[31] Both were more concerned over the impact that curtailed trade would have on supplying provisions for the people and for the military garrisons. As we saw in Chapter IV, rice imports were favored by the government. Fukien particularly, and Kwangtung to a lesser extent, did not produce enough rice to meet local demand, and both were forced to rely on imports from Formosa and Southeast Asia. Fearing that famine and poverty would result if the grain trade should cease, Wang and Tung urged the continuation of maritime commerce.[32]

The ideas expressed by Wang and Tung, while pertinent to the actual situation existing in Fukien in the early nineteenth century, were, nonetheless, reiterations of concepts pre-dating the Ch'ing. After Canton was closed to foreign commerce in the 1520s, local officials responded to deteriorating financial conditions in Kwangtung by petitioning the Court to permit the resumption of trade. Like Tung and Wang, they understood the role of trade in the provincial economy and supported it on those grounds.[33] The same arguments were again expounded during the seventeenth and eighteenth centuries as Chinese bureaucrats attempted to maintain sea communication between the southeastern coast and the *Nan-yang*. They were aware of the benefits commerce offered and presented their case in reasoned terms.

Lan Ting-yuan's[34] essay on the *Nan-yang*, written during the 1720s, is a link in the chain reaching back to the Ming memorialists and extending forward to the writings of Wang and Tung. He believed the *Nan-yang*

---

[30] *HCCSWP*: 85:12a.

[31] *The Indo-Chinese Gleaner* 10 (1819): 82.

[32] Ibid., *HCCSWP*: 85:11a-b.

[33] Chang T'ien-tse, *Sino-Portuguese Trade from 1514-1644* (Leyden: Brill, 1934), pp. 72-74; Elvin, *The Pattern*, p. 219.

[34] A native of Chang-p'u, Fukien, Lan was intimately involved in provincial affairs and was well grounded in the knowledge of China's coastal geography. He participated in piracy suppression and grain transport while holding office in Kwangtung. His attitude toward the maritime world was probably acquired during his early years in Fukien and during the ten years between 1710 and 1720 when he was in retirement in Chang-p'u caring for his mother. Situated as he was in the center of Sino-*Nan-yang* trading activity, he would have been constantly reminded of exactly how critical trade was to the Fukien economy. For his biography see Arthur Hummel, ed., *Eminent Chinese of the Ch'ing Period*, 2 vols. (Washington: U.S. Government Printing Office, 1943), vol. 1, pp. 440-41.

offered no threat to China's security, that trade enriched the people, that imports augmented internal insufficiencies, that local handicrafts were encouraged, and that provincial revenue was increased through the collection of customs duties.[35] Similar views were expressed by successive supporters of Chinese trade with Southeast Asia. Yang Lin,[36] Ts'ai Hsin,[37] Na-su-t'u,[38] and Ch'ing-fu,[39] to name but a few, recognized that foreign trade, through shipping and subsidiary occupations, was the principal form of employment along the coast, that it supplemented provincial revenue, and that the goods exchanged were of considerable

[35] *HCCSWP* : 83:13a-14a.

[36] *CHLC*: 162:12a-14b. Much of Yang's career was served in the southeastern provinces. He was involved in Kiangnan grain transport (1698), he was Commander-in-chief of the Fukien Land Forces (1711), Governor of Kwangtung (1715-1716), and the Liang-Kuang Governor-General from 1716 to 1724. During the debates in 1717 on prohibiting trade with the *Nan-yang*, he requested that trade with Annam be permitted: *KHSL*: 277:28b. He believed in fortifying strategic defenses, but did not see foreign trade and border defense as incompatible.

[37] Ts'ai, like Lan Ting-yuan, was a native of Chang-p'u hsien, Fukien. Although he was a supervisor in the school for the Emperor's sons for much of his career (1757-1785), he too spent over a decade during his middle years at home caring for his mother. His contact with the economic affairs of the coast stirred his interest in economic subjects. In his essay on the trade with the *Nan-yang*, he stressed the loss in revenue to the provincial treasury should trade be prohibited and the reliance of the Kwangtung and Fukien populations on overseas trade: *Chang-chou FC*: 1877:33:64a-65a; Hummel, *Eminent Chinese*, vol. 2, p. 734.

[38] While principally holding office in the capital (see *CSK*: 314:1188), Na-su-t'u did serve as the Liang-Kiang Governor-General (1737-1739), as the Min-Che Governor-General (1742-1744), and as the interim Governor-General of Liang-Kuang (1744-1745). He was concerned with the proper provisioning of the provinces where he served, with ensuring equitable taxation, and with abolishing taxes on fishing boats. See *CHLC*: 166:5a-10b.

[39] Ch'ing-fu's ideas about the role of foreign trade are somewhat more difficult to explain, for his experience in the maritime provinces was more limited than that of other officials who supported Chinese trade. He was the Governor-General of Liang-Kiang for a brief period in 1737 before Na-su-t'u took up the post and was later appointed the acting Liang-Kuang Governor-General (1741-1743). He also served as President of the Board of Revenue in 1733. Otherwise, he was located in Peking or was on military campaigns in the interior. And yet, his memorial of 1742 is one of the clearest statements of why Chinese trade with the *Nan-yang* should be permitted. He presents the comments by various officials opposed to one aspect or another of this trade and answers each fully with the arguments set out above: *Shih-liao hsun-k'an* 22 (Jan. 1, 1931): 803a-805a. For Ch'ing-fu's biography see Hummel, *Eminent Chinese*, vol. 2, p. 796; *CSK*: 303:1167.

value to the Chinese economy. Whether from active experience as provincial officials or from scrutiny of local conditions as natives of the area,
they advocated maritime trade for the multitude of financial advantages
it provided. Wang Chih-i and Tung Chiao-tseng were not, therefore,
setting out new or untried hypotheses in their case for preserving contacts
between China and the *Nan-yang*, but were voicing concepts which had
gained legitimacy through their repetition over several centuries.

While economic criteria were central to the writings of officials who
favored Chinese trade with Southeast Asia, border security or pacification proved to be the basis on which the government's commercial policy
was frequently determined. Concern with security was, of course, more
immediate during the seventeenth century before the southeastern coast
has been brought firmly under Manchu control. But it also appears to
have influenced later commercial decisions, particularly those regarding
the Western presence in China.[40] In this context, Chinese native trade was
permissible as long as it did not engender unrest along the maritime
frontier. Piracy and Chinese trade were closely linked in the minds of
some officials. Whenever the maritime borders were unsettled, these
officials quickly suggested prohibiting trade as a first step in regaining
order. This was true as late as the nineteenth century, long after the
Kwangtung-Fukien border posed any real political threat to Ch'ing rule.
The Court's early military experiences with the region clearly colored
later attitudes toward Chinese trade and immigration, but not, perhaps,
to the extent of confining it under an unduly repressive system.

The Chinese government's solution to the depredation of Japanese
pirates along the southeastern coast in the late Ming was to prohibit
foreign trade.[41] The Ch'ing Court responded similarly to the raids by
Coxinga (Cheng Ch'eng-kung) and his son, Cheng Ching, and to the anti-
Manchu activities during the Revolt of the Three Feudatories. Native
trade was prohibited in 1656 on the grounds that the Chengs could not
be eliminated until the merchants provisioning them had been banned
from access to the ocean.[42] By 1684 the disorder had been checked and

---

[40] Leonard, "Wei Yüan," pp. 48-49.

[41] Meilink-Roelofsz, *Asian Trade*, p. 74; Ray Huang, "Fiscal Administration during the
Ming Dynasty," in *Chinese Government in Ming Times*, ed. Charles Hucker (New York:
Columbia University Press, 1969), pp. 110-11.

[42] Fu, *A Documentary*, vol. 1, pp. 20-21. Edicts of a similar nature were issued over the
next twenty-odd years against merchants who, under cover of trade, supplied the off-
shore dissidents: ibid., pp. 28-29, 37, 50-51. The prohibition was relaxed somewhat in
1669 when ocean fishing was allowed: ibid., p. 46.

permission was obtained to establish maritime customs administrations in Kwangtung, Fukien, and Kiangnan.[43] Prohibitions against native trade and immigration to the *Nan-yang* were occasionally enacted in succeeding years, but the institutionalization of maritime trade under the *hai-kuan* system after 1684 marked the change to a more permissive outlook.

This is not to say that border security ceased thereafter to be of interest to the Court, but rather, that the southeast was regarded as sufficiently stable to sustain a well-organized and regulated maritime commerce. On various occasions during the Yung-cheng and Ch'ien-lung periods, decisions were made on the basis of how they might affect security.[44] Wang Chih-i's essay was an attempt to reconcile the continuation of trade with the suppression of piracy, while Tung Chiao-tseng maintained that the military situation no longer required restrictions on merchant vessels. As late as 1823, in fact, the Board of Rites stipulated that a problem involving Weng Jih-sheng, the Chinese interpreter for the Siamese tribute entourage, would be decided in a manner "consistent with the protection of our borders."[45]

Chinese trade with, and the immigration of various segments of the trading population to, Southeast Asia increased noticeably from the end of the K'ang-hsi period. Although some scholars have remarked upon the institution of a more restrictive policy toward trade during the Yung-cheng Emperor's reign,[46] this did not apply to Chinese native trade. Occasionally, restrictions were placed on the Sino-*Nan-yang* trade or immigration, but largely because of the potential alliance between merchants and pirates and because of the possible political threat from anti-Manchu enclaves and overseas Chinese. For instance, on March 7, 1717, Chinese merchants were forbidden to trade with Southeast Asia. In 1727, Chinese emigration was restricted by the reimposition of a three-year return date.[47] That the 1717 prohibition was not strictly enforced is

---

[43] Ibid., p. 61.

[44] Fu, *A Documentary*, vol. 1, pp. 158, 167, 200, 202-03; vol. 2, pp. 461 fn. 144, 515 fn. 71; Earl Pritchard, *Anglo-Chinese Relations during the Seventeenth and Eighteenth Centuries* (New York: Octagon Books, 1970), p. 127; Staunton, *Ta Tsing Leu Lee*, pp. 543-44; Boulais, *Manuel*, pp. 441, 437-38, 443, 446.

[45] *TCHTSL*: 1899:512:9b.

[46] See fn. 12 and Leonard, "Wei Yüan," p. 51.

[47] *KHSL*: 271:6a-7a. The first mention of possibly prohibiting the trade appeared on Dec. 9, 1716: *KHSL*: 270:16a; Fu, *A Documentary*, vol. 1, pp. 157-59; vol. 2, p. 515; Mancall,

evident from a comment by the Yung-cheng Emperor. He noted that in the years following this decision "only a few overseas Chinese returned to China *by the Chinese ships engaged in foreign trade*" [emphasis mine].[48] Later attempts to lure overseas Chinese home would indicate that the 1727 limitation was not observed either.

Overall, the government appears to have been favorably disposed toward Chinese trade with the *Nan-yang*, having taken into account, perhaps, the advice of its supporters. In 1718, at the behest of Yang Lin, the 1717 prohibition was modified and Chinese merchants were permitted to trade with Vietnam.[49] Because Siam's rice was said to be "cheap and plentiful," the K'ang-hsi Emperor in 1722 ordered that 300,000 piculs were to be shipped to the coastal provinces duty-free to ameliorate conditions there.[50] In 1724 Chinese sailors were discovered as crew members on Siamese tribute vessels. They were not retained in China but were allowed to return to Siam, ostensibly because of Siam's faithfulness as a vassal. The concession was actually granted because of the rice and other goods imported by the tribute vessel and its merchant convoy.[51] The *Nan-yang* was again opened to Chinese trade in 1727 at the request of the Min-Che Governor-General, Kao Ch'i-cho. His petition stressed the economic justifications for a formal renewal of trade. The Emperor's approval probably reflected the Court's cognizance of the *de facto* situation.[52]

Prohibitions against Chinese trade to Southeast Asia were once more counseled during the middle decades of the eighteenth century. Discussion arose when the Court requested provincial recommendations in the early 1740s about the advisability of stopping trade with the Dutch after their massacre of Chinese in Batavia in 1740.[53] Ch'ing-fu's summation of, and answer to, the opinions submitted by provincial officials is, perhaps,

"The Ch'ing," p. 89; Skinner, *Chinese Society*, p. 16. Skinner follows Chen Ta in giving 1729 as the year in which emigration was restricted. 1727 is correct.

[48] Fu, *A Documentary*, vol. 1, p. 158.

[49] *KHSL*: 277:28b; Mancall, "The Ch'ing," p. 88; Fu, *A Documentary*, vol. 1, p. 127.

[50] *KHSL*: 298:3a-b; Skinner, *Chinese Society*, p. 17; Mancall, "The Ch'ing," pp. 88-89. The edict does not mention, as Mancall asserts, that the rice was to be shipped in Siamese vessels.

[51] Skinner, *Chinese Society*, p. 17; *YCSL*: 25:20a-b.

[52] Fu, *A Documentary*, vol. 1, p. 157.

[53] Ibid., p. 173; Victor Purcell, *The Chinese in Southeast Asia* (London: Oxford University Press, 1951), pp. 467-70.

the most exhaustive treatment of the position favoring Sino-*Nan-yang* trade. In reply to Ts'e-leng,[54] who advocated prohibiting Chinese trade with the *Nan-yang* "in order to persuade the barbarians to repent and turn toward our civilization,"[55] Ch'ing-fu maintained that the latter could be achieved through spreading the Emperor's virtue. It would not be necessary to stop the trade which provided a living for the people of Kwangtung and Fukien.[56]

Li Ch'ing-fang[57] and Wang P'i-lieh[58] advocated limitations to some degree, although they did not want the *Nan-yang* trade totally closed as Ts'e-leng suggested. Li recognized that trade increased customs revenue and was important to the welfare of the people, but felt that trade with Batavia should be prohibited. The rest of the *Nan-yang* could remain open. Ch'ing-fu responded that, if trade were stopped with Batavia, other countries in Southeast Asia might fear similar consequences. Moreover, Batavia was a useful anchorage and ships should be permitted to call there in case of storms or trouble at sea.[59] Wang P'i-lieh suggested that the time limit within which merchants should return from abroad be more strictly enforced. Those who returned after two years might at some

[54] His career is rather obscure prior to 1741 when he was appointed the acting Min-Che Governor-General. He served as the acting Liang-Kuang Governor-General in 1743 and was appointed Governor of Kwang-tung in 1744, but was excused a month later. In 1745 he was reappointed the Liang-Kuang Governor-General. Toward the end of his career he was involved in pacification in Tibet and against the Eleuths (the

Central Asian frontier): Albert Hermann, *A Historical Atlas of China* (new edition) (Chicago: Aldine, 1966), map, pp. 48-49. For his biography see *CSK*: 320:1209; Hummel, *Eminent Chinese*, vol. 1, pp. 73, 220, 250.

[55] Fu, *A Documentary*, vol. 1, p. 173.

[56] Ch'ing-fu, "Ch'ien-lung ch'ao," p. 804a.

[57] Li's family was from An-ch'i hsien, Fukien. He rose through the ranks and became a Vice-President of the Board of War. His post in Fukien was that of Censor. He is cited in Li Yuan-tu, *Kuo-ch'ao hsien-cheng shih-lüeh* [Brief biographies of worthy officials of the Ch'ing dynasty], 60 *chüan* (Taipei: Wen-hai, 1967):7:21b.

[58] Wang was from Kiangsu and served as a Provincial Judge in Hunan and Fukien. He served in the Censorate and checked examination essays. His strict adherence to the time limitation for remaining abroad may be a by-product of his experience in the Censorate and as a judge. For his biography see Feng Chin-po, comp., *Kuo'ch'ao hua-shih* [A biography of Ch'ing dynasty painters], 17 *chüan* (Shanghai: Chung-hua shu-chü, 1941):11:5b-6a. For his complete memorial from which the excerpts cited by Ch'ing-fu were taken see: *MCSL:KP*, vol. 8, 707a-b.

[59] Ch'ing-fu, "Ch'ien-lung ch'ao," pp. 803a, 804a.

time be allowed to trade abroad; those who returned after three to four years would never again be allowed to leave China. To this Ch'ing-fu agreed. He did not, however, specify the length of time merchants could trade overseas, only that "they should not stay there long." The solution was for officials to maintain vigilance over the trade at their ports.[60]

The debates of the 1740s culminated in the memorial by Ch'en Hung-mou[61] requesting that Chinese merchants who had overstayed the three year limit imposed in 1727 be authorized to return "provided that their real reason for not returning within the time allowed was their inability to close their accounts."[62] Any merchant who wished to return could presumably have taken advantage of this loophole. The Court's approval of Ch'en's memorial indicates the continuing flexibility toward maritime commerce. Thus, while 1757 has traditionally been considered a turning point in Ch'ing commercial policy, this was true only with respect to Western trade. The Chinese and Asian junk trade was not confined to Canton but continued to expand steadily. The government thereafter appears to have made only sporadic attempts to force the junk trade to conform to previously enunciated regulations.[63] The government's leniency may have been a response to the more dramatic problems confronting the state in this period of increased Western encroachment. Governmental indifference and the willingness of certain bureaucrats to encourage Chinese maritime trade were important factors in its growth during the late eighteenth and early nineteenth centuries.

---

[60] Ibid., p. 804b.

[61] Ch'en was the Governor of Fukien from 1752 to 1754 and was prompted to submit his memorial after 1749 when an overseas Chinese merchant, Ch'en I-lao, was tried and banished upon his return to China. He believed this would frighten others from returning and advocated liberalization. For his biography, see Hummel, *Eminent Chinese*, vol. 1, pp. 86-87.

[62] Ch'en Hung-mou, "Notice Reminding Merchants Trading Overseas that They Are Free to Return Home, 1754," in T. F. Wade, *Key to the Tzu Erh Chi* (London: Trübner, 1867), p. 33; Fu, *A Documentary*, vol. 1, p. 193, vol. 2, p. 533, fn. 85; *CLSL*: 463:17a-18a.

[63] A number of examples from the nineteenth-century demonstrate this point. In 1807, Chinese were forbidden to sail Siamese trading vessels: *MCSL:KP*, vol. 6, 561b-62a. In 1815 they were forbidden to sail the tribute ships; *TCHTTL*: 1899:512:8b. These prohibitions seem to have been fairly ineffective as Chinese acted as supercargoes on Siamese vessels throughout the nineteenth century. Furthermore, Siamese vessels were not to participate in the coasting trade, but according to the testimony of the Ch'eng-hai hsien magistrate, these junks were often granted permits to carry goods to the provincial markets where a better price could be obtained: *MCSL:KP*, vol. 6, 561b-562a.

A hint was given above as to why some officials became active spokesmen for the Chinese native trade while others remained aloof or hostile. As Lan Ting-yuan noted, the restrictions upon maritime commerce were the products of ignorance: ignorance of China's neighbors and ignorance of the Chinese maritime coast.[64] His assessment is essentially fair, although he perhaps overlooked the politico-military context in which policy was designed. The men who planned policy for the central government were confronted by more far-reaching concerns than their provincial counterparts. Their preoccupation with frontier security and experiences with southern resistance to the imposition of Manchu rule may have made them wary of the possibility of continued dissent and disruption from that region. Even a suggestion of instability was enough to renew debate over the feasibility of imposing new restrictions.

Also implicit in Lan's criticism is the suggestion that ignorance on the part of officials may have been a product of their inexperience as local administrators. Wang Chih-i, Tung Chiao-tseng, Ts'ai Hsin, and Yang Lin, either through observation or government service, were familiar with the issues unique to the southeastern coast. In coping with the problems engendered by overpopulation, insufficient land, and the supply and maintenance of military patrols and fortifications, provincial officials were forced to rely on practical solutions. A vigorous native overseas trade was an obvious one. It brought wealth to the people, goods to exchange with other provinces, and it provided tax revenue. An official's experience and the scope of his decision-making powers were, therefore, of some consequence in shaping his attitudes toward the Chinese junk trade.

The bureaucrats who endorsed China's trade with Southeast Asia were often capable of swaying central government policy in the directions they wished to go. Trade was prohibited only if it was believed to contribute to political instability, as during the early years of the Ch'ing. The Court did not, however, maintain the isolationist stance in evidence during much of the Ming,[65] exhibiting instead a flexible approach to the maritime world.[66] This approach persisted throughout the eighteenth and

---

[64] *HCCSWP*: 83:13a.

[65] Wolters, *The Fall of Srivijaya*, chs. 3, 5.

[66] The K'ang-hsi Emperor was nonetheless alert to the dangers inherent in military complacency. He warned that even in times of peace the government should remain aware of possible threats to security. He was thus willing to endorse the prohibition against trade with the *Nan-yang* in 1717 because Java and Luzon were principal pirate

early nineteenth centuries, most noticeably in the Chinese treatment of Siam as a trading partner.

Siam furnished China with goods she needed. Rice was especially important, but other Siamese staples (see Chapter IV) were of almost equal value. As long as this trade supplied necessary goods and conformed to Chinese regulations, it was not burdened by onerous restrictions. Chinese memorialists advocating Sino-*Nan-yang* trade habitually remarked that rice production in Fukien and Kwangtung was not sufficient to meet demand. Only through imports from overseas could the deficits be made up.[67] Siam had the resources to meet this demand and the Chinese had the incentive to exploit it.

The force of tradition can clearly be seen in Ch'ing maritime policy decisions and in the ideas that produced or influenced them. Wang Chih-i and Tung Chiao-tseng premised the measures they advanced on concepts espoused long before their time. The logic of their economic analyses was convincing and must have been an element in retaining the relative freedom of native trade from restrictive Imperial enactments. The decline of the junk trade with the *Nan-yang* in the nineteenth century should not be attributed to governmental suppression, for it was largely a result of such external factors as steam competition, Western hegemony in Southeast Asia, and Siam's increasing commitment to Western forms of commercial enterprise. The impact of these factors in altering traditional economic patterns in the Asian maritime world will be examined in the final chapter.

lairs. If Chinese merchants joined with them, they might pose a threat to China's security: *KHSL*: 270:15b-16b.

[67] Fu, *A Documentary*, vol. 1, p. 157; Ch'ing-fu, "Ch'ien-lung ch'ao," p. 804b; *HCCSWP*: 85:11a.

7

CONCLUSION

China's traditional relationship with Siam was already showing signs of strain in the 1840s. Events in the 1850s were to weaken even further these fragile bonds and were to alter decisively the familiar patterns of diplomatic and commercial intercourse. The deterioration of the Sino-Siamese junk trade and the cessation of Siam's tribute missions to China coincided. These developments occurred partly as a result of the enlarged role assumed by Western powers in Asia after the Opium War and partly from the willingness of Siam's leaders to seek accommodation with Western nations. In a sense these stimuli were but two sides of the same coin, in that Siam might not have sought new alliances had the Western presence been less overwhelming. The impact of the Western intrusion and the extent to which the waning junk trade and Siam's departure from the Chinese tributary orbit were interrelated will be explored below.

China's defeat in the Opium War and the subsequent imposition of the Treaty of Nanking in 1842 were to have a profound effect on both her relations with the West and her relations with countries in Southeast Asia. The Sino-Asian junk trade had been capable of competing successfully with carriage by Western ships prior to this time largely because of the exclusive access to Chinese ports other than Canton enjoyed by junks. The treaty, by opening Amoy, Foochow, Ningpo, and Shanghai to Western shipping, largely nullified the junks' advantages and eliminated the need for Siam and other Asian states to rely on Chinese sailors and Chinese-style vessels to carry their trade with China. This meant, in effect, that the overseas Chinese who controlled various aspects of the foreign trade of the Southeast Asian countries where they had settled could now lade their cargoes on Western ships in transit between Europe and China, without fear of discrimination at the newly opened ports. Alternatively, Southeast Asians could build their own square-rigged sailing vessels and steamers, as the Siamese did, to carry their trade to the ports opened by the treaty.

The Siamese, who had begun constructing square-rigged vessels for the Siam-Singapore trade in the 1830s, now gradually increased the proportion of their trade with China carried in these ships. While Siam's share of the shipping at the treaty ports was small in comparison with that of Western merchants, the arrival and departure of Siamese vessels was regularly reported during the 1850s and 1860s.[1] A further stimulus to the use of Western-style vessels for transporting Siamese goods in addition to that supplied by the opening of the more important Chinese ports to them was the encouragement given to the construction of such ships by the Siamese king and nobility. A member of the prominent and powerful Bunnag family, Chuang, was an active sponsor of the new Western-style shipbuilding enterprises. As we saw above, members of the nobility were already employing these vessels for their trade with China in the 1840s.[2] Early in the Fourth Reign (1851-1868) Monkut abolished all state trade, with the result that the junks which had been used for this purpose were no longer needed.

The concessions obtained by Western shipping through the Treaty of Nanking and the Siamese elite's growing involvement in the learning of Western mechanical skills were critical factors in the transition from junk to Western forms of transport. The Bowring Treaty, negotiated between Siam and Great Britain in 1855, served to complete this shift. Articles similar to those in the Anglo-Chinese treaty of 1842 put British shipping, later extended to ships of other Western nations, on a basis of equality in Siam with that owned by Siamese and Chinese. Thus the preferential treatment of junks was abolished at both ends of the Sino-Siamese trading network. If one end had remained open, junk transport would, perhaps, have been maintained for a time; but after the much less expensive steamers came to dominate long-distance ocean transport, the junk's advantages largely disappeared.

---

[1] Great Britain: Board of Trade, *Abstract of Reports on the Trade*. In 1854-1855, Siam sent 11 square-rigged vessels to China (p. 47). In 1856, Shanghai reported the arrival of 7 Siamese ships and the departure of 8 (p. 60). In 1859, 9 Siamese ships entered and departed from Ningpo (p. 17); Great Britain: Foreign Office, *Commercial Reports from Her Majesty's Consuls in China, Japan, and Siam 1865*. Six Siamese vessels entered and left Shanghai in 1864 (p. 74). In 1863, 27 vessels arrived at Amoy from Siam and 22 departed (p. 168). In 1865, 19 entered and 18 departed from Ningpo (p. 36).

[2] CMH.R.3, #49, 1844.

[3] Historical examples of Siam's willingness to seek accommodation with other states are provided by O. W. Wolters, "Ayudhya and the Rearward Part of the World, *Journal of the Royal Asiatic Society*, pts. 3-4 (1968): 166-78.

Unlike China, which was forcibly drawn into relations with the West, Siam's leaders purposely chose a more conciliatory approach in meeting Britain's demands. Although the Chinese experience must have served as an object lesson to the Siamese, they were, nonetheless, already adept in the use of diplomacy, and demonstrated considerable flexibility when confronted by powers possessing obviously greater military might.[3] Their recognition of China's failure in this respect may explain the growing disenchantment with Siam's position in the Chinese tributary system. Dissatisfaction was expressed that China did not treat Siam as an equal, and that for Siam to maintain her status as a vassal state was to court the ridicule and disdain of the West.[4] Implicit in this attitude was the fear that Siam, as a tributary to China, would appear weak, thereby increasing the likelihood of her being made a pawn in Western power politics in Southeast Asia. From an economic standpoint, it was also felt that close ties with the West and concessions to Western trading interests would yield greater economic benefits in the long run than those derived from state and tributary trade with China.[5] The Siamese perception of Siam's place in the Asian world changed as the traditional economic and diplomatic structure was altered by the Western intrusion. Siam's vigorous response to British overtures hastened the process by removing the final advantages enjoyed by the Chinese native trade at Bangkok. As Siam moved closer to the West, her disengagement from the Chinese tributary system became inevitable.

The current literature on the tributary system is somewhat ambiguous as to the distinction between tributary and private trade. As a result, tribute missions have been portrayed in part as a cloak for trade with China and in part as a means of facilitating the operation of that trade. The fact that the frequency of Siam's tributary missions increased considerably between the early eighteenth and the mid-nineteenth century has been attributed to a growing interest in trade by the Siamese and to the necessity of accommodating an expanded trade.[6] If an argument such as this were applied to Siam, it would imply that the tribute missions were

---

[4] *Prachum prakat ratchakan thi 4* [The collected edicts of the Fourth Reign], 4 vols. (Bangkok: Khurusapha, 1960-61), 1868, edict 309, p. 346.

[5] CMH.R.4, #113, 1854. The Siamese Minister of Foreign Affairs, in writing to John Bowring prior to his arrival in Bangkok, explained that, even though the trade between China and Siam was of long duration, the taxes on Siamese goods were now high and no profit was made. See also CMH.R.4, #98, 1856.

[6] Fairbank and Teng, "On the Ch'ing Tribute," pp. 199-200, 206; Skinner, *Chinese Society*, pp. 24-26.

ended in the 1850s only because the junk trade generally, and that accompanying the tribute missions, was no longer regarded as sufficiently profitable to make the missions worthwhile. If Siamese trade could be advanced by the new conditions arising from the treaty provisions, i.e. the admittance of Siamese square-rigged vessels into the open ports, then Siam's compliance with tribute ideology[7] would become pointless.

One must ask, in fact, whether there was any connection between the tributary system and the Siamese junk trade with China other than that actually attached to missions. Since Siamese trade, because it was carried in Chinese vessels and handled by Chinese seamen, was treated as though it were Chinese trade, the answer must be no. Tribute's role in the Chinese cosmology was to justify and uphold the Chinese belief in Chinese superiority and in the universality of the Emperor's rule. This was supported on the diplomatic level by adhering to a specified set of forms, the most important of which was the presentation of tribute by the representatives of rulers who saw political benefits in the relationship. The presentation of tribute was the significant aspect of the ideology, and the tributary trade accompanying missions was considered a reward for faithfulness; it was of little consequence as an isolated activity.[8]

But the ambiguity revealed in the writings of modern historians of the tributary system reinforces the confusion as to whether or not trade, other than that actually carried by the tribute missions, was included within this framework. On the one hand, trade—presumably all trade—and tribute are described as "cognate aspects of a single system of foreign relations"[9] and that China's early overseas trade had been subsumed under the tributary system.[10] On the other hand, the Chinese native trade is credited with having executed the first breach in the tribute system precisely because it operated *outside* the boundaries of the system. It has been argued that when Chinese themselves began to trade directly with

[7] John K. Fairbank, "A Preliminary Framework," in *The Chinese World Order*, ed. John K. Fairbank (Cambridge: Harvard University Press, 1968), p. 4; Fairbank and Tent, "On the Ch'ing Tribute," p. 141; Fairbank, *Trade and Diplomacy*, p. 31.

[8] Fairbank, *Trade and Diplomacy*, p. 33.

[9] Ibid.

[10] Ibid., p. 36; Fairbank, "A Preliminary," p. 4: The statement that "economic relations could be formally permitted only within this (the tributary) political framework" leaves one with the impression that Fairbank is referring to all economic relations. Similar confusion exists in Mancall's discussion, "The Ch'ing Tribute System," pp. 75-77.

countries in Southeast Asia, the rulers of the countries where they traded no longer found it necessary to send their own vessels to China, and that this, furthermore, eliminated the need for sending tribute missions.[11] Chinese merchants operating in foreign lands were said to be "quite beyond control through tributary forms."[12]

It has been pointed out in the preceding chapters, however, that Chinese trade with Southeast Asia had been in existence, with few interruptions, since well before the Ch'ing dynasty. Chinese were permitted to go abroad without any reference to the tribute system, and their trade was administered under a different set of regulations from those pertaining to the trade accompanying tribute envoys. There was no contradiction between trade with Southeast Asia and tributary values, because the former was conducted by Chinese and carried in vessels recognized as Chinese. Had the Siamese attempted to trade in their own ships manned by their own nationals and succeeded in doing so, the tribute system might indeed have been abused. But such was not the case. The Sino-Siamese junk trade was able to exist in harmony with the tributary system primarily because the dimensions of the tributary system did not extend to Chinese who went abroad to trade or Chinese living in foreign countries who traded with China. If Siam ceased sending tribute missions for economic reasons, it was because they recognized the decreasing importance of state and tributary trade at Canton rather than because their junk trade at other Chinese ports had declined.

Chinese society has often been portrayed by modern historians as reflecting certain anti-commercial biases. These biases, they assert, were important in maintaining the primacy of the ceremonial over the economic purpose of the tributary missions. Confucian ideology has been regarded as antagonistic to merchants, whose activities were considered parasitic rather than productive. The Chinese belief in their country's self-sufficiency is further cited as underlying their antipathy to commercial

---

[11] Fairbank, *Trade and Diplomacy*, pp. 36-37. But as Fairbank points out, the Chinese must have been aware that Chinese merchants were trading with the countries of Southeast Asia, since they included former tributaries under the heading of trading nations in the Administrative Statutes of 1818. It should also have been obvious to the Chinese in this instance that tribute had been eclipsed by trade, and that considerable contact was taking place outside the auspices of the tributary framework.

[12] Fairbank and Teng, "On the Ch'ing Tribute," p. 205. Mancall asserts much the same thing with regard to ports of trade. Trade was permitted on China's frontiers because it could be controlled under Chinese supervision. Chinese were, however, prohibited from trading abroad because there "the government could not define normative or expected behavior patterns" ("The Ch'ing Tribute System," p. 81).

development showing that overseas trade was therefore of little concern in formulating decisions of state.[13] On the basis of the evidence presented in this essay, such assumptions have no validity with regard to the junk trade. While official Ch'ing commercial policy vacillated from permissiveness to prohibition, the native trade with Southeast Asia was never prohibited for long nor did it suffer undue governmental exploitation.

The commodities obtained via the Sino-Siamese and other Sino-Southeast Asian trade were useful to the regional economies of China's southeastern coast, and the importation of these goods over several centuries would suggest that China was not entirely self-sufficient economically, as often claimed. The articles of commerce shipped from Southeast Asia during the Ch'ing were primarily staples. Official distrust of foreign trade may well have arisen from recognition that the manufactures and opium imported by Western ships were not needed.[14] Many Chinese appreciated the contributions of the junk trade to the economy of the provinces on China's maritime border. As we have seen, arguments in its support emphasized the employment it provided coastal dwellers, its stimulating effect on local handicrafts, and the provincial revenue it engendered. That the junk trade remained relatively free from restrictive enactments is best demonstrated by its growth during the eighteenth and nineteenth centuries. Had the government intended to prohibit its development, the task would have been easier than circumscribing Western merchants who were backed by the possible threat of military force.

We can, therefore, eliminate governmental antipathy as an explanation for the gradual demise of the Sino-Siamese junk trade. As early as the 1840s, in fact, a Chinese official, fearful that Chinese junks would be displaced by Western ships, forbade Chinese merchants to consign their goods in square-rigged vessels for shipment from Singapore.[15] In the years after the Foreign Inspectorate of Customs was established, Western observers noted that officials at the native customs stations outside the jurisdiction of the Inspectorate consistently offered lower tariffs to junk

---

[13] Fairbank, *Trade and Diplomacy*, p. 33; Mancall, "The Ch'ing Tribute System," p. 89 and *passim*. For an alternative perspective on Chinese commercial thought see Thomas Metzger, "The State and Commerce in Imperial China," *Asian and African Studies* 6 (1970): 23-46.

[14] Metzger, "The State," p. 29; *HCCSWP*: 26:15b. The importation of opium was seen as particularly damaging to the Chinese economy because its sale led to the depletion of the country's monetary reserves.

[15] Wong Lin Ken, "The Trade of Singapore," pp. 123-24.

captains in the hope that they would report their cargoes at the native collectorates rather than at those under Western supervision. Shippers would benefit by paying a smaller sum in duties and the collectorate officers would themselves benefit by retaining the income they had customarily derived from the native trade.[16] These examples indicate that at least some Chinese port authorities continued to take an interest in the overseas trading activities of Chinese merchants and to support the long-standing carriage by junk.

At the same time, the Chinese attempted to regain Siam's allegiance as a vassal by dispatching a series of letters in 1862 from the Governor-General's office in Kwangtung, and from the hong merchant in charge of Siamese affairs in Canton, to the Siamese Minister of the Treasury. The correspondence requested that Siam resume her tribute missions now that peace had been restored in the Canton area and the safety of future missions could be assured.[17] But the Siamese government did not respond positively to these overtures nor was the junk trade revived.

The rapid deterioration of the junk trade appears to have resulted not from an absence of Chinese governmental encouragement but from that trade's failure to serve its original purpose. The economic situation that had prevailed in the traditional Asian commercial world and that had promoted the growth of the junk trade was, by the middle years of the nineteenth century, being replaced by new trading conditions and patterns that made reliance on shipping by junk superfluous.

[16] Banister, "A History of the External Trade of China," p. 144.

[17] Thiphakorawong, *The Dynastic Chronicles*, vol. 2, pp. 281, 300-01.

APPENDIX A
SINO-SIAMESE EXPORT TRADE 1800-1850

Sec. 1: *Siamese Exports to China*

Sec. 2: *Chinese Exports to Siam*

Note: The figures under "cost" reflect a range of prices for the products listed. They are approximate, having been drawn from a variety of sources (see Appendix A, Bibliography). While many of the prices are more representative of 1850 figures, the high and low for a given product have been provided where possible. The figures under "quantity exported" are also approximate. As with cost, they are often indicative of the quantities exported during the 1840s and 1850s.

Cost has been given in *baht* and quantity in piculs unless otherwise specified.

\#   = piece
1 *baht* = Sp. $.50

Sec. 1: Siamese Exports to China, 1800-1850

Name	Siam: Cost High-Low	China: Cost High-Low	Quantity Exported	Value	Source
Anchors	32.5#		limited number		G_{3-4}
Bark:					
Red Mangrove *Palong* or *Plong*[a]	1.25 -.75	4.25-2.75	large quantity		H_1,T,BB,CC,DD, G_{3-4}
Banjamin					
1st quality	60-50	200-60	150	15,000	C,D,J,K_1,T,V,X,BB,CC, DD
2nd quality	45-40	90-50	150	10,500	
3rd quality	25-20	40-16	100	2,500	
Betel-nut	4-2	7-4	large quantity		E,G_{3-4},H_1,I,M,T,V,X,Z
Beche-de-mer:[b]					
Black	65-60	160-30	250	25,000	C,E,H_1,M,T,U,V,X,BB, CC
White	40-14	20-10	400	6,000	
Birds (preserved)	.35#-.3#		100,000#		T
Birds' Nests:					
1st quality	8,000-3,000	8,000-6,000	4	28,000	E,H_1,K_1,M,T,U,V,X, BB,CC
2nd quality	6,000-1,500	6,000-2,500	25	100,000	
3rd quality	4,000-1,000	4,000-1,000	30	60,000	
Bones:					
Elephant		7-6.5		3,000	T,BB,CC,DD
Ox and Buffalo	1.5-1		20,000		
Tiger	35-30		150		
Cardamom:[c]					
1st quality	400-200		250-500		C,D,G_{3-4},H_1,J,T,W, BB,CC,DD
2nd quality	200-100		200		
3rd quality	150-20		200		
Copper	55-45		small quantity		D,P,V,CC,DD

Name	Siam: Cost High-Low	China: Cost High-Low	Quantity Exported	Value	Source
Cotton:					
Clean	26-8		30,000		A,B,C,D,G$_4$,H$_1$,K$_1$, M, T,BB,CC,DD
Seed	8-3		30,000		
Cushions and Mattresses	.5#-.375# 8#-4#		500,000# 4,000#		J,T,CC
Cutch (Terra Japonica)		14-8			E,G$_2$,K$_1$,U,X
Deer Sinews	30-16		1,000		H$_1$,T,BB
Dragon's Blood	50-20	200-120	700	112,000	E,T,U,V,X
Feathers:					
Peacock.	.3#- .28#		6,000#		G$_2$,H$_1$,T,BB,CC,DD
Kingfisher	25		400		
Fish:					
Dried	8-7				E,G$_3$,K$_1$,T,X,BB,CC, DD
Salt			large quantity		
Maws	60-50	180-80			
Gamboge:					
1st quality	60-50	120-100	200	22,000	A,C,D,E,G$_{1-2}$,J,K$_{1-2}$,M, T,U, V,X,BB,CC,DD
2nd quality	55-40		200		
3rd quality	40-30		200		
Hides and Pelts:					
Buffalo and Cow	8-1.75	12	30,000	360,000	B,C,D,G$_3$,H$_1$,J,K$_{1-2}$,T, BB,CC,DD
Rhinoceros	12		4,000		
Elephant	5.5		5,000		
Deer	.26#-.18#		100,000#		
Tiger	1#		600#		
Fish	.2#		70,000#		

Name	Siam: Cost High-Low	China: Cost High-Low	Quantity Exported	Value	Source
Horns:					
Rhinoceros	500#-50#	600#	limited quantity		C,D,F,G$_{1-4}$,H,K,T,U, X, V,BB,CC,DD
Deer	24-8	120	limited quantity		
Ox and Buffalo	6-4				
Indigo	.125/pot				A,K$_1$,M,BB
Iron	6-3	5	20,000	100,000	E,K$_1$,T,BB
Ivory^d	160-130	240-140	500-1,000	135,000	D,E,F,G$_{1-4}$,H$_1$,I,J,K$_1$,M, T,U,V,X,BB,CC,DD
Lead					D,I,BB,DD
Meat (Dried)	9-6	17-10	7,000	91,000	G$_3$,T,CC,DD
Oil:					C,D,T,BB,DD
Wood	8-3				
Coconut	10-7		5,000		
Pepper:^{e}					A,B,C,D,E,F,G$_{1-4}$,H$_1$,J, K$_{1-2}$,L,M,Q,T,V,W,X, BB,CC,DD
Black	15-8	16-13	60,000	870,000	
Long	20-18		500		
White	26-18		1,000		
Pots and Pans	10-4		large quantity		J,T,BB,CC
Prawns	10-8		2,000		T,BB
Rattan	5	7	a quantity		G$_3$
Rice:					See Chapter IV
Hulled	1.28-.72	7-3	200,000	1,000,000	
Paddy			(to meet demand)		
Rudders	150#-100#		limited quantity		G$_{3-4}$
Salt	.24-.1		50,000		D,F,K$_1$,T,V,BB,CC,DD

Name	Siam: Cost High-Low	China: Cost High-Low	Quantity Exported	Value	Source
Sharks' fins					
White	65-55	90-55	500	35,000	E,M,T,U,V,X,CC
Black	24-20	50-16	600	18,000	
Shoes (Chinese-style)			200,000 pr.		T
Sprouts (bean)			large quantity		H_1
Sticklac	18-7		16,000		$C,D,G_4,H_{1\text{-}2},J,K_1,T,BB$
Sugar:					
1st quality	8-7				$A,C,D,G_4,H_1,J,K_1,M,$ $O,Q,T,U,V,W,AA,BB,$ CC,DD
2nd quality	7-6		30,000-70,000		
3rd quality	6-5				
Red cane	.75				
Tin	32-20	45-40	6,000	252,000	$C,D,G_1,G_{3\text{-}4},H_1,I,K_{1\text{-}2},$ L,M,T,V,BB,CC,DD
Tumeric	6-5		3,000		T
Wood:					
Agila:f					
1st quality	1,000-350		20		G_2,H_1,J,T,V,BB,CC,DD
2nd quality	400-250		100		
3rd quality	200-50		800		
Ebony	2.5	4	5,000	20,000	E,G_2,J,N,T,BB,CC
Redwood	1.5-.75	5-3.5	40,000	160,000	$E,G_{3\text{-}4},H_1,K_1,Q,T,BB,$ CC,DD
Sandalwood (*Pradu*)g	5#		a quantity		$G_{3\text{-}4}$
Sapan	4.5-1	9-4	100,000	600,000	$C,D,E,F,G_{1\text{-}4},H,I,J,K_1,$ $M,N,Q,T,U,V,X,BB,$ CC,DD
Teak			a late export		D,H_1,K_1,T,AA

[a] The Latin name for *plong* (prong) is not available. It may be some form of mangrove since the tree is said to grow in salty water and that the wood was used for house construction, floor boards, etc.

[b] The price in China of black beche-de-mer was ordinarily about 100 *baht*. The 30 *baht* figure is unusually low.

[c] The value figure of 140,000 *baht* is the average annual amount Siam was said to sell to China: (K₁, p. 44).

[d] The price for tusk in G_3 (74.75 *baht*) is much lower than the prices provided in other sources. This may reflect the monopoly price at which the king purchased them, or they may have been poor quality tusk.

[e] Black pepper is listed by Malloch at 12-14 *baht*/picul and in G_4 at 7 *baht*/picul. Malloch gives 18-20 *baht*/picul for long pepper, while G_4 says the cost was 12 *baht*/picul. The prices for pepper in the Thai documents would indicate that buyers for the royally-sponsored trading vessels could obtain better prices than Malloch was aware of. The time differential (1844 vis-à-vis 1850) is not significant since pepper prices remained relatively constant over time. Moreover, by 1844, the monopoly on pepper had been abolished, so that the monopoly price would not have been a factor.

[f] Also known as eagle, aloes, and garoo wood.

[g] Sandalwood is known as *pradu* in Thai (*Pterocarpus santalinus*) or red sandalwood. A similar wood (*Mansonia gagei*) was often substituted and sent to China from Siam.

Sec. 2: Chinese Exports to Siam, 1800-1850

Name	China: Cost High-Low	Siam: Cost	Quantity Exported	Value	Source
Aloes (red)		25	300	7,500	T
Aniseed	28-17	10	100	1,000	E,T,U,X
Brimstone			500		T
Camphor[a]	84-22	13.3	150	1,995	E,K₁,T,V
Cassia oil	400-300		small quantity		E,T.U
Ceremonial & Temple Items:					
Mock gold leaf		2	3,000 books	6,000	G_4,T
Gold leaf			large quantity		G_4,T
Artificial flowers			48,500#		G_4,T
Gongs		2#	15,000#	30,000	T
Joss sticks			large quantity		E,H_1,T
Incense rods			large quantity		H_1,T
China root	7		500		E,T,V,X
Chinaware:[b]					D,H_1,T,U,V,X, CC
Rice plates		.125#	50,000#	6,250	
Spittoons		.5#	5,000#	2,500	
Betel dishes		.75#	20,000#	15,000	
Butter-type dishes		.5#	2,000#	1,000	
Oil pots		.125#	10,000#	1,250	
Hair oil dishes		.5#	3,000#	1,500	
Round betel dishes		.125#	100,000#	13,500	
Tobacco dishes		.25#	50,000#	12,500	
Lip salve dishes		.25#	50,000#	12,500	
Cups		.05#	500,000#	25,000	
Meat dishes		1#	10,000#	10,000	

Name	China: Cost High-Low	Siam: Cost High-Low	Quantity Exported	Value	Source
Cups with covers		.07#	50,000#	3,500	
Teapots		.5#	30,000#	15,000	
Cinnamon (Hainan)			500		T
Clove oil	100/catty–90/catty		small quantity		E,T
Copper-, Brass-, Pewterware:[c]					G_4,T,X
Wire			2,000		
Table lamps		.75#	500#	375	
Bed furniture			2,000		
Locks		.25#	30,000#	7,500	
Bangles		.125#	30,000#	3,750	
Candlesticks		.5#	5,000#	2,500	
Stands & dishes (copper)			500		
Stands & dishes (brass)		60	200	12,000	
Utensils		100	200	20,000	
Boxes with covers		.25#	50,000#	12,500	
Dishes with tops		.25#	50,000#	12,500	
Square brass boxes		.75#	25,000#	18,750	
Brass lanterns			130#		
Crapes:					
Shawls	8#–4#	6#–5#	20,000#	100,000	D,E,H_1,T
Unfinished		8#–2#	2,000#	10,000	
Cubebs	44–36		small quantity		E,T,U,X
Earthenware:					E,G_4,H_1,T
Rice bowls & basins		.125#	1,000,000#	125,000	
Plates, cups, saucers				50,000	

Name	China: Cost High-Low	Siam: Cost High-Low	Quantity Exported	Value	Source
Bottles with stoppers		.125#	5,000#	625	H[1],T,U,X,Z
Scent bottles		.125#	5,000#	625	
Jars with lids			200#		
Fans:					
Ivory (inferior-best)		3#-.25#	20,000#	30,000	T
Paper		.063#	10,000#	625	
Foodstuffs:					
Sea moss		6	3,000	18,000	
Roots			large quantity		
Hams		4	1,000	4,000	T
Furniture:					
Cane blinds		5	1,000#	1,500	
Rattan floor mats		.5#	300	100	
Wooden armchairs		2#-.5#	200#	1,250	
Bamboo couches & chairs			1,000#		
Gall-nuts[d]	16-8	28-12	100	1,900	T,DD
Glass & glassware:[e]					G[4],O,T
Earrings and rings		.063#	40,000#	2,500	
Betel boxes		.125#	2,000#	250	
Tumblers		.25#	30,000#	7,500	
Wine glasses		.03#	50,000#	1,500	
Mirrors		3#-1#	500#	1,000	
Lamps		.375#	3,000#	1,125	
Chandeliers		20#-5#	50#	600	
Vials with stoppers		.02#	50,000#	1,000	
Candlesticks		.125#	5,000#	625	
Glues and gums	20-18		500		E,T,X,Z

Name	China: Cost High-Low	Siam: Cost High-Low	Quantity Exported	Value	Source
Gold- & silverware:					G₄,Y,Z
Betel boxes			small quantity		
Trays			small quantity		
Tea caddies			small quantity		
Granite slabs			small quantity		E,G₄,S,T,U,X,Z
Grass cloth:					T,X,Z
Unfinished		16#–8#	2,000#	24,000	
Handkerchiefs		4#	200#	800	
Hats (straw)			25,000#		T,Z
Ink:					E,T,Z
Fine and coarse	1,000–75		a quantity		
Marking				a quantity	
Mace	200		300		T
Metal goods:					T
Knives		.125#	30,000#	3,750	
Bed frames		4#	500#	2,000	
Chisels, saws, etc.			large quantity		
Lanterns		.25#	5,000#	1,250	
Razors		.125#	10,000#	1,250	
Spectacles		.125#	10,000#	1,250	
Pipes			100,000#		
Nankeens:f					E,H₁,T,U,V,X,Z
Medium-fine quality	2#–.9#	20.25#	10,000#	202,500	
Poor quality			20,000#		
Different colors		2.25#–1#	10,000#	15,000	
Paints &		8	500	1,200	T,Z
varnish			150		

Name	China: Cost High-Low	Siam: Cost High-Low	Quantity Exported	Value	Source
Paper:					
Writing			large quantity		H_1,T,Z
Writing books		.25#-.125#	500,000#	62,500	
Sacrificial paper			large quantity		
Match paper		7	500	3,500	
Preserves & candies:					
Pickled onion & garlic		.5 per jar	50,000 jars	25,000	D,E,H,$_1$K,$_1$T,U,V,X,Z,
Ginger preserves			large quantity		DD
Oranges		2 per basket	10,000 baskets	20,000	
Lychees		2 per basket	5,000 baskets	10,000	
Sweetmeats	30-14	30	100	3,000	
Quicksilver	260-160		750		H,$_1$T,U,X,CC
Rhubarb	130-44		500		E,T,U,V,X
Saffron			large quantity		T
Shoes	4/pr-1/pr		25,000 pr		H,$_1$T,U,Z
Silk piece goods:[g]					E,G$_4$,H,$_1$T,V,Z,CC
Flowered silk		10#-4#	5,000#	35,000	
Silk sarongs		6#-4#	2,000#	10,000	
Velvet		12#-6#	500#	4,500	
Dresses (silk, satin)		10-.5#	2,000#	100,000	
Theatrical dresses		50#-1#	500#	12,500	
Handkerchiefs		5#	3,000#	15,000	
Damask			5,000 yds.		
Silk thread			15		
Kwangtung silk			530 rolls		
Shanghai silk			200 rolls		
Dragon silk			300 rolls		
Silk camlets		1#-.75#	4,000#	3,000	
Flowered satin		12#-5#	5,000#	40,000	

Name	China: Cost High-Low	Siam: Cost High-Low	Quantity Exported	Value	Source
Fine satin		20	200#	4,000	G_4,S,T
Shanghai satin			460 rolls		
Colored satin			140 rolls		
Cotton (red)		6#-3.5#	3,000#	13,500	
Stone:					
Paving and building			large quantity		
Ornamental			a quantity		
Tea (black-good quality)			a quantity		D,H₁,Z,CC
Tiles:					G_4,S,T
Figurines, bottles, etc.			limited quantity		
Roofing and building			large quantity		
Toys and games:					G_4,T,Z
Children's toys		1#-.5#	large quantity		
Children's boxes			1,000#	750	
Puppet shows			large quantity		
Puzzles			large quantity		
Model boats		15#-10#	300#	3,750	
Dice and cards		.25/bx., pk.	40,000 bxs., pks.	10,000	
Tobacco	42-26		large quantity		T
Tutenague		20	5,000	100,000	E,H₁,L,T,V
Umbrellas (paper)	.24#-.14#	1#-.125#	10,000#	5,000	E,H₁,T,U
Vermicelli (lacksoy)		20	100	2,000	H₁,T
Vermillion			100		E,T,V,X
Wooden goods (misc.):					T
Boxes		.5#-.125#	10,500#	2,500	
Platters		.125#	20,000#	2,500	
Paint brushes			large quantity		

[a] The price of camphor dropped considerably between 1810 and 1855. Much of China's camphor was imported and more may have been available toward the middle of the century. This would help to account for the drop in price. The high of 84 *baht* is more reflective of prices during the earlier decades of the nineteenth century.

[b] The Siam-cost of Chinaware has been averaged from the figures supplied by Malloch.

[c] The Siam-cost of copper-, brass-, and pewterware has been averaged from figures supplied by Malloch.

[d] The only price available for gall-nuts in China comes from Williams, *Commercial Guide*, 1863, p. 129.

[e] The Siam-cost of glassware is an average, or the lower of Malloch's figures has been chosen.

[f] Malloch's prices for nankeens, a durable cotton fabric, appear to be high in comparison with such other imported fabrics as silk. His price of 20.25 *baht* per piece is comparable to a piece of fine satin. The cost of colored nankeens is more in line with the quality of the material generally, and might be used as the basis for determining the prices of the medium-fine and poorer grades of material.

[g] The China-cost of the silk piece-goods and clothing exported to Siam is difficult to estimate because only the prices of the higher-quality grades exported to the West are given in the nineteenth-century commercial guides and price currents.

Bibliography

The titles of sources consulted in compiling Appendix A are given in brief below. For full citations, see the Bibliography at the end of the monograph.

A   *Allen's Indian Mail*, 9 (1844), 263; 84 (1847), 527-28.

B   *The Asiatic Journal and Monthly Register*, n.s., 38 (1842), 134.

C   Bowring, *Siam*, vol. 1, 231-32; 254-55.

D   *The Burney Papers*, vol. 1, pt. 1, 169-70; vol. 2, pt. 4, 79-85, 97-109.

E   *Canton Register*, 12/14/1827, 4/5/1828, 4/4/1829, 6/18/1829, 8/17/1829, 2/2/1831, 6/24/1824.

F   *Chinese Repository*, 8 (1839), 130.

G   *Chotmaihet* (Documents, National Library, Bangkok):

G_1 CMH. Thonburi, #13, 1781.
G_2 CMH. R.I, #3, 1784; #4, 1786; #6, 1792.
G_3 CMH. R.II, #15, 1813; #5, 1820.
G_4 CMH. R.III, #49, 1844; #123, 1844.

H   Crawfurd, John:

H_1 *Embassy*, 408-13, 417-35.
H_2 *History*, vol. 3, 183.

I   Elmore, *Directory*, 305-10.

J   Finlayson, *Mission to Siam*, 169, 214-15, 255-63.

K   Great Britain:

K_1 *Abstract of Reports*: Siam, 7, 39-48, 143-44, 162-65, 334-35.
K_2 *Report from the Select Committee*, vol. 5 (1830), 310-12.

L   Greenberg, *British Trade*, 49, 81, 87.

M   Gutzlaff, *Journal*, 44, 110.

N   Hamilton, *East India Gazetteer*, 744.

O   Hirth, "Geographical Distribution," *China Review* 2,5 (1873-74), 306-09; 2,6 (1873-74), 376-82.

P   Hsieh, *Hsin-pien Hsien-lo kuo-chih*, 73-84.

Q   *Hunt's Merchants' Magazine* 1 (1840), 472-74; 2 (1847), 376.

R   Ingram, *Economic Change*, 9.

S   Malcom, *Travels*, vol. 2, 122.

T   Malloch, *Siam*, 34-51, 59-63.

U   Martin, *China*, vol. 2, 120-31, 138.

V   Milburn, *Oriental Commerce*, vol. 2, 441-42, 491, 504.

W   Moor, *Indian Archipelago*, 206, 226, 235-37.

X   Morrison, *Commercial Guide*, 1848, 139-83.

Y   National Archives, *Letter*, King Rama IV to Yam Ap Toot, 1853.

Z   Neale, *Residence in Siam*, 173-77.

AA   Neon Snidvongs, "Siam at the Accession," 26-27.

BB   Pallegoix, *Royaume Thai*, vol. 1, 324-29.

CC   Roberts, *Embassy*, 273-74, 311-18.

DD   *Singapore Chronicle*, 10/18/1832, 4/11/1833, 11/21/1833, 12/12/1833.

The following references should be consulted for the Chinese names and the uses of the products listed above:

Burkill, *A Dictionary of the Economic Products of the Malay Peninsula*, 1966.

Stuart, *Chinese Materia Medica*, 1911.

Watson, *The Principal Articles of Chinese Commerce*, 1930.

Yule and Burnell, *Hobson-Jobson*, 1903.

APPENDIX B
THE CARGO MANIFESTS OF FOUR SIAMESE STATE TRADING VESSELS

Sec. 1: An Aggregate of the Four Manifests

Sec. 2: The Manifest of the Sunhong Junk

Sec. 3: The Manifest of the Sunha Junk

Sec. 4: The Manifest of the Cinli Junk

Sec. 5: The Manifest of the Thepkosin, a Square-rigged Vessel

Note: These manifests are found in CMH. R.III, #49, 1844. The document is actually undated, but is filed with those under the year 1844. Internal evidence would indicate that it should be dated 1845.

The products shipped to China appear to have been tax or tribute goods, especially the pepper, cardamon, lac, and rhino horn. Or some may have been remittances to the Siamese nobles sponsoring the vessels from the commoners subordinate to them. Although the Sunhong junk is not said to have been sponsored by a member of the nobility, all of this trade should be classified as state trade.

Weight is expressed in hap (piculs) unless otherwise specified.

Unit price, investment, and tax rates are expressed in *baht*.

The tax rate is expressed in *baht* per hap unless otherwise specified.

1 tara of tin equals 3 hap.

In Sec. 5, all the figures except for goods marked by asterisks have been rounded to the nearest füang. In Sec. 1-4, the figures include bia.

In Sec. 1, the figure for long pepper includes 263.47 piculs carried by a convoy of small junks which accompanied the four state trading vessels.

Sec. 1: An Aggregate of the Four Manifests

I. Cargo	Weight	Unit Price	Cargo Investment	Tax Rate	Total Tax	Investment + Tax
Sapan wood	12,450	1.25	15,562.5	1.0	12,450	28,012.5
Pepper:						
Remaining from 1844	2,044.74	7.0	14,313.18	—	—	14,313.18
Treasury, tax-farm bought in 1845	4,800	7.125	34,200	—	—	34,200
Redwood	4,284.8	1.125	4,957.16	.75	6,650.4	16,075.4
	4,582.4	.875	4,467.95			
Plong	400	.9425	377			
	300	.9	270			
	234.37	.811	190.059	.325	519.84	1,754.72
	112	.893	99.9775			
	553.15	.538	297.84			
Lac	100.48	9.0	904.32	1.25	194.8125	1,542.0925
	55.37	8.0	442.96			
Long pepper	352.64	12.0	4,231.44	—	—	4,231.44
Red cane sugar	200	3.75	750	—	—	750
Tin (54 tara)	162	80/tara	4,320	3.0x162	486	4,806

Cargo	Weight	Unit Price	Cargo Investment	Tax Rate	Total Tax	Investment + Tax
Rhino horn	.35	8/catty	280	.5/catty	17.5	297.5
Pursat Cardamom	10.04	220	2,208.8	14.0	140.5	2,349.36
Dried betel	15.12	2.5	37.8	1.0	15.045	52.845
Rudders:						
2 large	140	110 each	220	70 each	140	
2 small	85	48 each	96	32 each	64	520
Anchors:						
1	30	36 each	36	5.5 each	5.5	
3	90	32 each	96	5.5 each	16.5	252
4	120	20 each	80	4.5	18	
Pradu planks (35)	100	4.5 each	157.5	0.5 each	17.5	175
Total Cargo	31,222.46		88,596.4		20,735.59	109,332.035

Cargo	Weight	Unit Price	Cargo Investment	Tax Rate	Total Tax	Investment + Tax
II. Expenses						
One square-rigged vessel expended for crew and misc. expenses		5,536.936	12,856.691			12,856.691
Three junks expended for crew and misc. expenses		7,319.755				
Total Weight	31,222.46				Total Investment	122,188.726

Sec. 2: The Manifest of the Sunhong Junk

I. Cargo	Weight	Unit Price	Cargo Investment	Tax Rate	Total Tax	Investment + Tax
Sapan wood	3,000	1.25	3,750	1	3,000	6,750
Pepper: Payment in						
kind	221.55	7.125	1,578.544	—	—	12,112.5
Treasury	589.2	7.125	4,196.768	—	—	
Bought	889.43	7.125	6,337.189	—	—	
Redwood	1,700	1.15	1,955	.75	1,275	3,230
Plong	400	.9425	377	.325	130	507
Lac	50.42	9	453.78	1.25	63.025	516.805
Long Pepper	35.65	12	427.8	—	—	427.8
Total Cargo	6,886.25		19,076.08		4,468.025	23,544.105

Cargo	Weight	Unit Price	Cargo Investment	Tax Rate	Total Tax	Investment + Tax
II. Expenses						
Captain's salary			233			
Loading			1,208.625			
Boi chan (?)						
Misc.		425.5	1,101.24			
Hoi sit (?)		675.75	2,542.875			2,542.875
III. Goods						
Consigned	825					
Lata, crew goods	220.3 / 1,045.3					
Total Weight	7,931.55				Total Investment	26,086.98

Sec. 3. The Manifest of the Sunha Junk

I. Cargo	Weight	Unit Price	Cargo Investment	Tax Rate	Total Tax	Investment + Tax
Sapan wood	3,200	1.25	4,000	1.0	3,200	7,200
Pepper	1,700	7.125	12,112.5	—	—	12,112.5
Redwood	1,500	1.15	1,725	.75	1,125	2,850
Plong	300	.9	270	.325	97.5	367.5
Long pepper	20	12	240	—	—	240
Lac	50.06	9	450.54	1.25	62.5	513.115
Red cane sugar	200	3.75	750	—	—	750
Rudders (2)	140	110 each	220	70 each	140	360
Pradu planks (35)	100	4.5 each	157.5	.5 each	17.5	175
Total Cargo	7,210.06		19,925.54		4,642.5	24,568.115

Cargo	Weight	Unit Price	Cargo Investment	Tax Rate	Total Tax	Investment + Tax
II. Expenses						
Captain's salary			308			
Loading			1,189.5			
Boi chan (?)			1,065			
			2,562.5			2,562.5
III. Goods						
Consigned	795					
Lata, crew goods	346					
	1,121					
Total Weight	8,331.06				Total Investment	27,130.615

Sec. 4: The Manifest of the Cinli Junk

I. Cargo	Weight	Unit Price	Cargo Investment	Tax Rate	Total Tax	Investment + Tax
Sapan wood	2,000	1.25	2,500	1.0	2,000	4,500
Pepper	1,400	7.125	9,975	—	—	9,975
Redwood	668	1.163	777*	.75	501	1,278
Plong	234.37	.811	190.059	.2625**	76.17	266.23
Tin (34 tara)	102	80/tara	2,720	3x102	306	3,026
Rhino horn	.35	8/catty	280	.5/catty	17.5	297.5
Total Cargo	4,404.72		16,442.059		2,900.67	19,342.73
II. Expenses						
Captain's salary			669.7638			
Loading			971.8662			
Boi chan (?):						
Misc.		168				
Boi chan (?):		404.75	572.75			
			2,214.38			2,214.38
III. Goods						
Consigned	566.28					
Lata, crew goods	205.42					
	771.70					
Total Weight	5,176.42					
					Total Investment	21,557.11

* rounded   ** should be .4

Sec. 5. The Manifest of the Thepkosin, a Square-rigged Vessel

I. Cargo	Weight	Unit Price	Cargo Investment	Tax Rate	Total Tax	Investment + Tax
Sapan wood	4,250	1.25	5,312.5	1	4,250	9,562.5
Pepper	2,044.74	7	14,313.125	—	—	14,313.125
Redwood	4,582.40	.875	4,467.75			
	416.8	1.125	500.125	416.8	1.125	500.125
Pursat Cardamom*	10.04	220	2,208.8	14	140.5	2,349.36
Lac	55.37	8	442.875	1.25	69.125	512
Dried Betel*	15.12	2.5	37.8	1	15.045	52.845
Long pepper	33.52	12	402.125	—	—	402.125
Tin (20 *tara*)	60	80/*tara*	1,600	3x60	180	1,780
Plong*	553.15	.538	297.84	.325	216.182	613.999
	112	.893	99.9775			
Rudders (2)	85	48 each	96	32 each	64	160
Anchors:						
1	30	36 each	36	5.5 each	5.5	
3	90	32 each	96	5.5 each	16.5	
4	120	20 each	80	4.5 each	18.0	252
	12,458.14		29,991.25		8,724.227	38,715.204

Cargo	Weight	Unit Price	Cargo Investment	Tax Rate	Total Tax	Investment + Tax
II. Expenses						
Captain			5,536.875			5,536.875
Misc.						
Total Weight	12,458.14			Total Investment		44,252.079

*Have not been rounded to fűiang.

APPENDIX C
THE FEES AND DUTIES ON SIAMESE JUNKS
AT CANTON IN 1813

Source: CMH. R.2, #15, 1813

Explanation:

Part I. Duties on first opening the ship's hold:
   A. Probably refers to the duty on cargo.
   B1-2. Appears to be the breakdown of the cumshaw into entry and exit fees.
   C-E. No equivalent suggested.

Part II. Fees payable at the Capital:
   A. May refer to the fees paid to customs officials so they would not enter goods on which a high duty was assessed in the collectorate's books.
   B1-3. No equivalent suggested.
   B4. Is possibly the fee paid to the compradore to defray expenses of theatrical exhibitions.
   C-E. No equivalents suggested.

Note Many of the terms used in this document cannot be translated into English, nor has it been possible to locate equivalent Chinese terms. Few analogies to the duties levied either on Chinese junks or Western ships can be drawn. Furthermore, the document is not explicit as to whether the recorded charges are those for all the junks which sailed to Canton in 1813 or those levied on only one vessel. The overall total, figured from the sum of each entry, would seem to eliminate the latter possibility. It is highly unlikely that one junk would be charged $23,811.53, especially as that amount was equal to the total cargo investment of a large Siamese square-rigged vessel sailing to China in 1844 (see Appendix B, sec. 5). Finally, the figure for the total duties actually paid is nearly obliterated, but the few remaining legible numbers indicate that it is not a simple addition of all the separate entries. The junks (or junk) may, therefore, have paid either more or less than the $23,811.53 arrived at from the individual entries.

The document from which this list was taken states that seven junks sailed to Canton, but as one was a tribute vessel, it would have been exempt from duty. If the $23,811.53 is divided by six, each junk would have paid $3,968 in duties and fees, an inordinately large amount when one considers that a Western square-rigged vessel of comparable size (412 tons) would have paid $4,775 (Phipps, *A Practical Treatise on the China and Eastern Trade*, p. 143. His figure only reflects the port charges and does not take into account duties on goods. The total expenses for a Western ship may, therefore, have been much higher.) In light of the references to the parity that was said to exist between Chinese and Siamese shipping (FO 17/9, p. 46; *Canton Register*, 11/3/1832), however, a lower figure than $3,968 for these Siamese vessels might have been anticipated.

I.   Duties on first opening the ship's hold

A.   Selling goods (fees)   10,966.615 *baht*
B.   Entrance and exit fees
     1. All upstream (fees) 7,823.655 *baht*
     2. All downstream (fees) 8,746.615 *baht*   16,570.27
C.   Sign/placard/flag (fee)?   3,704.025
D.   Distributed to the *Sinlo* (chopboat
     or linguist?)   4,503.6
E.   *Pan Ju* gets/uses   1,839.2175

II. Fees payable at the Capital (Kuang-chou?)

A.   *Pang* (hide?) To hide the (real value of
     six kinds of goods)   2,813.7628
B.   1. All up and downstream fees   4,995.1252
     2. Distributed to *Sinlo* over
        (the above?)   104

3. Sailors not unloading, so money called for	16	5,157.1252
4. Sailors' subscription for *Ming-i* (play)	42	
C. *Pang* (?)		
1. *Yong* (?)	308.6525	
2. *T'a*	154.4447	463.0972
D. Freight dues/registration fees (hush money?)		1,270.5
E. *Pan Ju* uses		335.2175
Overall Total		47,623.18 *baht*

GLOSSARY

Chinese Names and Terms

Ao-men (Macao)　　澳門
Chang-chou　　漳州
ch'ang-kuan　　常關
Chang-lin　　樟林
Chang Shih-ch'eng　　張師誠
Chao-ch'ing　　肇慶
Ch'ao-chou　　潮州
chen　　鎮
Ch'en Ch'ang-hsü　　陳長緒
Chen-hai　　鎮海
Ch'en Hung-mou　　陳宏謀
Ch'en K'un-wan　　陳坤萬
Ch'eng-hai　　澄海
cheng-k'ou　　正口
cheng-o　　正額
cheng-shui　　正稅
cheng-shui k'ou　　正稅口
cheng-shui kuei-yin　　正稅規銀
chi-ch'a k'ou　　稽查口
ch'i-min　　耆民
Chi-shan　　佶山
chia　　家
chia-pan ch'uan　　夾板船
chiang-men　　江門
Chieh-yang　　揭陽
ch'ien-liang　　錢糧
Chin chü shun　　金聚順

Chin hsieh shun　　金協順
Chin kuang shun　　金廣順
Ch'ing-fu　慶復
Ching-hai　靖海
Ch'ing lan　清瀾
ch'ing-tan　清單
chiu-che　九折
Ch'iung-chou　瓊州
ch'u-hai　出海
ch'u-hai mao-i hsiang-liao　出海貿易香料
ch'u-yang　出洋
ch'uan　船
ch'uan-chao　船照
Ch'üan-chou　泉州
ch'uan-chu　船主
erh-liao　二繚
erh-ting　二碇
fan-ch'uan　番船
fan min-jen wu-p'iao szu-ch'u k'ou-wai che　　凡民人無票私出口外者
fan-ts'ao ch'uan　販艚船
fen-k'ou　分口
fen-t'ou　分頭
Fu-ch'ao hang　福潮行
Fu-chou　福州
Fu-t'ien　福田
Hai-ch'eng　海澄
hai-ch'uan　海船
hai-k'ou　海口
hai-kuan　海關
Hai-nan hang　海南行
hai-po　海波
Hai-yang　海陽
hang-shang　行商
hang-yung　行用
heng-yang ch'uan　橫洋船
Hsi-nan hai　西南海
Hsi-pei hai　西北海
hsi-pu　西部
Hsi-yang　西洋
Hsia-men　廈門
Hsiang-shan　香山
hsiao-k'ou　小口
Hsin Shih-jui　辛時瑞

hsün-ch'a 巡查
hua p'i ku 花屁股
Huang Kuan 黃官
Hui-lai 惠來
hung-t'ou 紅頭
huo-ch'ang 火長
i-, erh-, san-ch'ien 一，二，三遷
I-shun hang 怡順行
i-ting 一碇
Jao-p'ing 饒平
jen-hu k'uei-tui k'o-ch'eng 人戶虧兌課程
Ju-shun hang 如順行
kang-shou 綱首
Kao-chou 高州
kua-hao k'ou 掛號口
kuan-ch'uan 官船
kuan-shui 關稅
kuei-yin 規銀
kung-hang 公行
Lan Ting-yuan 藍鼎元
lao-erh 老二
lao-san 老三
lao-ta 老大
li 利
Li Ch'ing-fan 李清芳
Liu Ju-hsin 劉如新
lü-t'ou 綠頭
mai-pan 買辦
mao-i 貿易
min-ch'uan 民船
Na-su-t'u 那蘇圖
Nan-ao 南澳
Nan-hai 南海
Nan-pei hang 南北行
Nan-pu 南部
nan-ts'ao 南艚
Nan-yang 南洋
Ning-po 寧波
o-shui 額稅
pa-che 八折
p'ai-chao 牌照
pai-ti ch'uan 白底船
pao-shang 保商

pei-ts'ao　　北艚
Pen-kang hang　　本港行
pen-sheng ch'u-yang fa-ko wai-kuo　　本省出洋發 各外國
pih-tow-chuen　　白頭船
p'u-chia　　舖家
P'u-ch'ien　　舖前
pu-t'ou　　埠頭
San-shui　　三水
sha-ch'uan　　沙船
Shan-t'ou　　山頭
shang-ch'uan　　商船
Shang-hai　　上海
shang-hang　　商行
shang-jen she-li t'ou-mai　　商人射利偷賣
Shao-hsing ch'uan　　紹興船
shih-li (szele)　　事例
shui-tse　　稅則
shun　　順
Su-chou　　蘇州
szu-ch'u wai-ching chi wei-chin hsia-hai　　私出外境及違禁下海
szu-ch'ung ya-hang pu-t'ou　　私充牙行埠頭
szu-tsao hai-ch'uan　　私造海船
ta-kuan　　大關
ta-liao　　大繚
t'ai-chi　　太極
t'ang-ch'uan　　糖船
Teng Chang-chieh　　登彰傑
tien-chia　　店家
T'ien-chin　　天津
ting-o　　定額
to-kung　　舵工
t'ou　　偷
t'ou-meng　　頭猛
t'ou yüeh pien huan　　偷越邊關
tsa-shih　　雜事
ts'ai-fu　　財副
Ts'ai Hsin　　蔡新
ts'ao-pai ch'uan　　艚舶船
Ts'e-leng　　策楞
tsung-han　　總捍
tsung-k'ou　　總口
Tu-li yüeh hai kuan pu ta-jen　　督理粵海關部大人
T'ung-an　　同安

tung-chia　　東家
Tung Chiao-tseng　　董教增
Tung-lung kang　　東隴港
Tung-nan yang　　東南洋
t'ung-shih　　通事
Tung-yang　　東洋
Wai-yang hang　　外洋行
Wan-chü hang　　萬聚行
Wang Chih-i　　汪志伊
Wang P'i-lieh　　王丕烈
Wu Ching　　吳竟
wu-ts'ao　　烏艚
Wu Yang　　吳陽
ya-kung　　押工
Yang-chiang　　陽江
yang-ch'uan　　洋船
Yang-hang　　洋行
Yang Hua　　楊華
Yang Lin　　楊琳
Yang Wu-chen　　楊武鎮
Yang Yu　　楊由
yin-shui　　引水
ying-yü　　盈餘　or　贏餘
yü-chuan　　漁船
Yü-lin　　榆林
yu-mien　　優免
Yüeh hai kuan chien-tu　　粵海關監督
yung　　永

BIBLIOGRAPHY

Archival Materials - Thailand

National Archives

Original contemporary documents that were consulted fall into the
following categories:
Ledger copies of Ministry of War records, Fourth Reign (1851-1868).
Letters of King Rama IV (1851-1868).

National Library

Original documents from the last years of the Thonburi period through
the first four reigns of the Bangkok period (1775-1868) were
consulted. These documents are unpaginated and the entire
document has been cited in the footnotes under the heading:
Chotmaihet Ratchakan thi 1-4.

Asian Language Sources

Anuman Rajadhon, *Phya. Tamnan Sunlakakon* (History of the
Customs Department). Bangkok: privately published, 1939.
Chaen Patchusanon. *Prawat Kanthahanrua Thai* (A history of Thai
naval affairs). Bangkok: Krom Saraban Thahanrüa, 1966.
Chang-chou fu-chih 漳洲府志. (Prefectural gazetter of Chang-chou).
Comp. by Shen Ting-chün 沈定均. 50+1 *chüan*. 1877
Chang Hsieh 張燮. *Tung-hsi yang-k'ao* 東西洋考 (An investigation
of the Eastern and Western Oceans). 12 *chüan*. Ts'ung-shu chi-
ch'eng. Shanghai: Shang-wu yin-shu kuan, 1936. Orig. pub. 1618.

Chang Li-ch'ien 張禮千. *Tung-hsi yang-k'ao chung chih chen-lu* 東西洋考中之針路. (Studies on the routes in the "tung-hsi yang-k'ao"). Singapore: Nan-yang shu-chu, 1947.

Chang Mei-hui 張美惠. "Ming-tai Chung-kuo jen tsai hsien-lo chih mao-i" 明代中國人在暹邏之貿易(Chinese traders in Siam during the Ming dynasty), *Wen-shih -che hsüeh-pao* 文史哲學報, no. 3, (1951), 161-176.

Chang Te-ch'ang 張撽昌. "Chin-tai Chung-kuo te huo-pi" 近代中國的貨幣(Trading coins of the Ch'ing dynasty). *Jen-wen k'o-hsüeh hsüeh-pao* 人文科學學報, 1 (1942), 73-92.

_____. "Ch'ing-tai Ya-p'ien chan-cheng ch'ien chih Chung-Hsi yen-hai t'ung-shang" 清代鴉片戰爭前之中西沿海通商 (Sino-Western coastal trade in the Ch'ing period prior to the Opium War). *Ch'ing-hua hsüeh-pao* 10 (1935), 97-145.

Ch'ao-chou fu-chih 潮洲府報 (Prefectural gazetteer of Ch'ao-chou). Comp. by Chou Shih-hsün 周碩勳. 42+2 *chüan*. 1762.

Ch'ao-yang hsien-chih 潮陽縣志 (County gazetteer of Ch'ao-yang). Comp. by Chou Heng-chung *et al.* 周恆重. 22+1 *chüan*. 1884.

Che-chiang t'ung-chih 浙江通志 (Provincial gazetteer of Chekiang). Comp. by Shen I-chi *et al.* 沈翼機. 280+3 *chüan*. 1899. Shanghai: Shang-wu yin-shu kuan, 1934

Chen-hai hsien-chih 鎮海縣志 (County gazetteer of Chen-hai). Comp. by Yü Yüeh *et al.* 俞樾. 40 *chüan*. 1879.

Ch'en Lun-chiung 陳倫炯. *Hai-kuo wen-chien lu* 海國聞見錄(A record of things seen and heard in the maritime countries). 1 *chuan*. Maps 1 *chüan*. Taipei: T'ai-wan yin-hang, 1958. Author's preface 1730.

Ch'en T'i-ch'iang 陳體強. *Chung-kuo wai-chiao hsing-cheng* 中國外交行政(The administration of China's foreign affairs). Chungking: Shang-wu, 1945.

Ch'en Yen 陳衍. *Fu-chien t'ung-chih lieh-chuan hsüan* 福建通志列傳選(Selected biographies from the Fukien provincial gazetteer). 6 *chüan*. 3 vols. in 1. Taipei: T'ai-wan ying-hang. 1964.

Ch'eng-hai hsien-chih 澄海縣志 (County gazetteer of Ch'eng-hai). Comp. by Li Shu-chi *et al.* 李書吉. 26+1 chüan. 1814.

(Kuo-ch'ao) Ch'i-hsien lei-cheng ch'u-pien (國朝) 耆獻類徵初編 (A classified compendium of eminent Ch'ing personalities, main series). Comp. by Li Huan 李桓. 720 *chüan*. 1884-1890.

Chia-ch'ing ch'ung-hsiu i t'ung-chih 嘉慶重修一通志 (The Chia-
ch'ing revision of the Imperial Gazetteer). 560 *chüan*. Ssu-pu
ts'ung-k'an hsü-pien. Shanghai: Shang-wu yin-shu kuan, 1934.

Chiang-nan t'ung-chih 江南通志 (Provincial gazetteer of Kiangnan).
Comp. by Yin-chi-shan *et al.* 尹繼善. 200+4 *chüan*. 1736.

Chieh-yang hsien-chih 揭陽縣志 (County gazetteer of Chieh-yang).
Comp. by Liu Yeh-ch'in *et al.* 劉業勤. 8+1 *chüan*. 1779.

Chin-men chih 金門志 (Gazetteer of Quemoy). Comp. by Lin K'un-
huang *et al.* 林焜熿. 16 *chüan*. Taipei: T'ai-wan yin-hang, 1960.
Orig. pub. 1774.

Ch'ing -fu 慶復. "Ch'ien-lung ch'ao wai-yang t'ung-shang an" 乾隆
朝外洋通商案 (Cases on foreign trade in the Ch'ien-lung period)
Shih-liao hsün-k'an 史料旬刊, 22 (Jan. 1, 1931), 803a-805a.

Ch'ing-shih kao 清史槁 (A draft history of the Ch'ing dynasty).
Chao Erh-hsün ed. 趙爾巽. 534 *chüan*. n.p. Lien-ho shu-tien,
1942. Orig. pub. 1928.

Ch'ing-tai wai-chiao shih-liao 清代外交史料 (Documents on the
foreign relations of the Ch'ing dynasty). 10 *ts'e*. Peiping: Ku-
kung-po wu-yüan, 1932-33.

Ch'iung-chou fu-chih 瓊洲府志 (Prefectural gazetteer of Ch'iung-
chou). Comp. by Tu Kuang-wen *et al.* 杜廣文. 44+1 *chüan*. 1890.
Orig. pub.1841.

Ch'ou-pan i-wu shih-mo 籌辦夷務始末 (The complete account of
our management of barbarian affairs). 260 chüan. Taipei: Wen-
hai, 1970-71. Facs. rep. 1930 ed.

Chou Yü-ching 周玉津. Shang-yeh shih 商業史 (History of trade).
Taipei: privately published, 1963.

(Ch'in-ting) Chung-shu cheng-k'ao 欽定中樞政考 (Regulations of the
central administration). Comp. by Ming-liang *et al.* 明亮. 32
chüan. Taipei: Hsüeh-hai, 1968. Orig. pub. 1825.

En-p'ing hsien-chih 恩平縣志 (County gazetteer of En-p'ing). Comp.
by Yü P'i-ch'eng et al. 余丕承. 25+1 *chüan*. 1934.

Fang Kuan-ch'eng 方觀承. *Liang-che hai-t'ang t'ung-chih* 兩浙海塘
通志(A comprehensive history and geography the sea-walls of
the two Chekiangs). 8 *ts'e*. 1751.

Feng Ch'eng-chün 馮承鈞. *Chung-kuo nan-yang chiao-t'ung shih*
中國南洋交通史(A history of commerce between China and
the South Seas). Shanghai: Shang-wu yin-shu kuan, 1937.

_____. *Hai-lu chu* 海錄注(A commentary on the "Record of the
Seas"). Peking: Chung-hua shu-chü, 1955.

Feng Chin-po, comp. 馮金伯. *Kuo-ch'ao hua-shih* 國朝畫識 (A biography of Ch'ing dynasty painters). 17 *chüan*. Shanghai: Chung-hua shu-chü, 1941.

Feng-hsun hsien-chih 豐順縣志 (County gazetteer of Feng-hsun). Comp. by Ko Shu 葛曙. 8+1 *chüan*. 1746.

Fu-chien hsü-chih 福建續志 (A supplementary gazetteer of Fukien Province). Comp. by Ch'en T'ing-fang *et al.* 沈廷芳. 92+5 *chüan*. 1768.

Fu-chien sheng-li 福建省例 (Laws and regulations of Fukien Province). 34 *chüan*. 8 vols. in 3. Taipei: T'aiwan yin-hang, 1964. Orig. pub. 1752 Repr. 1872.

Fu-chien t'ung-chih 福建通志 (Provincial gazetteer of Fukien). Comp. by Ho Yü-lin 郝玉麟. 78+5 *chüan*. 1737.

Fu-chien t'ung-chih 福建通志 (Provincial gazetteer of Fukien). Comp. by Ch'en Shou-ch'i *et al.* 陳壽祺. 278 + 6 *chüan*. 1868.

Fu I-ling 傅衣凌. *Ming-Ch'ing shih-tai shang-jen chi shang-yeh tzu-pen* 明清時代商人及商業本· (Merchants and mercantile capital in Ming and Ch'ing times). Peking: Jen-min ch'u-pan she, 1956.

"The Hoppo Book of 1753." Chinese text with an English introduction. Manuscript no. 9. The Hirth Collection, Staatsbibliothek Preussischer Kulturbesitz, Berlin.

Hsia-men chih 廈門志 (Gazetteer of Amoy). Comp by Chou K'ai 周凱.16 chüan. 5 vols. in 2. Taipei: T'ai-wan yin-hang, 1961. Orig pub. 1832.

Hsiang Ta 向達. *Liang-chung hai-tao chen-ching* 兩種海道針經 (Two sailing manuals with compass bearings). Peking: Chung-hua shu-chü, 1961.

Hsiao-fang hu-chai yü-ti ts'ung-ch'ao 小方壺齋輿地叢鈔 (Collected texts on geography from the Hsiao-fang hu studio). Comp. by Wang Hsi-ch'i 王錫祺. Pt. 1: 12 *chih*: Pt. 2 (supplement): 12 *chih*; Pt. 3 (second supplement): 12 *chih*. Shanghai: Chu-i t'ang 著易堂, 1877-97.

Hsieh Ch'ing-kao 謝清高. *Hai-lu* 海錄 (A maritime record). 2 *chüan*. 1842. Pai-pu ts'ung-shu chi-ch'eng. Taipei: I-wen, 1968.

Hsieh Yu-jung 謝猶榮. *Hsin-pien Hsien-lo kuo-chih* 新編暹羅國志 (A new edition of the gazetteer of Siam). Bangkok: I-pao she, 1953.

Hsü Chi-yü 徐繼畬. *Ying-huan chih-lüeh* 瀛環志略(A brief discussion of the ocean circuit). 10 *chüan*. 1850.

(Ch'in-ting) Hu-pu tse-li 欽定戶部則例 (The precedents of the Board of Revenue). 134 *chüan*. 1791.

_____. 100 *chüan*. 1874.

Huang-ch'ao chang-ku hui-pien 皇朝掌故彙編(Collected historical records of the Ch'ing dynasty). Comp. by Chang Shou-yung *et al.* 張壽鏞. 100+2*chüan*. n.p., Ch'iu-shih shu-she 求實書社, 1902.

Huang-ch'ao cheng-tien lei-tsuan 皇朝政典類纂 (Classified compendium of the administrative statutes of the Ch'ing dynasty). Comp. by Hsi Yü-fu 席裕福. 500 *chüan*. Shanghai: T'u-shu chi-ch'eng chü, 1903.

Huang-ch'ao ching-shih wen-pien 皇朝經世文編(Essays on statecraft during the Ch'ing dynasty). Comp. by Ho Ch'ang-ling *et al.* 賀長齡.120 *chüan*. Taipei: Shih-chieh, 1964. Orig. pub.1873.

Huang-ch'ao hsü wen-hsien t'ung-k'ao 皇朝續文獻通考 (Ch'ing supplement to the encyclopedia of historical records). Comp. by Liu Chin-tsao 劉錦藻. 400 *chüan*. Shanghai: Shang-wu yin-shu kuan, 1936.

Kotmai tra sam duang (The Law of the Three Seals). Bangkok: Khurusapha,1962. Tai laws codified in 1805.

(Ch'in-ting) Ku-chin t'u-shu chi-ch'eng 欽定古今圖書集成 (Imperial encyclopedia). Ed. by Ch'en Meng-lei et al. 陳夢雷. 10,000 *chüan*. Shanghai: Chung-hua, 1934. Facs. rep. 1726 ed.

Kuan-cheng 關政 (Tariffs). Nanking: Hsing-cheng yüan. Hsin-wen chü, 1947.

Kuang-chou fu-chih 廣州府志 (Prefectural gazetteer of Kuang-chou). Comp. by Chang Ssu-yen 張嗣衍. 60+1 chüan. 1759.

_____. Comp. by Shih Teng et al. 史澄. 163 *chüan*. 1879.

Kuang-tung t'ung-chih 廣東通志(Provincial gazetteer of Kuangtung). Comp. by Ho Yü-lin *et al.* 郝玉麟. 64 *chüan*. 1731.

_____. Comp. by Juan Yüan *et al.* 阮元. 334+1 *chüan*. 4 vols. Taipei: Chung-hua ts'hung-shu, 1959. Orig. pub. 1822. Repr. 1864.

(Ch'in-ting) Li-pu tse-li 欽定禮部則例 (The precedents of the Board of Rites). Comp. by T'e-teng-o *et al.* 特凳額. 202 *chüan*. 1844.

Li Yuan-tu 李元度. *Kuo-ch'ao hsien-cheng shih-lüeh* 國朝先正事略 (Brief biographies of worthy officials of the Ch'ing dynasty). 60 *chüan*. Taipei: Wen-hai, 1967.

Liang Chia-pin 梁嘉彬. *Kuang-tung shih-san hang k'ao* 廣東十三行考(A study of the thirteen hong of Kwangtung). Nanking: Kuo-li pien-i kuan 國立編譯館, 1937.

Ling Ch'un-sheng *et al.* 凌純聲 eds. *Chung-T'ai wen-hua lun-chi* 中泰文化論集 (Essays on Sino-Thai culture). Taipei: Chung-hua wen-hua ch'u-pan, 1958.

Lu Chi-fang 盧濟芳. "Ch'ing Kao-tsung shih-tai te Chung-Hsien kuan-hsi" 清高宗時代的中暹關係 (Sino-Siamese relations in the Ch'ien-long period), *Li-shih hsüeh-pao* 2 (1974), 385-412.

Lu Tz'u-yün 陸次雲. *Pa-hung i-shih* 八泓譯史 (A geography of the world). 4 *chüan*. Ts'ung-shu chi-ch'eng ch'u-pien. Ch'angsha: Shangwu yin-shu kuan, 1939., Author's preface 1683.

Lung-ch'i hsien-chih 龍溪縣志 (County gazetteer of Lung-ch'i). Comp. by Wu I-hsieh 吳宜燮. 26 *chüan*. Taipei: Ch'eng-wen ch'u-pan she, 1967. Orig. pub. 1879.

Ming-Ch'ing shih-liao. Keng-pien 明清史料 庚編 (Historical materials of the Ming and Ch'ing periods. Series G). Taipei: Chung-yang yen-chiu yüan, n.d.

————. *Ting-pien.* 丁編 (Series D). Shanghai: Shang-wu yin-shu kuan, n.d.

Nan-yang ti-li 南洋地理 (A geography of the Southern Ocean). Comp. by Shen Chüeh-ch'eng *et al.* 沈厥成. 2 vols. Taipei: Shang-wu yin-shu kuan, 1938.

Ning-po fu-chih 寧波府志 (Prefectural gazetteer of Ningpo). Comp. by Ts'ao Ping-jen *et al.* 曹秉仁. 36+1 *chüan*. 1741 rev. ed.

Pao Tsun-p'eng 包遵彭. *Cheng-Ho hsia hsi-yang chih pao-ch'uan k'ao* 鄭和下西洋之寶船考 (On the treasure ships of Cheng Ho which went to the western ocean). Taipei: Chung-hua tsung-shu pien shen-wei yüan-hui, 1961.

P'eng Hsin-wei 彭信威. *Chung-kuo huo-pi shih* 中國貨幣史 (A history of Chinese currency). Shanghai: Shang-hai jen-min ch'u pan she, 1965.

P'eng Ning-ch'iu 彭甯求. *Li-tai kuan-shih cheng-shui chi* 歷代關市征稅記 (Customs duties in successive dynasties). Ts'ung-shu chi-ch'eng ch'u-pien. Ch'angsha: Shang-wu yin-shu kuan, 1939.

P'eng tse-i 彭澤益. "Ch'ing-tai Kuang-tung yang-hang chih-tu te ch'i-yüan" 清代廣東洋行制度的起源 (The rise of the co-hong in Kwangtung during the Ch'ing dynasty), *Li-shih yen-chiu*, 1 (1957), 1-24.

Prachum prakat ratchakan thi 4 (The collected edicts of the Fourth Reign). 4 vols. Bangkok: Khurusapha, 1960-61.

Shang-hai hsien-chih 上海縣志 (County gazetteer of Shanghai). Comp. by Ying Pao-shih *et al.* 應寶時. 32+2 chüan. 1871.

Su-chou fu-chih 蘇州府志(Prefectural gazetteer of Soochow). Comp. by Li Ming-huan 李銘皖. 150 chuan. 1877.

(Ch'in-ting) Ta-Ch'ing hui-tien 欽定大清會典 (Administrative statutes of the Ch'ing dynasty). 80 *chüan*. 1813 [1818?].

_____. 100 *chüan*. 1899. Taipei: Ch'i-wen, 1963.

(Ch'in-ting) Ta-Ch'ing hui-tien shih-li 欽定大清會典事例 (Administrative statutes and precedents of the Ch'ing dynasty). 250 *chüan*. 1733.

_____. 1,220 *chüan*. 1899. Taipei: Ch'i-wen, 1963.

Ta-Ch'ing li-ch'ao shih-lu 大清歷朝實錄 (Veritable records of the Ch'ing dynasty). 4,485 *chüan*. Taipei: Hua-wen shu-chü, 1964. Orig. pub. 1937-38.

Ta-Ch'ing lü-li 大清律例 (The statutes and sub-statutes of the Ch'ing dynasty). Ed. by San t'ai *et al.* 三泰. 2 *ts'e*. 1740.

Ta-Ch'ing lü-li t'ung-k'ao 大清律例通考 (A comprehensive survey of the statutes and sub-statutes of the Ch'ing dynasty). Comp. by Wu T'an 吳壇. 40 *chüan*. 1886.

T'ang Hsiang-lung 湯象龍. "Shih-pa shih-chi chung-yeh Yüeh hai-kuan te fu-pai" 十八世紀中葉粵海關的腐敗 (The corruption of the Kwangtung maritime customs in the mid-18th century), *Jen-wen k'o-hsüeh hsüeh-pao* 1 (1942), 129-35.

T'ien Ju-k'ang 田汝康. "*Shih-ch'i shih-chi chih shih-chiu shih-chi chung-yeh Chung-kuo fan-ch'uan tsai tung-nan Ya-chou hang-yun ho shang-yeh shang de ti-wei*" 十七世紀至十九世紀中葉中國帆船在東南亞洲航運和商業上的地位 (The place of Chinese sailing ships in the maritime trade of Southeast Asia from the mid- 17th to the mid- 19th centuries). Shanghai: Jen-min ch'u-pan she, 1957.

T'ung-an hsien-chih 同安縣志 (County gazetteer of T'ung-an). Comp. by Wu T'ang 吳堂. 30+1 *chüan*. 1798. Rep. 1885.

_____. Comp. by Lin Hsüeh-tseng et al. 林學曾. 42+1 *chüan*. 1929.

T'ung Meng-cheng 童蒙正. *Kuan-shui kai-lun* 關稅概論 (An essay on customs duty). Shanghai: Shang-wu yin-shu kuan, 1946.

Wang Ch'ao-tsung 王朝宗. *Hai-wai fan-i lu* 海外番夷錄(A record of the overseas barbarians). 2 *ts'e*. 1844.

Wang Chih-ch'un 王之春, ed. *Kuo-ch'ao t'ung-shang shih-mo chi* 國朝通商始末記(A complete account of the foreign trade with various countries by the Ch'ing dynasty). 20 *chüan*. Taipei: Wen-hai, 1966. Author's preface. 1880.

Wang Hsiao-t'ung 王孝通. *Chung-kuo shang-yeh shih* 中國商業史(A history of Chinese commerce). Shanghai: Shangwu yin-shu kuan,1936.

Wang Ta-hai 王大海. *Hai-tao i-chih* 海島逸誌(An informal treatise on the islands of the sea). 6 *chüan*. 1791. *Hsiao-fang hu-chai yü-ti ts'ung-ch'ao*. Pt. 1, *chih* 10.

Wei Yuan 魏源. *Hai-kuo t'u-chih* 海國圖志 (An illustrated treatise on the maritime kingdoms). 60 *chüan*. 2nd ed. Yangchou: Ku-wei t'ang, 1847.

Wen-hsien ts'ung-pien 文獻叢編 (Collectanea of historical records). Peiping: Ku-kung-po wu-yüan, 1930-1943.

Wong Po-shang 黃菩生. "Ch'ing-tai Kuang-tung mao-i chi ch'i tsai chung-kuo ching-chi shih shang chih i-i" 清代廣東貿易及其在中國經濟史上之意義 (The historical significance of Kwangtung trade during the Ch'ing dynasty), *Ling-nan hsüeh-pao*, 3.4 (1935), 157-96.

Wu-pei chih 武備志 (A treatise on armament technology). Comp. by Mao Yuan-i 茅元儀. 240 *chüan*. 1664.

Ya-p'ien chan-cheng 鴉片戰爭 (The Opium War). Ed. by Ch'i Ssu-ho *et al.* 齊思和. 6 vols. Shanghai: Jen-min ch'u-pan she, 1957.

Yang-chiang hsien-chih 陽江縣志 (County gazetteer of Yang-chiang). Comp. by Chang I-ch'eng 張以誠. 39+1 *chüan*. 1925.

Yen Ju-i 嚴如熤. *Yang-fang chi-yao* 洋防輯要(Essentials of maritime defense). 24 *chüan*. 1838.

Yü Ch'ang-hui 俞昌會. *Fang-hai chi-yao* 防海輯要 (Essentials of coastal defense). 18+1 *chüan*. 1842.

Yüeh hai-kuan cheng-shou ko-hsiang kuei-kung yin-liang keng-ting tse-li 粵海關征收各項歸公銀兩更定則例 (Amended regulations for harbor dues, taxes, etc. of the Canton maritime customs, arranged by places). Canton, 1749.

Yüeh hai-kuan chih 粵海關志(Gazetteer of the maritime customs of Kwangtung). Comp. by Liang T'ing-nan 梁廷楠. 30 *chüan*. 4 vols. Taipei: Ch'eng-wen ch'u-pan she, 1968. Orig. pub. 1838.

Yüeh hai-kuan kuei-li 粵海關規例 (Canton customs house regulations). 2 *pen*. Canton, 1759.

Yüeh-tung sheng-li hsin-tsuan 粵東省例新纂 (A new edition of the statutes of Kwangtung). Comp. by Ning Li-t'i *et al.* 寧立梯. 8 *chüan*. 2 vols. Taipei: Ch'eng-wen ch'u-pan she, 1968. Orig. pub. 1846.

Western Language Sources

Abeel, David. *Journal of a Residence in China and the Neighboring Countries from 1830 to 1833*. London: James Nisbet and Co., 1835.

A.C.D. "Notes on Chinese Commercial Law," *The China Review*, 2 (1873-1874), 144-48.

Allen's Indian Mail, and Register of Intelligence. London: Wm. H. Allen and Co., Nos. 1-20 (1843-44); Nos. 44-139 (1846-49). Nos. 1-20 under the title *Indian Mail, and Register of Intelligence*.

Artz, Frederick. *Reaction and Revolution, 1814-1832*. New York: Harper & Row, 1963.

(*The*) *Asiatic Journal and Monthly Register for British India and Its Dependencies*. London: Parbury, Allen & Co. Vols. 1-28 (1816-29); New Series, vols. 1-40 (1830-43).

Assey, Charles. *On the Trade to China and the Indian Archipelago*. London: Rodwell and Martin, 1819.

Audemard, L. *Les Jonques Chinoises*. 6 vols. Rotterdam: Publicaties van Het Museum Voor Land- en Volkenkunde, 1957.

Bangkok Calendar. Bangkok: American Missionary Association Press, 1865, 1871.

Banister, T. R. "A History of the External Trade of China, 1834-81," China. The Maritime Customs. I.-Statistical Series: No. 6, *Decennial Reports . . . 1922-31*, Vol. 1, pp. 1-193.

Bannister, Saxe, ed. and tr. *A Journal of the First French Embassy to China, 1698-1700*. London: Thomas Cautley Newby, 1859. Trans. from an unpublished manuscript.

Barrow, John. *A Voyage to Co-chin China, in the Years 1792 and 1793*. London: T. Cadell and W. Davies, 1806.

Battelle Memorial Institute, Columbus, Ohio. *Blue Book of Coastal Vessels*: *Thailand*. Bangkok: Joint Thai-U.S. Military Research and Development Center, 1967.

Bodde, Derk, and Morris, C. *Law in Imperial China*. Cambridge: Harvard University Press, 1967.

Boulais, Le P. Guy. *Manuel du Code Chinois*. Shanghai: Catholic Mission Press, 1924.

Bowring, John. *The Kingdom and People of Siam*. 2 vols. London: John W. Parker and Son, 1857.

Boxer, C. R. "Notes on Chinese Abroad in the Late Ming and Early Manchu Periods Compiled from Contemporary European Sources (1500-1750)," *T'ien Hsia Monthly*, 9.5 (Dec. 1939), 447-68.

British Relations with the Chinese Empire in 1832. London: Parbury, Allen & Co., 1832.

Brunnert, H. and Hagelstrom, V. *Present Day Political Organization of China*. Trans. from the Russian by A. Beltchenko and E. E. Moran. Shanghai: Kelly and Walsh, 1912.

Burkill, I. H. *Dictionary of the Economic Products of the Malay Peninsula*. 2 vols. Kuala Lumpur: Ministry of Agriculture & Co-operatives, 1966.

(The) Burney Papers. 4 vols. in 5 pts. Farnborough, Hants: Gregg International Publishers Ltd., 1971.

(The) Canton Press. Macao, 1835-1844. Vols. 1-9.

Canton Register. Canton, 1827-1841. Vols. 1-14.

Chang, Chung-li. *The Income of the Chinese Gentry*. Seattle: University of Washington Press, 1962.

Chang, T'ien-tse. *Sino-Portuguese Trade from 1514-1644*. Leyden: E. J. Brill Ltd., 1934.

Chang, Yu-kwei. *Foreign Trade and Industrial Development of China*. Washington: The University Press of Washington, 1956.

Chatterton, E. Keble. *Sailing Ships, The Story of Their Development from the Earliest Times to the Present Day*. London: Sidgwick & Jackson, Ltd., 1914.

Ch'en, Hung-mou. "Notices Reminding Merchants Trading Overseas That They Are Free to Return Home, 1754," in T. F. Wade, *Key to the Tzu Erh Chi*. London: Trübner, 1867, pp. 33-34.

Ch'en, Kenneth. "*Hai-lu*, Fore-runner of Chinese Travel Accounts of Western Countries," *Monumenta Serica*, 7 (1942), 208-26.

Chen, Shao-kwan. *The System of Taxation in China in the Tsing Dynasty, 1644-1911*. London: Longmans, Green & Co., 1914.

Chen, Ta. *Emigrant Communities in South China*. New York: Secretariat, Institute of Pacific Relations, 1940.

China. Imperial Maritime Customs. I.-Statistical Series: No. 6, *Decennial Reports on the Trade, Navigation, Industries, etc. of the Ports Open to Foreign Commerce in China & Corea, 1882-91*. Shanghai: Statistical Dept. of the Inspectorate General of Customs, 1893.

_____. _____. I.-Statistical Series: No. 6, *Decennial Reports on the Trade, Navigation, Industries, etc. of the Ports Open to Foreign Commerce in China, 1892-1901*. 3 vols. Shanghai: Statistical Dept. of the Inspectorate General of Customs, 1904.

_____. _____. III.-Miscellaneous Series: No. 10, *Names of Places on the China Coast and the Yangtze River*. Shanghai: Statistical Dept. of the Inspectorate General of Customs, 1904.

_____. _____. Statistical Series: No. 7, *Native Customs Trade Returns*. Nos. 1-3. Shanghai: Statistical Dept. of the Inspectorate General of Customs, 1904.

_____. _____. III.-Miscellaneous Series: No. 3, *Port Catalogues of the Chinese Customs' Collection at the Austro-Hungarian Universal Exhibition, Vienna, 1873*. Shanghai: Imperial Maritime Customs' Press, 1873.

"The Chinese Empire in Its Foreign Relations," *The Bombay Quarterly Review*, 3 (1856), 234-35.

The Chinese Repository. Canton: Office of the Chinese Repository, 1832-1851. Vols. 1-20.

Cordier, Henri. "Les Merchands Hanistes de Canton," *T'oung Pao*, 3 (1902), 281-315.

Couveur, F. S. *Géographie Ancienne et Moderne de la Chine*. Hien Hien: Imprimerie de la Mission Catholique, 1917.

Cowan, C. D., ed. "Early Panang and the Rise of Singapore," *Journal of the Malayan Branch of the Royal Asiatic Society*, 23.2 (1950), 1-210.

Crawfurd, John. *History of the Indian Archipelago*. 3 vols. Edinburgh: Archibald Constable & Co., 1820.

_____. *Journal of an Embassy to the Courts of Siam and Cochin China*. Kuala Lumpur: Oxford University Press, 1967. Orig. pub. 1828.

Davis, John F. *China: A General Description of That Empire and Its Inhabitants*. 2 vols. London: John Murray, 1857.

_____, tr. "Extracts from the Peking Gazette," *Transactions of the Royal Asiatic Society of Great Britain and Ireland*. 2 (1830), 86-89.

Dermigny, Louis. *La Chine et l'Occident: Le Commerce à Canton au XVIIIe Siècle 1719-1833*. 3 vols; 1 album. Paris: École Pratique des Hautes Études, 1964.

A Description of the Royal Chinese Junk, 'Keying'. London: Printed for the proprietors of the Junk, 1848.

Dobell, Peter. *Travels in Kamtchatka and Siberia; with a Narrative of a Residence in China*. 2 vols. London: Henry Colburn and Richard Bently, 1830.

Donnelly, Ivon. *Chinese Junks, A Book of Drawings in Black and White*. Shanghai: Kelly & Walsh, Ltd., 1920.

_____. *Chinese Junks and Other Native Craft*. Shanghai: Kelly & Walsh, Ltd., 1924.

_____. "Early Chinese Ships and Trade," *The Mariner's Mirror*, 11 (1925), 344-54.

_____. "Foochow Pole Junks," *The Mariner's Mirror*, 9 (1923), 226-31.

_____. "Historical Aspects of Chinese Junks and Maritime Trade," *The Orient*, 5.10 (May 1955), 72-85.

Dutch Papers: Extracts from the "Dagh Register" 1624-42. Bangkok: Vajiranana National Library, 1915.

Elmore, H. M. *The British Mariner's Directory and Guide to the Trade and Navigation of the Indian and China Seas*. London: T. Bensley, 1802.

Elvin, Mark. *The Pattern of the Chinese Past*. Stanford: Stanford University Press, 1973.

Fairbank, John K. "The Early Treaty System in the Chinese World Order," in *The Chinese World Order*, John K. Fairbank, ed. Cambridge: Harvard University Press, 1968, pp. 257-75.

———— "A Preliminary Framework," in *The Chinese World Order*, John K. Fairbank, ed. Cambridge: Harvard University Press, 1968, pp. 1-19.

————. *Trade and Diplomacy on the China Coast*. 2 vols. in 1. Cambridge: Harvard University Press, 1969. Orig. pub. 1953.

————, and Teng, S. Y. "On the Ch'ing Tributary System," *Ch'ing Administration: Three Studies*. Harvard-Yenching Institute Studies, No. 19. Cambridge: Harvard University Press, 1960. Orig. pub. 1941.

Finlayson, George. *The Mission to Siam and Hue the Capital of Cochin China, in the Years 1821-22*. London: John Murray, 1926.

The Foreign Trade of China Divested of Monopoly, Restriction, and Hazard, by Means of Insular Commercial Stations. London: Effingham Wilson, 1832.

Fox, Grace. *British Admirals and Chinese Pirates, 1832-1869*. London: Kegan Paul, Trench, Trubner & Co., Ltd., 1940.

Frankfurter, O. "King Monkut," *The Journal of the Siam Society*, 1 (1904), 191-206.

Freedman, Maurice. *Lineage Organization in Southeastern China*. London: The Athlone Press, 1958.

Fu, Lo-shu. *A Documentary Chronicle of Sino-Western Relations (1644-1820)*. 2 vols. Tucson: University of Arizona Press, 1966.

"General Description of Shanghai and Its Environs, Extracted from Native Authorities," in *Medhurst's Chinese Miscellany*. Shanghai: Mission Press, 1850. Sep. pag.

Great Britain. Board of Trade. *Abstract of Reports on the Trade of Various Countries and Places, for the Year 1854*. (Gt. Br. Parliament. Papers by Command. 1856-[61?].)

————. Foreign Office. *Commercial Report by Her Majesty's Consul-General in Siam for the Year 1875*. (Gt. Br. Parliament. Papers by Command. Siam. No. 1, 1876.)

————. Foreign Office. *Commercial Reports from Her Majesty's Consuls in China, Japan, and Siam, 1865*. (Gt. Br. Parliament. Papers by Command. 1866.)

————. Foreign Office. *Correspondence Respecting Diplomatic and Consular Expenditure in China, Japan, and Siam*. (Gt. Br. Parliament. Papers by Command. China. No. 5, 1870.)

————. Parliament. House of Commons. *Select Committee on Commercial Relations with China*. (Gt. Br. Parliament. Reports and Papers. 1847 [H.C.] 654.)

_____. Parliament. House of Commons. Select Committee on the East India Company's Affairs. *Report from the Select Committee Appointed to Inquire into the Present State of the Affairs of the East India Company, and into the Trade between Great Britain, the East Indies, and China.* (Gt. Br. Parliament. Sessional papers. 1830, Vol. 5, [H.C.] 644.)

_____. Parliament. House of Commons. Select Committee on Foreign Trade. *Third Report from the Select Committee Appointed to Consider of the Means of Improving and Maintaining the Foreign Trade of the Country: East Indies and China.* (Gt. Br. Parliament Sessional Papers. 1821, Vol. 6 [H.C.] 746.)

_____. Parliament. House of Lords. Select Committee on Foreign Trade. *Report [Relative to the Trade with the East Indies and China] from the Select Committee of the House of Lords, Appointed to Inquire into the Means of Extending and Securing the Foreign Trade of the Country, and to Report to the House; together with the Minutes of Evidence. . . .* (Gt. Br. Parliament. Sessional papers. 1821, Vol. 7 [H.L.] 476.)

Greenberg, Michael. *British Trade and the Opening of China 1800-1842.* Cambridge: Cambridge University Press, 1951.

Gréhan, M. A. *Le Royaume de Siam.* Paris: Challamel Ainé, 1870.

Gutzlaff, Charles. *China Opened.* 2 vols. London: Smith, Elder & Co., 1838.

_____. *The Journal of Two Voyages along the Coast of China, in 1831 & 1832.* New York: John P. Haven, 1833.

_____. *A Sketch of Chinese History, Ancient and Modern: Comprising a Retrospect of the Foreign Intercourse and Trade with China.* 2 vols. London: Smith, Elder and Co., 1834.

Hamilton, Walter. *The East India Gazetteer.* London: John Murray, 1815.

Hao, Yen-p'ing. *The Comprador in Nineteenth Century China: Bridge between East and West.* Cambridge: Harvard University Press. 1970.

Herrmann, Albert. *An Historical Atlas of China* (new ed.). Chicago: Aldine Publishing Co., 1966.

Hinton, Harold. *The Grain Tribute System of China (1845-1911).* Cambridge: Harvard University Press, 1956.

Hirth, Friedrich. "The Geographical Distribution of Commercial Products in Kwangtung," *The China Review,* 2.5 (1873-74), 306-09; 2.6 (1873-74), 376-82.

_____. "The Hoppo-Book of 1753," *Journal of the North-China Branch of the Royal Asiatic Society,* 17 (1882), 221-35.

_____. "The Port of Hai-k'ou," *The China Review,* 1.2 (1872), 124-27.

_____, and Rockhill, W. W., trans. *Chau Ju-kua; His Work on the Chinese and Arab Trade in the Twelfth and Thirteenth Centuries, Entitled 'Chu-Fan-Chi'.* St. Petersburg: Printing Office of the Imperial Academy of Sciences, 1911.

Hornell, J. "The Origin of the Junk and Sampan," *The Mariner's Mirror*, 20 (1934), 331-37.

Hoshi, Ayao. *The Ming Tribute Grain System*. Trans. by Mark Elvin. Michigan Abstracts of Chinese and Japanese Works on Chinese History, No. 1. Ann Arbor: University of Michigan Press, 1969.

Hou, Chi-ming. *Foreign Investment and Economic Development in China 1840-1937*. Cambridge: Harvard University Press, 1965.

Hsieh, Kuo-ching. "Removal of Coastal Population in the Early Tsing Period," *The Chinese Social and Political Science Review*, 15 (1932), 559-96.

Huang, Ray. "Fiscal Administration during the Ming Dynasty," in *Chinese Government in Ming Times*, Charles Hucker, ed. New York: Columbia University Press, 1969, pp. 73-128.

Hughes, George. *Amoy and the Surrounding Districts*. Hongkong: De Souza & Co., 1872.

Hummel, Arthur, ed. *Eminent Chinese of the Ch'ing Period*. 2 vols. Washington: U.S. Government Printing Office, 1943.

Hunt's Merchants' Magazine and Commercial Review. Conducted by Freeman Hunt. New York: Privately published, 1839-1859. Vols. 1-4. Original title, *The Merchants' Magazine and Commercial Review*.

Illustrated Catalogue of the "Maze Collection" of Chinese Junk Models in the Science Museum, London. n.p. 1938.

The Indo-Chinese Gleaner. Malacca: Anglo-Chinese Press. No. 10 (1819); Nos. 12-13 (1820); Nos. 16-17 (1821); Nos. 19-20 (1822).

Ingram, James. *Economic Change in Thailand since 1850*. Stanford: Stanford University Press, 1955.

Jobé, Joseph, ed. *The Great Age of Sail*. Greenwich: New York Graphic Society Ltd., 1967.

Journal of the Indian Archipelago and Eastern Asia. Singapore. Vols. 1-9 (1847-1855); New Series Vols. 1-4 (1856-1862).

Kato, Shigeshi. "On the Hang or the Associations of Merchants in China," *Memoirs of the Research Department of the Toyo Bunko* 8 (1936), 45-83.

King, Frank. *Money and Monetary Policy in China 1845-1895*. Cambridge: Harvard University Press, 1965.

Koenig, Jean G. "Journal of a Voyage from India to Siam and Malacca in 1779," *Journal of the Straits Branch of the Royal Asiatic Society*, 26 (Jan. 1894), 58-201; 27 (Oct. 1894), 57-125.

Komai, Yoshiaki, trans. "Tung Hsi Yang K'ao," *The Kyoto University of Foreign Studies Academic Bulletin*, 9 (1967), 135-59; 10 (1968), 113-25; 11 (1970), 77-88; 12 (1971), 115-43.

Kuwabara, Jitsuzo. "On P'u Shou-keng a man of the Western Regions, who was the Superintendent of the Trading Ships' Office in Ch'üan-chou towards the end of the Sung Dynasty, together with a general sketch of Trade of the Arabs in China during the T'ang and Sung eras," *Memoirs of the Research Department of the Toyo Bunko*, 2 (1928), 1-79; 7 (1935), 1-104.

La Loubère, Simon de. (*A New Historical Relation of*) *The Kingdom of Siam*. 2 vols. in 1. London: Oxford University Press, 1969. Repr. of 1693 ed.

Landström, Björn. *The Ship*. Trans. from *Skeppet* by M. Phillips. London: Allen & Unwin, 1961.

Leonard, Jane. "Chinese Overlordship and Western Penetration in Maritime Asia: A Late Ch'ing Re-appraisal of Chinese Maritime Relations," *Modern Asian Studies*, 6 (1972), 151-174.

_____. "Wei Yüan and the *Hai-kuo t'u-chih*: A Geopolitical Analysis of Western Expansion in Maritime Asia." Unpublished Ph.D. dissertation, Cornell University, 1971.

Lopez, Robert and Raymond, Irving, eds. *Medieval Trade in the Mediterranean World*. New York: W. W. Norton & Co., 1965.

Ma Huan; see J. V. G. Mills.

Makepeace, W. and Brooks, G. *et al.*, eds. *One Hundred Years of Singapore*. 2 vols. London: John Murray, 1921.

Malcom, Howard. *Travels in South-Eastern Asia Embracing Hindustan, Malaya, Siam and China*. 2 vols. Boston: Gould, Kendall, & Lincoln, 1839.

Malloch, D. E. *Siam, Some General Remarks on Its Productions*. Calcutta: Baptist Missionary Press, 1852.

Mancall, Mark. "The Ch'ing Tribute System: An Interpretive Essay," in *The Chinese World Order*, John K. Fairbank, ed. Cambridge: Harvard University Press, 1968, pp. 63-89.

Mandelslo, John Albert de. *The Voyages and Travels of J. Albert de Mandelslo into the East-Indies 1638-1650*. Trans. by John Davies. London: Thomas Dring & John Starkey, 1662.

Martin, R. Montgomery. *China; Political, Commercial, and Social*. 2 vols. London: James Madden, 1847.

_____. *Reports, Minutes and Despatches, on the British Position and Prospects in China*. London: Harrison and Co., 1846.

Mayers, W. F. "Chinese Junk Building," *Notes & Queries on China & Japan*, 1.12 (1867), 170-73.

Meilink-Roelofsz, M. A. P. *Asian Trade and European Influence in the Indonesian Archipelago between 1500 and about 1630*. The Hague: Martinus Nijhoff, 1962.

Metzger, Thomas. "Ch'ing Commercial Policy," *Ch'ing-shih wen-t'i*, 1.3 (Feb. 1966), 4-10.

_____. "The State and Commerce in Imperial China," *Asian and African Studies*, 6 (1970), 23-46.

Milburn, William. *Oriental Commerce.* 2 vols. London: Black, Parry, & Co., 1813.

Mills, J. V. G. *Ma Huan, Ying-yai sheng-lan, 'The Overall Survey of the Ocean's Shores'* [1433]. Cambridge: Cambridge University Press, 1970.

Moor, J. H. *Notices of the Indian Archipelago, and Adjacent Countries.* Singapore, 1837.

Morrison, J. R. *Chinese Commercial Guide.* Canton, 1834.

_____. *Chinese Commercial Guide.* Canton: Chinese Repository, 1848.

Morse, Hosea B. *The Gilds of China.* London: Longmans, Green, and Co., 1933.

_____. *The Trade and Administration of the Chinese Empire.* London: Longmans, Green, and Co., 1908.

Murphey, Rhoads, ed. *Nineteenth Century China: Five Imperialist Perspectives.* Michigan Papers in Chinese Studies, No. 13. Ann Arbor: The University of Michigan Center for Chinese Studies, 1972.

Neale, Arthur. *Narrative of a Residence at the Capital of The Kingdom of Siam.* London: Office of the National Illustrated Library, 1852.

Needham, Joseph. *Science and Civilization in China.* Vol. 4, pts. 1 & 3. Cambridge: Cambridge University Press, 1962, 1971.

Neon Snidvongs. "Siam at the Accession of King Monkut: Relations with the West," in *Thang maitri kap farang nai ratchakan thi 4.* Bangkok: Privately published, 1959, pp. 1-70.

Newbold, T. J. *Political and Statistical Account of the British Settlements in the Straits of Malacca.* 2 vols. London: John Murray, 1839.

Notices concerning China, and the Port of Canton. Malacca: Mission Press, 1823.

Oey, Giok P. "Record of the Southern Ocean." Unpublished M.A. dissertation, Cornell University, 1953.

Pallegoix, Jean Baptiste. *Description du Royaume Thai ou Siam.* 2 vols. Paris, 1854.

Paris, Pierre. "Quelques Dates pour une Histoire de la Jonque Chinoise," *Bulletin de l'École Française d'Extrême-Orient*, 46 (1952), 267-78.

Philastre, P. L. F. *Le Code Annamite.* 2 vols. Taipei: Ch'eng-wen, 1967. Orig. pub. 1909.

Phipps, John. *A Practical Treatise on the China and Eastern Trade.* Calcutta: Baptist Mission Press, 1835.

Poujade, Jean. *Les Jonques des Chinois du Siam.* Paris: Gauthier-Villars, 1946.

Pritchard, Earl. *Anglo-Chinese Relations during the Seventeenth and Eighteenth Centuries*. New York: Octagon Books, 1970.

Purcell, Victor. *The Chinese in Southeast Asia*. London: Oxford University Press, 1951.

R., J., supercargo. "Diary of a Journey Overland, through the Maritime Provinces of China, from Manchao on the South Coast of Hainan, to Canton, in the Years 1819 and 1820," in *New Voyages and Travels*, 6 (1822), 1-116.

Raffles, Stamford. "The Maritime Code of the Malays," *Journal of the Straits Branch of the Royal Asiatic Society*, 3 (1879), 62-84.

Rawski, Evelyn. *Agricultural Change and the Peasant Economy of South China*. Cambridge: Harvard University Press, 1972.

Records of the Relations between Siam and Foreign Countries in the 17th Century. 5 vols. Bangkok: Vajiranana National Library, 1915.

Roberts, Edmund. *Embassy to the Eastern Courts of Cochin-China, Siam, and Muscat*. New York: Harper & Brothers, 1837.

The Siam Repository. Bangkok: S. J. Smith's Office, 1869-1874. Vols. 1-6.

Sigaut, E. "A Northern Type of Chinese Junk [the low-decked Tsingtao freighter]," *The Mariner's Mirror*, 46 (1960), 161-74.

The Singapore Chronicle and Commercial Register. Singapore: Singapore Chronicle Press, 1831-1833. New Series. Vols. 1-3.

Skinner, G. William. *Chinese Society in Thailand*. Ithaca: Cornell University Press, 1957.

Sirr, Henry C. *China and the Chinese: Their Religion, Character, Customs and Manufactures*. 2 vols. London: Wm. S. Orr & Co., 1849.

Slade, John. *Notices on the British Trade to the Port of Canton*. London: Smith, Elder, and Co., 1830.

Smith, Adam. *An Inquiry into the Nature and Causes of the Wealth of Nations*, Edwin Cannan, ed. 2 vols. New Rochelle: Arlington House, 1966.

Smyth, H. Warington. *Mast and Sail in Europe and Asia*. London: John Murray, 1906.

Spicer, Stanley. *Masters of Sail, the Era of Square-rigged Vessels in the Maritime Provinces*. Toronto: Ryerson Press, 1968.

Staunton, George, trans. *Ta Tsing Leu Lee: Being the Fundamental Laws, and a Selection from the Supplementary Statutes of the Penal Code of China*. London: T. Cadell and W. Davies, 1810.

Stuart, G. A. *Chinese Materia Medica*. Shanghai: American Presbyterian Mission Press, 1911.

Suebsaeng Promboom. "Sino-Siamese Tributary Relations, 1282-1853." Unpublished Ph.D. dissertation, University of Wisconsin, 1971.

Sun, E-tu Zen. "The Board of Revenue in Nineteenth-Century China," *Harvard Journal of Asiatic Studies*, 24 (1962-63), 175-228.

_____, and Sun Shiou-chuan, trans. *T'ien-kung k'ai-wu, Chinese Technology in the Seventeenth-Century*. University Park: The Pennsylvania University Press, 1966.

Thiphakorawong, Cawphaja. *The Dynastic Chronicles, Bangkok Era, the Fourth Reign, B.E. 2394-2411 (A.D. 1851-1868)*. 2 vols. Chadin Flood, trans. with the assistance of E. T. Flood. Tokyo: Center for East Asian Cultural Studies, 1965.

Ting, V. K. and Donnelly, Ivon. "Things Produced by the Works of Nature," *The Mariner's Mirror*, 11 1935), 234-50.

Tông-Phúc-ngoan and Duòng-van-châu. *Xiêm-La-Quóc Lô-Trình Tâp-Luc* (Collected Records of Itineraries to Siam). An English introduction by Ch'en Ching-ho. Hong Kong: The Chinese University of Hong Kong, 1966.

"Trade to all the Ports of the Chinese Empire." Great Britain. Foreign Office. Papers in the Public Record Office. Series: Foreign Office 17. China No. 9. 1835. 1-72.

Tsiang, T. F. "The Government and the Co-hong of Canton, 1839," *Chinese Social and Political Science Review*, 15.4 (1932), 602-7.

Van der Heide, J. H. "The Economical Development of Siam during the Last Half Century," *Journal of the Siam Society*, 3.2 (1906), 74-101.

Van der Sprenkel, Sybille. *Legal Institutions in Manchu China*. London: The Athlone Press, 1962.

Vella, Walter. *Siam under Rama III, 1824-1851*. Locust Valley, N.Y.: J. J. Augustin Inc., 1957.

Wada, Sei. "The Philippine Islands as Known to the Chinese before the Ming Period," *Memoirs of the Research Department of the Toyo Bunko*, 4 (1929), 121-166.

Wang, Gungwu. "Early Ming Relations with Southeast Asia: A Background Essay," in *The Chinese World Order*, John K. Fairbank, ed. Cambridge: Harvard University Press, 1968, pp. 34-62.

_____. "The Nanhai Trade," *Journal of the Malayan Branch of the Royal Asiatic Society*, 31.2 (1958), 1-135.

_____. *A Short History of the Nanyang Chinese*. Singapore: Eastern University Press, Ltd., 1959.

Waters, D. W. "Chinese Junks: The Antung Trader," *The Mariner's Mirror*, 24 (1938), 49-67.

_____. "Chinese Junks: The Hangchow Bay Trader and Fisher," *The Mariner's Mirror*, 33 (1947), 28-38.

_____. "Chinese Junks: The Pechili Trader," *The Mariner's Mirror*, 33 (1947), 62-87.

_____. "Chinese Junks: The Twaqo," *The Mariner's Mirror*, 32 (1946), 155-67.

Watson, Andrew, trans. *Transport in Transition: The Evolution of Traditional Shipping in China.* Michigan Abstracts of Chinese and Japanese Works on Chinese History. No. 3. Ann Arbor: University of Michigan Center for Chinese Studies, 1972.

Watson, Ernest. *The Principal Articles of Chinese Commerce.* Shanghai: Statistical Dept. of the Inspectorate General of Customs, 1930.

Wenk, Klaus. *The Restoration of Thailand under Rama I, 1782-1809.* Tucson: University of Arizona Press, 1968.

White, Ann B. "The Hong Merchants of Canton." Unpublished Ph.D. dissertation, University of Pennsylvania, 1970.

Wilkinson, Endymion. "Studies in Chinese Price History." Unpublished Ph.D. dissertation, Princeton, 1970.

Williams, S. Wells. *A Chinese Commercial Guide.* Canton: Chinese Repository, 1856.

_____. *The Chinese Commercial Guide.* Hong Kong: A. Shortrede & Co., 1863.

Wilson, Constance M. "State and Society in the Reign of Monkut, 1851-1868: Thailand on the Eve of Modernization." Unpublished Ph.D. dissertation, Cornell University, 1970.

Winstedt, Richard. "Old Malay Legal Digests and Malay Customary Law," *Journal of the Royal Asiatic Society,* pt. 1-2 (1945), 17-29.

_____ and De Jong, P. E. "The Maritime Laws of Malacca," *Journal of the Malayan Branch of the Royal Asiatic Society,* 29.3 (1956), 22-59.

Wolters, O. W. "Ayudhya and the Rearward Part of the World," *Journal of the Royal Asiatic Society,* pts. 3-4 (1968), 166-78.

_____. *Early Indonesian Commerce.* Ithaca: Cornell University Press, 1967.

_____. *The Fall of Srivijaya in Malay History.* Ithaca: Cornell University Press, 1970.

Wong Lin Ken. "The Trade of Singapore, 1819-1869," *Journal of the Malayan Branch of the Royal Asiatic Society,* 33.4 (1960), 1-315.

Worcester, G. R. G. *The Junks and Sampans of the Yangtze.* 2 vols. Shanghai: Statistical Dept. of the Inspectorate General of Customs, 1947.

_____. *Sail and Sweep in China.* London: Her Majesty's Stationery Office, 1966.

_____. "Six Craft of Kwangtung," *The Mariner's Mirror,* 45 (1959), 130-44.

Wyatt, David K. "Family Politics in Nineteenth Century Thailand," *Journal of Southeast Asian History,* 9.2 (Sept. 1968), 208-28.

Yang, C. and Hau, H. B. *Statistics of China's Foreign Trade during the Last Sixty-five Years.* [Shanghai]: Academia Sinica, 1931.

Yule, Henry and Burnell, A. C. *Hobson-Jobson.* London: John Murray, 1903.

CHINESE MONEY, WEIGHTS, AND MEASURES

Money: 10 cash (*li* 厘)   = 1 candareen (*fen* 分)
        10 candareen   = 1 mace (*ch'ien* 錢)
        10 mace   = 1 tael (*liang* 兩)
         1 tael   = Sp. $1.40

The following format is used in the text to express denominations of Chinese currency:
        T.M.C.C.
        0.0.0.0.

To convert 2.5.3.0 into Spanish dollars:
        2 tael   = 2.80
        5/10 x 1.40/1   = .70   = Sp. $3.54
        3/100 x 1.40/1   = .042

Weights: 1 catty   = 1.3 lb.
          100 catties = 1 picul = 133.33 lbs.

Measures: 1 *ts'un* (寸) = 1 inch
           10 *ts'un*   = 1 *ch'ih* (尺)
           10 *ch'ih*   = 1 *chang* (丈)

When lengths have been converted to inches or feet in the text and footnotes, a Chinese equivalent, i.e. 1 *Chinese* inch, 1 *Chinese* foot (10"), is the measure referred to. Local usage and custom dictated the number of inches in a Chinese foot and the variation was wide. In Chang-chou, for example, there were 11 inches in the shipbuilders' foot, while at Shanghai there were 16 inches.

SIAMESE MONEY AND WEIGHTS

Money:

			Expressed as decimals of *baht*:		
800 *bia*	= 1 *füang*		1 *bia.*	=	.00015625
2 *füang*	= 1 *salüng*		1 *füang*	=	.125
4 *salüng*	= 1 *baht*		1 *salüng*	=	.25
4 *baht*	= 1 *tamlüng*		1 *baht*	=	1.0
20 *tamlüng*	= 1 *chang*		1 *tamlüng*	=	4.0
			1 *chang*		= 80.0

In nineteenth-century documents, sums are usually expressed in the following fashion:

	chang		4	
tamlüng	*baht*	3	2	
				= 334.875 *baht*
füang	*salüng*	1	3	
bia		0		

At 1850 rates: 2 *baht* = Sp. $1.00

Weights:

1 *chang*	= 1.3 lb.
100 *chang*	= 1 *hap* = 1 picul = 133.33 lbs.
100 *hap*	= 1 *tara*

For weighing tin, 1 *tara* = 3 *hap*

Salt and rice were measured according to the *coyan*: 1 *coyan* = 25 piculs.

The number of piculs in a Siamese *coyan* often varied, however, between 20 and 27.

Textiles were measured according to the *corge*: 1 *corge* = 20 pieces.

ABBREVIATIONS USED IN FOOTNOTES

CCSL	*Chia-ch'ing shih-lu* (Veritable records of the Chia-ch'ing reign period)
CHLC	*Kuo-ch'ao ch'i-hsien lei-cheng ch'u-pien* (Ch'ing biographies, first supplement
CLSL	*Ch'ien-lung shih-lu* (Veritable records of the Ch'ien-lung reign period)
CMH.R.	*Chotmaihet Ratchakan thi 1-4* (Official documents in the National Library, Bangkok. Reigns 1-4)
CSK	*Ch'ing-shih k'ao* (Draft history of the Ch'ing Dynasty)
FO 17/9	"Trade to All the Ports of the Chinese Empire"
FC	*Fu-chih* (Prefectural gazetteer)
FCSL	*Fu-chien sheng-li* (Laws and Regulations of Fukien)
HC	*Hsien-chih* (County gazetteer)
HCCSWP	*Huang-ch'ao ching-shih wen-pien* (Essays on statecraft during the Ch'ing Dynasty)
HMC	*Hsia-men chih* (Gazetteer of Amoy)
HPTL	*Hu-pu tse-li* (Precedents of the Board of Revenue)
JAS	*Journal of Asian Studies*
JMBRAS	*Journal of the Malayan Branch of the Royal Asiatic Society*
JNCBRAS	*Journal of the North-China Branch of the Royal Asiatic Society*
JSBRAS	*Journal of the Straits Branch of the Royal Asiatic Society*
KHSL	*K'ang-hsi shih-lu* (Veritable records of the K'ang-hsi reign period)
MCSL:KP	*Ming-Ch'ing shih-liao keng-pien* (Historical materials of the Ming and Ch'ing. Series G)
MCSL:TP	*Ming-Ch'ing shih-liao ting-pien* (Historical materials of the Ming and Ch'ing. Series D)
TC	*T'ung-chih* (Provincial gazetteer)
TCHT	*Ta-ch'ing hui-tien* (Administrative statutes of the Ch'ing Dynasty)

TCHTSL	*Ta-ch'ing hui-tien shih-li* (Administrative statutes and precedents of the Ch'ing Dynasty)
TCLL	*Ta-ch'ing lü-li* (Ch'ing statutes and sub-statutes)
YCSL	*Yung-cheng shih-lu* (Veritable records of the Hung-cheng reign period)
YHKC	*Yüeh hai-kuan chih* (Gazetteer of the maritime customs of Kwangtung)

SOUTHEAST ASIA PROGRAM PUBLICATIONS

Cornell University

Studies on Southeast Asia

Number 28   *The Hadrami Awakening: Community and Identity in the Netherlands East Indies, 1900-1942.* Natalie Mobini-Keseh. 1999. 174 pp. ISBN 0-87727-727-3

Number 27   *Tales from Djakarta: Caricatures of Circumstances and their Human Beings.* Pramoedya Ananta Toer. 1999. 145 pp. ISBN 0-87727-726-5

Number 26   *History, Culture, and Region in Southeast Asian Perspectives,* rev. ed., O. W. Wolters. 1999. 275 pp. ISBN 0-87727-725-7

Number 25   *Figures of Criminality in Indonesia, the Philippines, and Colonial Vietnam,* ed. Vicente L. Rafael. 1999. 259 pp. ISBN 0-87727-724-9

Number 24   *Paths to Conflagration: Fifty Years of Diplomacy and Warfare in Laos, Thailand, and Vietnam, 1778-1828,* Mayoury Ngaosyvathn and Pheuiphanh Ngaosyvathn. 1998. 268 pp. ISBN 0-87727-723-0

Number 23   *Nguyễn Cochinchina: Southern Vietnam in the Seventeenth and Eighteenth Centuries,* Li Tana. 1998. 194 pp. ISBN 0-87727-722-2

Number 22   *Young Heroes: The Indonesian Family in Politics,* Saya S. Shiraishi. 1997. 183 pp. ISBN 0-87727-721-4

Number 21   *Interpreting Development: Capitalism, Democracy, and the Middle Class in Thailand,* John Girling. 1996. 95 pp. ISBN 0-87727-720-6

Number 20   *Making Indonesia,* ed. Daniel S. Lev, Ruth McVey. 1996. 201 pp. ISBN 0-87727-719-2

Number 19   *Essays into Vietnamese Pasts,* ed. K. W. Taylor, John K. Whitmore. 1995. 288 pp. ISBN 0-87727-718-4

Number 18   *In the Land of Lady White Blood: Southern Thailand and the Meaning of History,* Lorraine M. Gesick. 1995. 106 pp. ISBN 0-87727-717-6

Number 17   *The Vernacular Press and the Emergence of Modern Indonesian Consciousness,* Ahmat Adam. 1995. 220 pp. ISBN 0-87727-716-8

Number 16   *The Nan Chronicle,* trans., ed. David K. Wyatt. 1994. 158 pp. ISBN 0-87727-715-X

Number 15   *Selective Judicial Competence: The Cirebon-Priangan Legal Administration, 1680–1792,* Mason C. Hoadley. 1994. 185 pp. ISBN 0-87727-714-1

Number 14   *Sjahrir: Politics and Exile in Indonesia,* Rudolf Mrázek. 1994. 536 pp. ISBN 0-87727-713-3

Number 13   *Fair Land Sarawak: Some Recollections of an Expatriate Officer,* Alastair Morrison. 1993. 196 pp. ISBN 0-87727-712-5

Number 12   *Fields from the Sea: Chinese Junk Trade with Siam during the Late Eighteenth and Early Nineteenth Centuries,* Jennifer Cushman. 1993. 206 pp. ISBN 0-87727-711-7

Number 11   *Money, Markets, and Trade in Early Southeast Asia: The Development of Indigenous Monetary Systems to AD 1400,* Robert S. Wicks. 1992. 2nd printing 1996. 354 pp., 78 tables, illus., maps. ISBN 0-87727-710-9

Number 10   *Tai Ahoms and the Stars: Three Ritual Texts to Ward Off Danger*, trans., ed. B. J. Terwiel, Ranoo Wichasin. 1992. 170 pp. ISBN 0-87727-709-5

Number 9   *Southeast Asian Capitalists*, ed. Ruth McVey. 1992. 2nd printing 1993. 220 pp. ISBN 0-87727-708-7

Number 8   *The Politics of Colonial Exploitation: Java, the Dutch, and the Cultivation System*, Cornelis Fasseur, ed. R. E. Elson, trans. R. E. Elson, Ary Kraal. 1992. 2nd printing 1994. 266 pp. ISBN 0-87727-707-9

Number 7   *A Malay Frontier: Unity and Duality in a Sumatran Kingdom*, Jane Drakard. 1990. 215 pp. ISBN 0-87727-706-0

Number 6   *Trends in Khmer Art*, Jean Boisselier, ed. Natasha Eilenberg, trans. Natasha Eilenberg, Melvin Elliott. 1989. 124 pp., 24 plates. ISBN 0-87727-705-2

Number 5   *Southeast Asian Ephemeris: Solar and Planetary Positions, A.D. 638–2000*, J. C. Eade. 1989. 175 pp. ISBN 0-87727-704-4

Number 3   *Thai Radical Discourse: The Real Face of Thai Feudalism Today*, Craig J. Reynolds. 1987. 2nd printing 1994. 186 pp. ISBN 0-87727-702-8

Number 1   *The Symbolism of the Stupa*, Adrian Snodgrass. 1985. Revised with index, 1988. 3rd printing 1998. 469 pp. ISBN 0-87727-700-1

SEAP Series

Number 17   *Gangsters, Democracy, and the State*, ed. Carl A. Trocki. 1998. 94 pp. ISBN 0-87727-134-8

Number 16   *Cutting Across the Lands: An Annotated Bibliography on Natural Resource Management and Community Development in Indonesia, the Philippines, and Malaysia*, ed. Eveline Ferretti. 1997. 329 pp. ISBN 0-87727-133-X

Number 15   *The Revolution Falters: The Left in Philippine Politics After 1986*, ed. Patricio N. Abinales. 1996. 182 pp. ISBN 0-87727-132-1

Number 14   *Being Kammu: My Village, My Life*, ed. Damrong Tayanin. 1994. 138 pp., 22 tables, illus., maps. ISBN 0-87727-130-5

Number 13   *The American War in Vietnam*, ed. Jayne Werner, David Hunt. 1993. 132 pp. ISBN 0-87727-131-3

Number 12   *The Political Legacy of Aung San*, ed. Josef Silverstein. Revised edition 1993. 169 pp. ISBN 0-87727-128-3

Number 10   *Studies on Vietnamese Language and Literature: A Preliminary Bibliography*, Nguyen Dinh Tham. 1992. 227 pp. ISBN 0-87727-127-5

Number 9   *A Secret Past*, Dokmaisot, trans. Ted Strehlow. 1992. 2nd printing 1997. 72 pp. ISBN 0-87727-126-7

Number 8   *From PKI to the Comintern, 1924–1941: The Apprenticeship of the Malayan Communist Party*, Cheah Boon Kheng. 1992. 147 pp. ISBN 0-87727-125-9

Number 7   *Intellectual Property and US Relations with Indonesia, Malaysia, Singapore, and Thailand*, Elisabeth Uphoff. 1991. 67 pp. ISBN 0-87727-124-0

Number 6   *The Rise and Fall of the Communist Party of Burma (CPB)*, Bertil Lintner. 1990. 124 pp. 26 illus., 14 maps. ISBN 0-87727-123-2

Number 5   *Japanese Relations with Vietnam: 1951–1987*, Masaya Shiraishi. 1990. 174 pp. ISBN 0-87727-122-4

| Number 3 | *Postwar Vietnam: Dilemmas in Socialist Development*, ed. Christine White, David Marr. 1988. 2nd printing 1993. 260 pp. ISBN 0-87727-120-8 |
| Number 2 | *The Dobama Movement in Burma (1930–1938)*, Khin Yi. 1988. 160 pp. ISBN 0-87727-118-6 |

Translation Series

Volume 4	*Approaching Suharto's Indonesia from the Margins*, ed. Takashi Shiraishi. 1994. 153 pp. ISBN 0-87727-403-7
Volume 3	*The Japanese in Colonial Southeast Asia*, ed. Saya Shiraishi, Takashi Shiraishi. 1993. 172 pp. ISBN 0-87727-402-9
Volume 2	*Indochina in the 1940s and 1950s*, ed. Takashi Shiraishi, Motoo Furuta. 1992. 196 pp. ISBN 0-87727-401-0
Volume 1	*Reading Southeast Asia*, ed. Takashi Shiraishi. 1990. 188 pp. ISBN 0-87727-400-2

CORNELL MODERN INDONESIA PROJECT PUBLICATIONS
Cornell University

Number 75	*A Tour of Duty: Changing Patterns of Military Politics in Indonesia in the 1990s.* Douglas Kammen and Siddharth Chandra. 1999. 99 pp. ISBN 0-87763-049-6
Number 74	*The Roots of Acehnese Rebellion 1989–1992*, Tim Kell. 1995. 103 pp. ISBN 0-87763-040-2
Number 73	*"White Book" on the 1992 General Election in Indonesia*, trans. Dwight King. 1994. 72 pp. ISBN 0-87763-039-9
Number 72	*Popular Indonesian Literature of the Qur'an*, Howard M. Federspiel. 1994. 170 pp. ISBN 0-87763-038-0
Number 71	*A Javanese Memoir of Sumatra, 1945–1946: Love and Hatred in the Liberation War*, Takao Fusayama. 1993. 150 pp. ISBN 0-87763-037-2
Number 70	*East Kalimantan: The Decline of a Commercial Aristocracy*, Burhan Magenda. 1991. 120 pp. ISBN 0-87763-036-4
Number 69	*The Road to Madiun: The Indonesian Communist Uprising of 1948*, Elizabeth Ann Swift. 1989. 120 pp. ISBN 0-87763-035-6
Number 68	*Intellectuals and Nationalism in Indonesia: A Study of the Following Recruited by Sutan Sjahrir in Occupation Jakarta*, J. D. Legge. 1988. 159 pp. ISBN 0-87763-034-8
Number 67	*Indonesia Free: A Biography of Mohammad Hatta*, Mavis Rose. 1987. 252 pp. ISBN 0-87763-033-X
Number 66	*Prisoners at Kota Cane*, Leon Salim, trans. Audrey Kahin. 1986. 112 pp. ISBN 0-87763-032-1
Number 65	*The Kenpeitai in Java and Sumatra*, trans. Barbara G. Shimer, Guy Hobbs, intro. Theodore Friend. 1986. 80 pp. ISBN 0-87763-031-3
Number 64	*Suharto and His Generals: Indonesia's Military Politics, 1975–1983*, David Jenkins. 1984. 4th printing 1997. 300 pp. ISBN 0-87763-030-5

Number 62 *Interpreting Indonesian Politics: Thirteen Contributions to the Debate, 1964–1981,* ed. Benedict Anderson, Audrey Kahin, intro. Daniel S. Lev. 1982. 3rd printing 1991. 172 pp. ISBN 0-87763-028-3

Number 61 *Sickle and Crescent: The Communist Revolt of 1926 in Banten,* Michael C. Williams. 1982. 81 pp. ISBN 0-87763-027-5

Number 60 *The Minangkabau Response to Dutch Colonial Rule in the Nineteenth Century,* Elizabeth E. Graves. 1981. 157 pp. ISBN 0-87763-000-3

Number 59 *Breaking the Chains of Oppression of the Indonesian People: Defense Statement at His Trial on Charges of Insulting the Head of State, Bandung, June 7–10, 1979,* Heri Akhmadi. 1981. 201 pp. ISBN 0-87763-001-1

Number 58 *Administration of Islam in Indonesia,* Deliar Noer. 1978. 82 pp. ISBN 0-87763-002-X

Number 57 *Permesta: Half a Rebellion,* Barbara S. Harvey. 1977. 174 pp. ISBN 0-87763-003-8

Number 55 *Report from Banaran: The Story of the Experiences of a Soldier during the War of Independence,* Maj. Gen. T. B. Simatupang. 1972. 186 pp. ISBN 0-87763-005-4

Number 52 *A Preliminary Analysis of the October 1 1965, Coup in Indonesia (Prepared in January 1966),* Benedict R. Anderson, Ruth T. McVey, assist. Frederick P. Bunnell. 1971. 3rd printing 1990. 174 pp. ISBN 0-87763-008-9

Number 51 *The Putera Reports: Problems in Indonesian-Japanese War-Time Cooperation,* Mohammad Hatta, trans., intro. William H. Frederick. 1971. 114 pp. ISBN 0-87763-009-7

Number 50 *Schools and Politics: The Kaum Muda Movement in West Sumatra (1927–1933),* Taufik Abdullah. 1971. 257 pp. ISBN 0-87763-010-0

Number 49 *The Foundation of the Partai Muslimin Indonesia,* K. E. Ward. 1970. 75 pp. ISBN 0-87763-011-9

Number 48 *Nationalism, Islam and Marxism,* Soekarno, intro. Ruth T. McVey. 1970. 2nd printing 1984. 62 pp. ISBN 0-87763-012-7

Number 43 *State and Statecraft in Old Java: A Study of the Later Mataram Period, 16th to 19th Century,* Soemarsaid Moertono. Revised edition 1981. 180 pp. ISBN 0-87763-017-8

Number 37 *Mythology and the Tolerance of the Javanese,* Benedict R. O'G. Anderson. 2nd edition 1997. 104 pp., 65 illus. ISBN 0-87763-041-0

Number 25 *The Communist Uprisings of 1926–1927 in Indonesia: Key Documents,* ed., intro. Harry J. Benda, Ruth T. McVey. 1960. 2nd printing 1969. 177 pp. ISBN 0-87763-024-0

Number 7 *The Soviet View of the Indonesian Revolution,* Ruth T. McVey. 1957. 3rd printing 1969. 90 pp. ISBN 0-87763-018-6

Number 6 *The Indonesian Elections of 1955,* Herbert Feith. 1957. 2nd printing 1971. 91 pp. ISBN 0-87763-020-8

LANGUAGE TEXTS

INDONESIAN

Beginning Indonesian Through Self-Instruction, John U. Wolff, Dédé Oetomo, Daniel Fietkiewicz. 3rd revised edition 1992. 3 volume set. 1,057 pp. ISBN 0-87727-519-X

Indonesian Readings, John U. Wolff. 1978. 4th printing 1992. 480 pp. ISBN 0-87727-517-3

Indonesian Conversations, John U. Wolff. 1978. 3rd printing 1991. 297 pp. ISBN 0-87727-516-5

Formal Indonesian, John U. Wolff. 2nd revised edition 1986. 446 pp. ISBN 0-87727-515-7

TAGALOG

Pilipino Through Self-Instruction, John U. Wolff, Ma. Theresa C. Centano, Der-Hwa U. Rau. 1991. 4 volume set. 1,490 pp. ISBN 0-87727-524-6

THAI

A. U. A. Language Center Thai Course Book 1, J. Marvin Brown. Originally published by the American University Alumni Association Language Center, 1974. Reissued by Cornell Southeast Asia Program,1991. 267 pp. ISBN 0-87727-506-8

A. U. A. Language Center Thai Course Book 2, 1992. 288 pp. ISBN 0-87727-507-6

A. U. A. Language Center Thai Course Book 3, 1992. 247 pp. ISBN 0-87727-508-4

A. U. A. Language Center Thai Course, Reading and Writing Text (mostly reading), 1979. Reissued 1997. 164 pp. ISBN 0-87727-511-4

A. U. A. Language Center Thai Course, Reading and Writing Workbook (mostly writing), 1979. Reissued 1997. 99 pp. ISBN 0-87727-512-2

KHMER

Cambodian System of Writing and Beginning Reader, Franklin E. Huffman. Originally published by Yale University Press, 1970. Reissued by Cornell Southeast Asia Program, 3rd printing 1992. 365 pp. ISBN 0-300-01314-0

Modern Spoken Cambodian, Franklin E. Huffman, assist. Charan Promchan, Chhom-Rak Thong Lambert. Originally published by Yale University Press, 1970. Reissued by Cornell Southeast Asia Program, 3rd printing 1991. 451 pp. ISBN 0-300-01316-7

Intermediate Cambodian Reader, ed. Franklin E. Huffman, assist. Im Proum. Originally published by Yale University Press, 1972. Reissued by Cornell Southeast Asia Program, 1988. 499 pp. ISBN 0-300-01552-6

Cambodian Literary Reader and Glossary, Franklin E. Huffman, Im Proum. Originally published by Yale University Press, 1977. Reissued by Cornell Southeast Asia Program, 1988. 494 pp. ISBN 0-300-02069-4

HMONG

White Hmong-English Dictionary, Ernest E. Heimbach. 1969. 7th printing 1997. 523 pp. ISBN 0-87727-075-9

VIETNAMESE

Intermediate Spoken Vietnamese, Franklin E. Huffman, Tran Trong Hai. 1980. 3rd printing 1994. ISBN 0-87727-500-9

* * *

Southeast Asian Studies: Reorientations. Craig J. Reynolds and Ruth McVey. Frank H. Golay Lectures 2 & 3. 70 pp. ISBN 0-87727-301-4

Javanese Literature in Surakarta Manuscripts, Nancy K. Florida. Hard cover series ISBN 0-87727-600-5; Paperback series ISBN 0-87727-601-3. Vol. 1, *Introduction and Manuscripts of the Karaton Surakarta.* 1993. 410 pp. Frontispiece, 5 illus. Hard cover, ISBN 0-87727-602-1, Paperback, ISBN 0-87727-603-X

Sbek Thom: Khmer Shadow Theater. Pech Tum Kravel, trans. Sos Kem, ed. Thavro Phim, Sos Kem, Martin Hatch. 1996. 363 pp., 153 photographs. ISBN 0-87727-620-X

In the Mirror, Literature and Politics in Siam in the American Era, ed. Benedict R. O'G. Anderson, trans. Benedict R. O'G. Anderson, Ruchira Mendiones. 1985. 2nd printing 1991. 303 pp. Paperback. ISBN 974-210-380-1

To order, please contact:

Cornell University
SEAP Distribution Center
369 Pine Tree Rd.
Ithaca, NY 14850-2819 USA

Tel: 1-877-865-2432 (Toll free – U.S.)
Fax: (607) 255-7534

E-mail: SEAP-Pubs@cornell.edu
Web page (credit card orders): www.einaudi. cornell.edu:591/SEAPpubs

Orders must be prepaid by check or credit card (VISA, MasterCard, Discover).